The Theory of the Novel in Early German
Romanticism

Utah Studies
in Literature and Linguistics

edited by

Andrée M.L. Barnett
Robert E. Helbling – Luis Lorenzo-Rivero
Gerhard P. Knapp – Wolff A. von Schmidt

Vol. 11

Special Editor
Wolff A. von Schmidt

PETER LANG
Berne · Frankfurt am Main · Las Vegas

Diana Behler

The Theory of the
Novel in Early
German Romanticism

PETER LANG
Berne · Frankfurt am Main · Las Vegas

PREFACE

This publication grew out of my dissertation <u>The Romantic Theory of the Novel and its Implications for Thomas Mann's Zauberberg</u>, which I defended in December, 1969, at the University of Washington. As the title indicates, my thesis did not arise out of a merely theoretical interest in Romanticism as such, but had the more practical goal of applying the romantic theory of the novel to the interpretation of phenomena of modern literature. In other words, I assumed that the romantic theoreticians in their "divinatory criticism" had something to reveal to us about literary works of our own time, but did not attempt to ascertain direct influences. This was by no means an extravagant assumption, but has been a well established working concept utilized in a number of investigations, e. g.: Käthe Hamburger, <u>Thomas Mann und die Romantik</u> (Berlin, 1932); Renée Lang, <u>André Gide et la pensée allemande</u> (Paris, 1949); Henry Hatfield, "Castorp's Dream and Novalis," <u>History of Ideas News Letter I</u> (1954), 9-11; Erich Heller, <u>The Ironic German. A Study of Thomas Mann</u> (Boston, 1958); Hermann J. Weigand, <u>The Magic Mountain</u> (Chapel Hill, 1964); Hans Eichner, "Thomas Mann und die deutsche Romantik" in <u>Das Nachleben der Romantik in der modernen deutschen Literatur</u> (Heidelberg, 1969), 152-173. One can safely say that the literary theory of the <u>Athenäum</u> was prophetic, in that it anticipated many literary forms, devices, and features which did not actually appear in literary works until a much later date.

The same forward-looking thrust animates this study of the theory of the novel in early German Romanticism. However, the focus has shifted from a broad comparative perspective to a monographic one and has concentrated solely on the early romantic theory of the novel. I am still convinced of the legitimacy and value of applying critical concepts and theories devised by the members of the early romantic school to phenomena of modern or contemporary literature. Fruitful topics for such investigations would be an analysis of Nietzsche's idea of the Dionysiac in light of Friedrich and August Wilhelm Schlegel's writings on Greek literature, the comparison of basic devices in the contemporary theater of the absurd with ironic techniques which were à l'ordre du jour in early German romantic literature and poetry, the study of the use of the fragment by contemporary authors with a view to the theory of the fragment as it was developed by Novalis and Friedrich Schlegel, and research in the romantic background of the present-day emphasis on rhetoric and essayistic forms.

Yet this publication pursues a more modest goal and intends to establish a monographic basis for the concept of the novel among the early German Romantics. Three reasons have determined this scope. First, the sources for the theory of the novel in early German Romanticism have become so abundant, especially with the new editions of Friedrich Schlegel's and Novalis' posthumous writings, and are so complex because of their extravagant terminology and fragmentary presentation that they require an independent investigation.

Second, in spite of the most recent clarifications of the concept of Romanticism (<u>Romantic and its Cognates. The European History of a Word</u>, ed. Hans Eichner (Toronto, 1972); Raymond Immerwahr, <u>Romantisch. Genese und Tradition einer Denkform</u> (Respublica Literaria, Vol. 7, Frankfurt, 1972); Ernst Behler, "Kritische Gedanken zum Begriff der europäischen Romantik," in <u>Die europäische Romantik</u> (Frankfurt, 1972, pp. 7-43), the present use of the term in literary criticism is

5

still imbued with the traditional understanding of Romanticism as a movement of unrestrained imagination. Thus the realistic and classical elements of the romantic theory of the novel, as well as the emphasis given to form, structure, observation, and learning must be established as essential elements of this theory, a task best achieved through a monographic approach. Third, and from a more pragmatic point of view, this study intends to provide teachers and students with a succinct presentation of the often debated and perhaps most essential topic of early German romantic literary theory. This can now be achieved, as the re-edition of Novalis has come to its conclusion and all relevant posthumous manuscripts by Friedrich Schlegel have appeared. In similar fashion, I have presented Thomas Mann's theory of the novel in an independent study ("Thomas Mann as a Theorectician of the Novel," Colloquia Germanica, 1974, 1/2, pp. 52-88). The metaphysical implications of the early romantic theory of the novel involving the "Dichter-Priester" are not central to this presentation which is genre-oriented. My article on "Lessing's Legacy to the Romantic Concept of the Poet Priest," Lessing Yearbook IV (1972), pp. 67-93, does, however, investigate this topic.

Focusing a book on the theory of the novel in early German Romanticism on Friedrich Schlegel and Novalis is no limitation of the topic. In spite of his early essay "Etwas über William Shakespeare bei Gelegenheit Wilhelm Meisters" of 1796 and some reviews of contemporary novels in the Jenaische Allgemeine Literaturzeitung, August Wilhelm Schlegel never developed a coherent theory of the novel of his own. Since his Berlin lectures Ueber schöne Literatur und Kunst (1801-1804), even since his Jena lectures on Philosophische Kunstlehre (1798), but especially his Vienna lectures on Geschichte der dramatischen Kunst und Literatur (1808), he established himself as the most prominent theoretician of the drama, especially of tragedy. What August Wilhelm Schlegel says in his Berlin lectures about the epic, the romance, and the novel is not meant to be original, but intended, according to his own words, to summarize "alles Vernünftige und Gemässigte" of the doctrine of the Athenäum (Deutsche Literaturdenkmale, Vol. 17, p. LXIV). An examination of Tieck's writings and correspondence during the period of the early romantic school did not reveal material which would justify his appearance as a distinct theoretician of the novel in this study, nor do the writings of Schleiermacher, A. L. Hülsen, and the other members of what we consider the first romantic school in Germany. Nevertheless, observations on the novel by August Wilhelm Schlegel and Tieck have been dealt with in the introduction and at appropriate places in the text.

It is my particular pleasure to thank my colleagues William H. Rey, Raymond Immerwahr, and last but not least, Ernst Behler, for the inspirations they gave me while working on this monograph.

University of Washington

September, 1976   Diana I. Behler

TABLE OF CONTENTS

INTRODUCTION

Friedrich Schlegel and Novalis were the two leading critics of early German Romanticism for whom the novel was of special importance, even to the degree of constituting the epitome of what they projected in their literary theories. Schlegel's concept of the novel derives from his compilation of a comprehensive history of the epic genre, the novel representing the vehicle for modern expression. Although Schlegel saw forerunners of his projected ideal work in the past, he was not satisfied with former achievements, but utilized them as inspirations for sketching the blueprint of an "absolute novel", a universal work integrating various types of the novel with poetry in general to form a "mingled poem". The salient feature of this absolute novel is its outer comprehensiveness and encyclopedic character which achieves inner unity through the individuality of the author expressed in it. After having established such an all-encompassing ideal, however, Schlegel was to realize that the novel could not fulfill his expectations, and he soon shifted to other literary genres representing what he called "symbolic form". Yet for a crucial period of his life, more precisely, the period of the first romantic school (1796-1801) and the periodical Athenäum (1798-1800), the novel was for Schlegel the highest genre of literature, an ideal not achieved within his own time, but pointing to nineteenth and twentieth century literary manifestations.

Novalis has been unjustly viewed by critics as a representative of escape into flights of fantasy, an advocate of sheer poetic imagination having no basis in reality, and a subjective dreamer in the realm of infinity. Upon closer scrutiny, however, especially in light of recent critical text editions, Novalis' thoughts appear to be more complex and dualistic. Like Schlegel, he saw two central tendencies of the poetic drive, one towards universality and comprehensiveness and the other towards individuality and distinctiveness. Novalis envisioned the novel as that poetic totality capable of embracing philosophy and poetry, objectivity and subjectivity, universality and individuality, intellect and imagination. He too progressed beyond the confines of this genre and projected a fusion of the novel with the fairytale, an art form that was to penetrate a deeper sphere of reality and to achieve a greater synthesis of reality and ideality.

None of the romantic authors, however, actually carried out what was called for in the realm of the novel, especially if one regards the all-encompassing antitheses that are to be reconciled in this genre according to Aphorism 116 of the Athenäum. The task of the poetry of the novel ("Romanpoesie" equalling romantic poetry) was not only

Alle getrennte Gattungen der Poesie wieder zu vereinigen, und die
Poesie mit der Philosophie und Rhetorik in Berührung zu setzen.
Sie will, und soll auch Poesie und Prosa, Genialität und Kritik,
Kunstpoesie und Naturpoesie bald mischen, bald verschmelzen, die
Poesie lebendig und gesellig, und die Formen der Kunst mit gedie-
genem Bildungsstoff jeder Art anfüllen und sättigen, und durch die
Schwingungen des Humors beseelen. Sie umfasst alles, was nur poetisch
ist, vom grössten wieder mehre Systeme in sich enthaltenden
Systeme der Kunst, bis zu dem Seufzer, dem Kuss, den das dichtende
Kind aushaucht in kunstlosen Gesang. (1)

INTRODUCTION

This impression of a lack of fulfillment in the romantic age is intensified by a consideration of the manuscript sources from which the published aphorisms derive, in which the novel appears to be even more enormous in scope. Furthermore, no claim was made that any literary work of the time had satisfied the requirement of the task. With respect to the highly esteemed <u>Wilhelm Meister</u> of Goethe, Schlegel said:

> Ein vollkommener Roman müsste auch weit mehr romantisches Kunstwerk sein als <u>Wilhelm Meister</u>; moderner und antiker, philosophischer und ethischer und poetischer, politischer, liberaler, universeller, gesellschaftlicher. (2)

For these reasons, the main sources for my investigation are the theoretical reflections on the novel by the early romantics rather than their own creative endeavors in this genre, although these literary works can illuminate their postulates and will be taken as illustrations whenever this seems appropriate.

There are two further general considerations which have guided this presentation that require some introductory comments. The first concerns the notion of Romanticism as it is used in connection with the theory of the novel, and the second affects the use of the terms 'poetry' and 'prose' in this context. Since the novel is a work in prose, it is by no means self-evident that the novel should constitute the highest genre of poetry as it did for Friedrich Schlegel and Novalis during one period of their literary careers.

As to the general notion of Romanticism, this investigation takes the romantic demand for a fusion of philosophy and poetry literally by recognizing it as a call for both an intellectual <u>and</u> imaginative understanding of the world. In departing from the typical cliché of Romanticism, one realizes that Romanticism defies the simplistic definition of escape into the realm of imagination, transcendence, and chimeras that has long clouded its understanding and that it was fundamentally a very rational and sound endeavor. Recent scholarship has ventured into this new direction, and the results have brought about a significant change in our image of Romanticism, particularly that of the early theorists, such as the Schlegel brothers and Novalis. A shift of emphasis from the over-exaggerated fantastic sphere to the more rational and intellectual elements of this movement has indeed taken place. (3) Similarly, entrenched ideas about the relationship of Romanticism to Realism, according to which Romanticism is assumed to represent the polar contrast to Realism, require corrective revision through research.

A few examples can best illustrate the image of Romanticism that is reflected in my presentation. As evidence for the supposed opposition of Romanticism to Realism, the following aphorism by Novalis is often quoted: "Die Poesie ist das ächt absolut Reelle. Dies ist der Kern meiner Philosophie. Je poetischer, je wahrer." (4) Yet this conviction appears in another light, if one recognizes that Novalis' concept of poetry already constitutes a synthesis of both aspects of existence, the real and the ideal, the concrete and the imaginative. Indeed, this statement can easily be counterbalanced by others that emphasize the observative faculties of the poet and his contact with empirical reality, an aspect that will experience more detailed examination later. In one of his most famous fragments, Novalis said:

> Die Welt muss romantisiert werden. So findet man den ursprüng-
> lichen Sinn wieder. Romantisieren ist nichts, als eine qualitative
> Potenzierung. Das niedere Selbst wird mit einem besseren Selbst
> identifiziert. So wie wir selbst eine solche qualitative Potenzen-
> reihe sind. Diese Operation ist noch ganz unbekannt. Indem ich dem
> Gemeinen einen hohen Sinn, dem Gewöhnlichen ein geheimnisvolles
> Ansehen, dem Bekannten die Würde des Unbekannten, dem Endlichen
> einen unendlichen Schein gebe, so romantisiere ich es. (5)

The concluding part of this aphorism, however, depicts a movement directly opposite to that of romanticizing, and this interchangeability of directions assumes almost dialectical features:

> Umgekehrt ist die Operation für das Höhere, Unbekannte, Mysti-
> sche, Unendliche - dies wird durch diese Verknüpfung logarythmi-
> siert - Es bekommt einen geläufigen Ausdruck. romantische
> Philosophie.

The relativity and alternation of direction is clearly emphasized by the added phrase: "Wechselerhöhung und Erniedrigung." (6)

René Wellek considered Friedrich Schlegel as the first critic to apply the term "Realism" to literature. (7) Not only the illustrious instance in the "Rede über die Mythologie" where Schlegel prophesies the rise of a "neuer, ebenso grenzenloser Realismus" out of the lap of Idealism evidences this hypothesis, (8) but also numerous recently published aphorisms revealing his search for a higher "Indifferenzpunkt" (9) in which Realism and Idealism, "Realpoesie" and "Idealpoesie" merge together. Schlegel's Cologne lectures of 1804-1806 contain the perhaps most important and comprehensive discussion of Realism in the early nineteenth century. (10) To be sure, he did not visualize Realism as the observation of mere facts, but rather as a reality in which the Divine forms an integral part. The Schlegel brothers recognized that art in its essence is not mere naturalistic depiction of the real world, but is fundamentally a process by which nature is given shape. In his Berlin lectures on "Schöne Literatur und Kunst", August Wilhelm Schlegel said:

> Bei Natur denken sich viele nichts weiter, als das ohne Zutun mensch-
> licher Kunst Vorhandne. Wenn man nun zu diesem negativen Begriff
> der Natur, einen ebenso passiven von Nachahmen hinzufügt, so dass es
> ein blosses Nachmachen, Kopieren, Wiederholen bedeutet, so wäre die
> Kunst in der Tat ein brotloses Unternehmen. Man sieht nicht ein, da
> die Natur schon vorhanden ist, warum man sich quälen sollte, ein
> zweites jenem ganz ähnliches Exemplar von ihr in der Kunst zustande
> zu bringen, das für die Befriedigung unsers Geistes nichts voraus
> hätte, als etwa die Bequemlichkeit des Genusses [...] (11)

INTRODUCTION

Taking up this idea in his Vienna lectures on "Philosophie des Lebens", Friedrich Schlegel designates sculpture as the best example of this relationship between art and reality:

> Zum Beweise aber, dass es auch hier nicht die, wenngleich, noch so schwere und wundervolle Nachahmung der Wirklichkeit ist, welche das Ziel oder den Gegenstand und überhaupt das Prinzip dieser wie alle andern Kunst bildet, bleibt die Farbe mit allem ihrem Zauber, als zu täuschend und der Wirklichkeit zu nahe stehend, von der plastischen Kunst und ihrer körperlichen Darstellung ausgeschlossen, indem dadurch das künstlerische Ideal oder Götterbild, fast ebenso sehr wie durch eine mechanisch hervorgebrachte und nachgekünstelte Gliederbewegung, unfehlbar in eine Kinderpuppe verwandelt werden würde. Niemals also ist die Wirklichkeit und wirkliche Gestalt und ihre täuschende Nachahmung oder Nachbildung der eigentliche und nächste Zweck der bildenden Kunst; aber auch nicht immer ist die Schönheit der Form, wenigstens nicht allein und ausschliessend der einzige Zweck derselben; sondern nur bedingungsweise und mit Rücksicht auf die andern gegebenen Verhältnisse und Beziehungen des Ausdrucks, des Charakters, und der äussern Bestimmung und ganzen Bedeutung. Immer aber und überall ist es ein Gedanke, die Idee des Gegenstandes oder der Gestalt, als der innere Sinn und die innere Bedeutung desselben, worin das Wesentliche des Kunstwerkes besteht, und worauf die Kunst ausgeht; oder mit andern Worten, alle Kunst ist symbolisch. (12)

This interpenetration of the two realms is the heart of the romantic view of art and poetry.

With regard to the use of the terms poetry and prose in the context of the early romantic theory of the novel, I have taken the following considerations into account. Although the prose genres occupy a prominent position in the early romantic theory of literature, (13) originally they were not admitted to the domain of poetry, which like in classical "art poetique" embraced only the epic, lyric, and dramatic genres. The art of prose thus had a subordinated, secondary position from which it was not released until it gradually came to be evaluated as genuine poetry, one of the most essential developments in the formation of the early literary theory of German Romanticism and of prime concern for the evolving theory of the novel.

Reading the earliest treatises on literary theory of this movement, one has the impression that the superiority of poetry over prose was chiefly based on formalistic characteristics such as meter and rhythm. The early romantic definition of poetry thus strikes, at least at first glance, a surprisingly conservative note and appears to renounce the broad concept of poetry which had become prominent during the second half of the eighteenth century in Germany and France. According to this narrow concept of poetry, the novel could not really be considered as poetry, and indeed there was considerable hesitance and wavering among the early Romantics as to whether this essentially prosaic genre was entitled to the ennobling designation of poetry. In an article as late as 1808, Friedrich Schlegel depicted the historical origin of the novel thus:

Der Roman entstand ursprünglich bloss aus der Auflösung der
Poesie, da die Abfasser sowohl, als die Leser der Ritterbücher,
der metrischen Form müde, die Prosa bequemer fanden. Der
Inhalt blieb noch lange abenteuerlich, doch näherte auch er sich
immer mehr dem Prosaischen. (14)

Yet even during the earliest phase of the romantic literary theory, poetry
was not viewed as being entirely dependent on form. There are metric poetic productions such as didactic poems, which by nature are just as unpoetic as works of
prose. (15) On the other hand, the spirit of poetry was considered so universal and
pervasive that it could infiltrate the prose of the novel, and the poet often incorporated
his best poetic creations into the seemingly loose form of the novel just to demonstrate
that poetry was not bound to a particular external form or subject to any restriction.
(16) In the last analysis, there are two elements which determine the early romantic
concept of poetry, metrical form and inner spirit. Metrical form may even be relative,
secondary to inner spirit, perhaps constitute only "äusserer Schmuck der Poesie." (17)
As inner spirit, poetry is original and ineffable. (18) Yet poetry does not come into
existence by an expansion of prose towards the realm of poetry, but poetry exists
originally and independently. If poetry manifests itself in prose, then this is not because prose has risen to the level of poetry, but because poetry has permeated this
essentially unpoetic form of expression.

August Wilhelm Schlegel was the most outspoken representative of the strict
view of poetry, as is evident in his early studies, the Briefe über Poesie, Silbenmass
und Sprache of 1795, the essay Etwas über William Shakespeare bei Gelegenheit
Wilhelm Meisters of 1796, as well as in his review of Goethe's Hermann und Dorothea
of 1797. One can also include among these writings his posthumous Betrachtungen
über Metrik which because of their polemics against Klopstock's concept of poetry
form a parallel to his later dialogue Die Sprachen. Ein Gespräch über Klopstock's
grammatische Gespräche of 1798. (19). In all of these works, August Wilhelm Schlegel
opposes the unrestrained and exuberant notion of poetry as it had developed in the
movements of genius, Storm and Stress, and in the wake of Diderot's "Prinzip der
Natürlichkeit". He attempts to confine poetry again within a discipline, that of meter,
of "Silbenmass" and rejects "poetische Prosa". The poetic forms are for him
essential elements of poetry, and to abandon them would bring about the loss of
poetry itself. Answering the question "Ist das Silbenmass der Poesie wesentlich?",
he unequivocally maintains "dass der rhythmische Gang der Poesie dem Menschen
nicht weniger natürlich ist als sie selbst." (20)

A slight modification of this strict separation of poetry and prose in August
Wilhelm Schlegel's theory shows up when he turns to the genre of the novel. His
appreciation of the novel, however, is limited to a few masterpieces of the genre,
especially to Cervantes' Don Quixote, deemed "ein vollendetes Meisterwerk der
höheren romantischen Kunst," and Goethe's Wilhelm Meister, which appears to him
as a miracle among the "Hässlichkeit und Verworrenheit der gewöhnlichen Roman-
welt." (21) This transformation of August Wilhelm Schlegel's poetic doctrine, however, results from his broad historical evaluation of the epic genre and certainly
does not represent a break with his previous subordination of poetry to metric form.

Evidence for this view is provided by Schlegel's consideration of the epic,
especially the Homeric metric form ("Silbenmass"), as a bridge between epic poetry
and the prosaic novel, as he explains:

> Die Lehre vom epischen Rhythmus verdient eine genauere Ausein-
> andersetzung. Sie ist auch deswegen wichtig, weil sie Anwendung
> auf den Roman leidet. Ein Rhythmus der Erzählung, der sich zum
> epischen ungefähr so verhielte wie der oratorische Numerus zum
> Silbenmasse, wäre vielleicht das einzige Mittel, einen Roman nicht
> bloss nach der allgemeinen Anlage, sondern nach der Ausführung
> im einzelnen durchaus poetisch zu machen, obgleich die Schreibart
> rein prosaisch bleiben muss; und im Wilhelm Meister scheint dies
> wirklich ausgeführt zu sein. (22)

It is thus the "Prosarhythmus des Satzbaus" which entitles the novel to be considered
as poetic, examples of which are Cervantes' Don Quixote, but especially Goethe's
Meister.

August Wilhelm Schlegel's postulates provided the impetus for Novalis to re-
formulate the distinction between poetry and prose and to mediate between them in
their polar relationship, which he had originally established as strictly as August
Wilhelm Schlegel. "Poesie ist Poesie" he had said: "Von Rede- (Sprach)kunst
himmelweit verschieden." (23) In a letter of January 12, 1793, Novalis responded to
August Wilhelm Schlegel's review of Hermann und Dorothea, which had pleased him
because of its general views on "Bildung". He rejected, however, the concluding
remarks on Wilhelm Meister which established the epic "Rhythmus der Erzählung"
as a means "einen Roman nicht bloss nach der allgemeinen Anlage, sondern nach
der Ausführung im einzelnen durchaus poetisch zu machen, obgleich die Schreibart
rein prosaisch bleiben muss." With regard to such prose "die sich erweitern will
und der Poesie auf ihre Weise nachahmen," Novalis simply said: "Dennoch bleibt
sie Prosa - und also auf einen bestimmten Zweck gerichtet, beschränkte Rede-
Mittel." (24)

For Novalis, the mediation between prose and poetry was not the task of
prose, but rather of poetry. Whereas prose could not rise beyond itself to enter
the realm of poetry, poetry could usurp the sphere of prose and become "fähiger
zur Darstellung des Beschränkten." This expanded poetry ("erweiterte Poesie")
capable of absorbing prose was for Novalis "das höchste Problem des practischen
Dichters - ein Problem was nur durch Annäherung gelöst werden kann, und was zu
der höheren Poesie eigentlich gehört." (25)

These observations about the unification of poetry and prose already indicate
that they derive from Novalis' futuristic, eschatalogical, and messianic views,
according to which poetry and prose are opposite, but only in the first stage of
poetic formation. Novalis sees the coming of an age in which opposition develops into
mutual penetration, and only then shall we have true, achieved, and genuine poetry.
He muses:

Es wäre eine artige Frage, ob denn das lyrische Gedicht eigentlich
Gedicht, PlusPoësie, oder Prosa, Minuspoësie wäre? Wie man den
Roman für Prosa gehalten hat, so hat man das lyrische Gedicht für
Poësie gehalten - beydes mit Unrecht. Die höchste, eigentlichste
Prosa ist das lyrische Gedicht. (26)

He accentuates the re-evaluation of prose by the following speculation:

Die sogenannte Prosa ist aus Beschränckung der absoluten Extreme
entstanden. - Sie ist nur ad interim da und spielt eine subalterne,
temporelle Rolle. Es kommt eine Zeit, wo sie nicht mehr ist. Dann
ist aus der Beschränkung eine Durchdringung geworden. Ein wahr-
haftes Leben ist entstanden, und Prosa und Poësie sind dadurch auf
das innigste vereinigt, und in Wechsel gesetzt. (27)

This slow and hesitating overcoming of the subordination of prose to poetry
on the part of August Wilhelm Schlegel and Novalis was soon outpaced by an impetuous
and daring appreciation of the poetic possibilities of prose in the literary theory of
Friedrich Schlegel. In his literary views, Schlegel was strongly affected by classical
rhetoricans, especially by Dionysios of Halicarnassus whom he translated and
discussed in a publication for Wieland's Teutsches Museum of 1796 ("Kunsturteil des
Dionysios über den Isokrates" including a "Nachschrift des Uebersetzers"). Because
of this relationship Schlegel had no difficulty in recognizing a poetic character in
certain works of prose and appreciating what he called the "Kunst der schönen
Prosa". (28) Dionysios of Halicarnassus had paved the way for him by admitting that
Thucydides' historical prose works, the speeches by Isocrates, and Plato's dialogues
were poetry in the true sense. (29) As Schlegel emphasized, Dionysios said "dass die
Werke des Plato und Isokrates nicht wie geschriebene wären, sondern ausgehöhlter
und erhobner Bildnerarbeit glichen." Schlegel wanted to add "sie seien wie mit
Meissel und Feile hervorgetrieben und gerundet," and anticipating his brother's
analogy between the prosaic rhythm of Wilhelm Meister and the metrical numerus
of Homer, he commented:

Wie viel Betrachtungen kann es nicht allein erregen, dass die
Parisosen sich zum strengen Reim etwa so verhalten wie der
prosaische Numerus zum eigentlichen poetrischen Metrum, so
dass man die älteste hellenische Kunstprosa mit eben so viel
Recht gereimt, wie rhythmisch nennen könnte. (30)

In short, Schlegel recognized "wahre poetische Prosa" and "prosaische Poesie" from
the very beginning. He went so far as to say: "Alle Prosa ist poetisch [...] Sezt
man Prosa der Poesie durchaus entgegen, so ist nur die logische eigentliche Prosa."
Like Novalis he saw the full development of prose into poetry as a task of the future:
"Prosa ist derzeit noch nicht Kunst," he stated, but he believed to know how to
achieve this, commenting: "Was Prosa eigentlich sei, hat noch niemand gesagt." (31)

With regard to classical antiquity, Schlegel saw three prose genres capable of poetic qualities, i. e., history, rhetoric, and philosophy. The "poetische Kunstprosa" of the ancients found their correspondence, however, in the novel of the moderns, especially in Cervantes' Don Quixote, Boccaccio's Decamerone, and Goethe's Wilhelm Meister. "Der Roman ist die ursprünglichste, eigentümlichste, vollkommenste Form der romantischen Poesie," Schlegel said in his Paris lectures, and the prose of Cervantes was for him "die einzige moderne, die wir der Prosa eines Tacitus, Demosthenes oder Plato entgegenstellen können, eben weil sie so durchaus modern, wie jene antik und doch in ihrer Art ebenso kunstreich und aus-gebildet ist." This prose was for him "dem Roman, der die Musik des Lebens phantasieren soll [...] so eigentümlich angemessen wie die Prosa der Alten den Werken der Rhetorik und Historie."(32) In his notebooks he saw the principle of romantic prose as being identical to that of verse: "Symmetrie und Chaos, ganz nach der alten Rhetorik; im Boccaz diese beiden in Synthese sehr deutlich." Goethe's prose too was for him "rein poetische Poesie," and Wilhelm Meister "Poesie ohne Metrum". Yet this did not apply to all Moderns. Lessing was the exception. His Nathan was "metrische Prosa", but his writings were composed in "Konversationsprosa" and not in "grosse Kunstprosa".(33)

On the basis of these considerations, Schlegel never experienced the difficulty his brother and Novalis had to contend with, namely, to associate the novel with the beauty of poetry. Even such a prosaic business as literary criticism could very well rise to the heights of poetry for him, and in its last analysis had to, since according to Fragment 117 of the Lyceum: "Poesie kann nur durch Poesie kritisiert werden. Ein Kunsturteil, welches nicht selbst ein Kunstwerk ist [...] hat gar kein Bürger-recht im Reiche der Kunst."(34) The poetic quality of the novel, however, stems from its incorporating the two central elements of his concept of poetry, namely, rhetoric and music. The unity of the novel was for Schlegel a "musikalische und rhetorische," and he made rhetoric and music the essential elements of his definition of poetry: "Die Poesie ist eine unendliche Rhetorik und eine logische geistige Mu-sik."(35) Music was for him that art "die über das menschliche Herz eine über alles gehende Gewalt ausübt, das Gefühl in seinen verborgensten Tiefen mit unwidersteh-lichen Zwange ergreift, erhebt und veredelt, und so ihre bildende Kraft auf die Quelle und Wurzel alles Bewusstseins erstreckt." In another instance, he defined "logische Musik" as being analogous to mathematics, to arithmetic. Finally, by joining all these constituent parts together, Schlegel comes to the following concept of the novel:

Offenbar hat der Roman die ganze Form von Mathematik, Rhetorik und Musik. - Von Mathematik das Potenziren, Progression des Irrationalen, von Rhetorik die Figuren.

In order to emphasize the essentially poetic character of this genre, Schlegel adds: "Organon der Poesie."(36)

Only after the debate about the relationship between poetry and prose had thus been concluded, could the novel finally assume the eminent position of being the highest expression of poetry, at least for the period of the Athenäum according to the creed of two members of the early romantic school in Germany, namely, Friedrich Schlegel and Novalis.

PART ONE

FRIEDRICH SCHLEGEL

I. THE INTELLECTUAL BACKGROUND AND THE LITERARY DERIVATIONS OF FRIEDRICH SCHLEGEL'S THEORY OF THE NOVEL

In the latter years of the eighteenth century, a specific tendency among certain philosophers and critics in Germany can be noticed, a trend which led to the elevation of art and the artist, more specifically, of poetry and the poet, to the highest realm. This was not only to become the characteristic feature of the romantic movement, but it also permeated the intellectual atmosphere of a greater portion of the entire nineteenth century. The new emphasis has been interpreted as a reaction against the ideals of the Enlightenment and the deification of "le philosophe"(1), but also marks a decisive step beyond the preceding development of German philosophical thought of that period. Since Kant, the discipline of philosophy had been conceived of as having two major branches, theoretical and practical knowledge, whereby practical knowledge had been given distinct priority as is evidenced in the famous dictum of the "Primat der praktischen Vernunft". (2) Fichte had intensified this hierarchical evaluation by strongly emphasizing the ethical and moral attitudes toward the world. Since 1798 a predominantly aesthetic view comes into focus. In his private notebooks of the summer of 1798, a period of intimate communication, indeed communal life, among Fichte, Schelling, Novalis, and other members of the romantic circle in Dresden, Friedrich Schlegel remarked: "Dem Candide kann nur ein aesthetischer Optimismus entgegengesetzt werden; dass diese Welt die schönste sei." A bit later he continues:

> Die Schönheit liegt in der Art der Vorstellung und Anschauung und in der aesthetischen Ansicht der Welt sieht man wirklich alle Dinge in Gott. Die Aesthetik hat einen Mittelpunkt und der ist eben der - Menschheit, Schönheit, Kunst - goldnes Zeitalter ist das Centrum dieses Centrums. -(3)

We can hardly determine who of these authors actually initiated such thoughts. The inspiration for these reflections did not only derive from philosophical and theoretical meditations, but also from the more imaginative and poetic experience of the world, from Goethe's lyrics of nature, and last but not least, from a re-vivified communication with nature, as it was kindled by Herder and originated by Spinoza. (4) With regard to the new appreciation of the artist and the poet, one can refer to the theory of creative genius in the Storm and Stress movement, deriving from the writings of Shaftesbury, but in the last analysis, constituting the elements of ancient Platonic thought. (5)

Three authors in particular were responsible for elevating art and poetry to the highest level of human endeavor: Schelling, Friedrich Schlegel, and Novalis. The disentanglement of mutual influences among these three thinkers, who not only lived for a while in the same city and conversed frequently, but even dwelled under the same roof for certain periods of time, is indeed difficult. (6) Furthermore, the discovery of priorities in thought is especially complicated because of the situation concerning the texts, most of which have been transmitted to us in the form of manuscripts. Schelling's Philosophie der Kunst is available to us in the lectures of 1804-1805, edited only in 1859, and Novalis published very little of his work during his lifetime. Schlegel's aphorisms too remained primarily in manuscript form, and only a few were published in the Athenäum.

It can be taken for granted that Schelling took the decisive step in the philosophical domain by overcoming the distinction between theoretical and practical
knowledge in the culmination of aesthetics with the deification of the creative artist.
The most illuminating text in this context is to be found in the concluding passages
of his <u>System des transzendentalen Idealismus</u> of 1800, expressing a unique glorification of art and the artist. For Schelling, art is the sphere in which the Godly
itself makes its appearance and is "die einzige und ewige Offenbarung, die es gibt,
und dasjenige Wunder, das, wenn es auch nur einmal existiert hätte, uns von der
absoluten Realität jenes Höchsten überzeugen müsste."(7) However, in the same
degree to which art surpasses all intellectual activities of man, even religious experiences, so does the artist distinguish himself from other men and occupies, as
the vicar of the Divine, that extraordinary position that had hitherto been accorded
the priest. The artist appears in Schelling's presentation as the vessel of a super-
natural godly power, as the penetration of the Divine into our world. However
deliberate and intentional he might proceed in the creation of his work, he yet
appears to be "unter der Einwirkung einer Macht [...] die [...] ihn Dinge auszu-
sprechen oder darzustellen zwingt, die er selbst nicht vollständig durchsieht, und
deren Sinn unendlich ist." The artist discloses the ultimate meaning of the world;
he lifts the "unsichtbare Scheidewand" separating the real and the ideal spheres.(8)

Above all, it was Schelling's concern to demonstrate the superiority of art
above science and philosophy. He believed that the tasks of science and philosophy
do indeed coincide with that of art, yet while these two disciplines clumsily miss the
mark, art can master the attempt and reach the goal of a complete understanding
and presentation of the marvelous. Thus art becomes the model for science and
philosophy, or even more directly: "Wo die Kunst sei, soll die Wissenschaft erst
hinkommen."(9) Science and philosophy are to flow back together into that
common ocean out of which they first emerged. Since this transition cannot materialize
at once, however, Schelling postulates a medium, a "Mittelglied", permitting the
transformation of science and philosophy into art. This is the "new mythology" for
him, "nicht die Erfindung des einzelnen Dichters, sondern eines neuen, nur Einen
Dichter gleichsam vorstellenden Geschlechts", and he designates the creation of this
new mythology a "Problem, dessen Auflösung allein von den künftigen Schicksalen
der Welt und im weiteren Verlauf der Geschichte zu erwarten ist."(10)

As one easily realizes, Schelling formulates here ideas about art and the
artist which were on the agenda of the early romantic school and comprised an
essential aspect of the <u>Athenäum</u>. His <u>System des transzendentalen Idealismus</u>
was not to appear in print until 1800, but these concepts were fomenting among the
Romantics for some time prior to this date. In an intriguing footnote to his idea of a
new mythology, Schelling refers to a treatise on mythology which had been elaborated
by him several years earlier: "Die weitere Ausführung dieses Gedankens enthält eine
schon vor mehreren Jahren ausgearbeitete Abhandlung über Mythologie." (11) We are
perhaps not remiss in assuming that this early treatise on mythology can be detected
in a peculiar and much disputed fragment which was discovered only in 1917 and then
published under the title "Das älteste Systemprogramm des deutschen Idealismus".
Indeed, this enigmatic manuscript which was first attributed to Hegel, then to
Hölderlin, and is now generally considered Schelling's intellectual property, contains

the kernel of the enthusiastic concepts about art and the artist referred to at the beginning of this chapter. (12)

The part of the sketch that has been transmitted to us gives an interesting survey of the progression of German Idealism and the changing goals of this philosophical movement. In true Kantian manner, the author depicts a state of philosophy in which "die ganze Metaphysik künftig in die Moral fällt," and then describes in the Fichtean vein, the "einzig wahre und gedenkbare Schöpfung aus Nichts," namely, the emergence of the entire world out of a free and self-conscious being. Yet it is typical of Schelling to express the desire to give wings to "unsrer langsamen an Experimenten mühsam schreitenden Physik." The highest goal envisioned by Schelling is definitely the idea of beauty:

> Zuletzt die Idee, die alle vereinigt, die Idee der Schönheit, das Wort in höherem platonischem Sine genomen. Ich bin nun überzeugt, dass der höchste Akt der Vernunft, der, indem sie alle Ideen umfast, ein ästhetischer Akt ist, und dass Wahrheit und Güte, nur in der Schönheit verschwistert sind." (13)

This ideal of beauty forms the basis for this thinker's high estimation of poetry, which is indeed conceived of as the most sublime activity of man: "Die Poësie bekomt dadurch e[ine] höhere Würde, sie wird am Ende wieder, was sie am Anfang war - Lehrerin der ‹Geschichte› Menschheit; denn es gibt keine Philosophie, keine Geschichte mehr, die Dichtkunst allein wird alle übrigen Wissenschaften u. Künste überleben." (14) This fragment also constitutes the first sketch of the idea of a new mythology: "Zuerst werde ich hier von einer Idee sprechen, die soviel ich weiss, noch in keines Menschen Sin gekomen ist--wir müssen eine neue Mythologie haben, diese Mythologie aber muss im Dienste der Ideen stehen, sie mus e[ine] Mythologie der Vernunft werden." (15) Schelling's new mythology, however, embraces both aesthetic and philosophical aspects and in his opinion thereby constitutes religion:

> Ehe wir die Ideen ästhetisch, d. h. mythologisch machen, haben sie für das Volk kein Interesse; und umgekehrt, ehe die Mythologie vernünftig ist, muss sich der Philosoph ihrer schämen. So müssen endlich Aufgeklärte und Unaufgeklärte sich die Hand reichen, die Mythologie muss philosophisch werden, und das Volk vernünftig, und die Philosophie muss mythologisch werden, um die Philosophen sinnlich zu machen. Dann herrscht ewige Einheit unter uns [...] Ein höherer Geist vom Himmel gesandt, muss diese neue Religion unter uns stiften, sie wird das letzte, grösste Werk der Menschheit sein. (16)

This programmatical system not only projects the blueprint of Schelling's intellectual development from his philosophy of nature to his philosophy of art, but also anticipates central ideas of romantic poetics and aesthetics of the Athenäum. Three major topics in particular come to mind in this respect: the famous romantic postulate of a fusion of philosophy and poetry; the assumption that this fusion leads to a new mythology; and finally, the belief that the new mythology constitutes the core of a new religion to be expressed in poetry. (17) These ideas were cherished by Friedrich Schlegel and Novalis who even intensified them to such a degree that they were to find expression in the postulates of the poet-priest and the project of creating a new Bible. Such expectations place the highest demand on poetry and literature, and interestingly enough, these ideas are pertinent to the romantic theory of the novel, now envisioned as the literary vehicle for the new religion: "Als Roman wird die neue Bibel kommen," Schlegel said, and considering the absolute character of the novel, he observed: "Der Roman ist offenbar absolutes System, ein Buch im höchsten Sinne." (18)

During the romantic era, the opinion was widespread that the novel enjoyed a particularly eminent position within the genres of poetry. The stimulus for this emphasis on the novel can certainly be traced back to Friedrich von Blanckenburg's "Versuch über den Roman"(19), but finds perhaps a more plausible explanation in the seventh and eighth sections of Herder's Briefe zur Beförderung der Humanität which Schlegel read and reviewed.(20) The predominance of the novel is not less conspicuous in Herder's earlier work: Ueber die Wirkung der Dichtkunst auf die Sitten der Völker of 1778, in the third section of which two basic forms of the modern novel are distinguished, the one idealistic, in the vein of Richardson, and the other realistic and "true to nature" developed by Fielding.(21) The actual flourishing of the novel as a favored genre was to come about in the romantic age, however, and can be detected in Schelling's Philosophie der Kunst of 1802-03, in August Wilhelm Schlegel's aesthetic writings, and most significantly in Jean Paul's Vorschule der Aesthetik of 1804.(22) Just as the first section of this book centers in "humoristische Dichtkunst" (7th Program), the second section culminates in a discussion about the novel. Repercussions of Jean Paul's extensive discussion of the novel can still be found in the third chapter of Hegel's Aesthetik where the novel, just like the epic, requires "die Totalität einer Welt- und Lebensanschauung, deren vielseitiger Stoff und Gehalt innerhalb der individuellen Begebenheit zum Vorschein kommt."(23) Since the necessary prerequisites from which the classical epic arose, "der breite Hintergrund einer totalen Welt", are lacking for the modern novel, however, this philosopher thinks little of the novel in comparison to the classical epic and concedes tragedy the highest place among the modern poetic arts. Thus with Hegel, we are at the turning point in the history of the theory of the novel, a critical juncture that paves the way for the future and also brings the previous chapter of German aesthetics to a close. These aspects can be illuminated through Georg Lukács and Arthur Schopenhauer.

When Georg Lukács states in his early work Die Theorie des Romans: "die grosse Epik gestaltet die extensive Totalität der Lebensverhältnisse",(24) he seems to share Hegel's predilection for "Totalität einer Welt und Lebensanschauung" upon which the classical epic was founded and which the modern novel lacks. However, he departs from his master by conceiving of the novel as a form of "grosse Epik", although he would admit to him that for the modern world "die extensive Totalität des Lebens nicht mehr sinnfällig gegeben ist", that for us the essential meaning of life has become problematical. Yet there is still a predilection for totality, and it is essentially the novel that seeks a closed system of life: "der Roman sucht gestaltend die verborgene Totalität des Lebens aufzudecken und aufzubauen." (25) To be sure, it cannot achieve this goal without some cracks and flaws, crevices that can only be bridged by irony, but precisely this characteristic indicates why Lukács considered romantic irony in a world without God as the only possible foundation for a genuine and total creation, a creation to be achieved in the novel. (26) In other words, Lukács carries the romantic ideal of the novel into the future, even through Hegel's barriers, but it is also true that Hegel brought the reign of the romantic novel to an end, an actuality that can be demonstrated by his great opponent Schopenhauer. In Schopenhauer's hierarchy of aesthetic values, music attains the highest prize, residing far above the poetic ideal of the Romantics. The novel is only one genre among the forms of objective poetic creation, along with epos and drama, and even here, it does not find too prominent a place: "Als der Gipfel der Dichtkunst, sowohl in Hinsicht auf die Grösse der Wirkung, als auf die Schwierigkeit der Leistung, ist das Trauerspiel anzusehen und ist dafür anerkannt." (27) This quotation is taken from the first edition of the original version of Die Welt als Wille und Vorstellung of 1818. Within the two decades from the end of the eighteenth century to the beginning of Schopenhauer's rise, the romantic novel had worn out its glamour, although its ideal was later to be revivified.

During the period of the reign of the novel as a theoretical ideal, there was surely no author who had contributed more to its flourishing than the young Friedrich Schlegel. In his early characterizations of Homer's epics, Schlegel had already emphasized a feature that the Hegelian and Marxist critics later called the "extensive Totalität des Lebens", when he mentioned that Homer's poetry contained "zwar keine systematische Enzyklopädie, aber doch eine sehr umfassende und reichhaltige Ansicht der hellenischen Welt jener Zeit." (28) But within this classical framework, Schlegel also observed more modern, subjective features which are clearly indicative of his later theory of the novel, and in a more contemporary understanding, even of modern film techniques. Surprisingly enough, Schlegel speaks of the "sinnliche Einheit" of the epic, the distinction between "epische Harmonie" and "dramatische Vollendung", of a "fliessendes Gemälde", the unlimited scope, the striving for "Fülle und sinnliche Harmonie" without a beginning or an end, but having the beginning in the middle. (29) Furthermore, he stresses the "grenzenlose Aussicht", the "Erwartung ins Unendliche", the "epischer Strom", as well as the incitements of the marvelous and the adventuresome. (30) With these insights on the basis of Homer, Schlegel was already close to the idea of the "romance" in its medieval expression, and here we are certainly at the incipience of his forthcoming concept of the novel. Further inspirations for his later idea of the novel can be seen in Vergil's Aeneid, which appeared to him as an "Urbild der verhältnismässig besten Mischung der römischen Kultur und der hellenischen Bildung", altogether not as a "reines, echtes Epos": "Das Rhetorische und Tragische hat man im Ganzen und im Einzelnen oft bemerkt, und die lyrischen Stellen bieten sich auch sichtbar und zahlreich genug dar." (31) In addition, the Aeneid is praised as the national poem of the Romans--an attribute later to be bestowed upon novels. (32) Yet the most interesting aspect of these detections of classical patterns for the medieval romance is that almost a century before Erwin Rohde's Der Griechische Roman, Schlegel discovered the romances of Achilles Tatius, Chariton, Heliodorus, Longus, and Xenophon of Ephesus as precursors to the romantic novels. (33) Since the second century A. D., these authors created romantic compositions in prose, but the fragments show that this literary form originated at an earlier date. Presumably, the romantic novel was developed from their semi-historical, semi-mythical accounts of legendary heroes and famous men, such as Alexander the Great. All of these novels, including the Daphnis and Chloe of Longus, show similarities of content and style: a young man and his bride are tested with respect to moral rectitude and physical courage by a prolonged series of adventures, and during their wanderings across many lands they encounter friends and enemies, stock characters having little individuality. The elements of these adventures consist in love, excitement, descriptions of battles, and compelling moments of truth. (34) Also among the Romans, Schlegel found antecedents to the medieval romance, although there was no continuous tradition of prose fiction in this literature. Some authors, however, under the influence of the Greeks, developed character sketches, and Petronius wrote a novel utilizing a mixture of prose and verse recounting the adventure of three disreputable young men. And then there was Apuleius' Golden Ass. (35) One can safely assume that Schlegel, through his extensive studies in preparation for his book Geschichte der Poesie der Griechen und Römer, was acquainted with these sources.

Raymond Immerwahr directed attention to Schlegel's dependence on the English concept of romance as it derived from actual romances of various European literatures. (36) Schlegel was well acquainted with Geoffrey Chaucer and what he called die "Altenglische Literatur." (37) The old French inspirations of his idea of the novel, although somewhat late in occurrence and not so conspicuous at the beginning, are most clearly manifested in a letter to August Wilhelm Schlegel of January 15, 1803, in answer to his brother's request for a report on old "Roman-manuskripte" in the French national library:

> Der Reichtum ist so gross, dass ich nicht recht einsehe, wie Du
> diese Schätze nutzen könntest, ohne selbst herzukommen. Nur
> allein auf der Nationalbibliothek ist der Vorrat sehr gross. Romane
> vom Tristan und die von Lanzelot öfter als ich notiert habe, von je-
> dem leicht ein 6 etwa. Ich setze Dir bloss den Titel des Tristan her,
> der mir der älteste scheint, d. h. nach dem Titel, wegen des Zu-
> satzes traduit du latin nro. 6776. LE ROMAN DE TRISTAN DE
> LATIN PAR LE Sr LUCES DU CHATEL DU GATS. - Der PERCE-
> FOREST (doch wohl Parcival?) kommt fast ebenso oft vor. Dann
> noch Roman de Joseph d'arimathie (von der Stiftung des Graals)
> Roman d'artus - des chevaliers de la table ronde - de la destruction
> de la table ronde - Roman de Merlin - Roman de Meliadus - Histoire
> de St Graal jusqu'à la mort de Lancelot et d'Artus - Roman de
> Genevre - Roman de Giron - d'Agravains - Bans et Beors - Barans -
> Berinus. - Ob der Otiurl zu dieser Fabel gehört, wirst Du besser
> wissen als ich; den Titurel habe ich unter diesem Namen noch nicht
> gefunden. Nun nimm noch dazu, dass die Kataloge alle sehr schlecht
> sind; nichts ist gewöhnlicher als die Anzeige - plusieurs Romans en
> rime - Deux Romans tres anciens [...] (38)

Another important source for Schlegel's projection of the novel is to be found in Spanish "Ritterbücher", and among them, there is none that granted more inspiration than the Amadis novel, the first modern version of which was published in 1508 by Garci Ordoñez de Montalvo, but which Schlegel claims to have known in an earlier medieval form. (39) Still in his later lectures on world literature, he says about the chivalric novels of the Spaniards:

> Ihre Ritterbücher von meist selbst erfundenem Inhalt, der den
> übrigen Nationen fremder blieb, zeichneten sich aus, wenigstens
> das älteste und bekannteste derselben, der Amadis, durch eine
> gebildetere und schöne Schreibart und durch den vorherrschenden
> Hang zu sanften und idyllischen Darstellungen. (40)

With regard to the novels of the Spaniards, Schlegel also emphasized the pastoral genre: "an die Ritterbücher schloss sich schon früh bei den Spaniern und Portugiesen, der Schäferroman als eine beliebte Gattung an." But one is certainly not far afield in assuming that among all these national sources--Greek, Latin, Old English, Old French, Spanish, and Portuguese--there was none so influential as Boccaccio among the Italians and Cervantes among the Spaniards.

To be sure, for Schlegel, Dante will always be the "heilige Stifter und Vater der modernen Poesie,"(41) but Boccaccio is the author whose "Verstand eine unversiegbare Quelle merkwürdiger, meistens wahrer und sehr gründlich ausgearbeiteter Geschichten für die Dichter jeder Nation stiftete und durch kraftvollen Ausdruck und grossen Periodenbau die Erzählungssprache der Konversation zu einer soliden Grundlage für die Prosa des Romans erhob."(42) From the modern vantage point, one might object to calling Boccaccio a novelist, and even if we remain within the sphere of Germanics, Schlegel's discussions of Boccaccio have gained recognition as contributions to the theory of the "Novelle" rather than to the "Roman", as in the recent studies of Benno von Wiese and K. K. Polheim.(43) However, there are some features in Schlegel's characterization of Boccaccio that transcend the limitations of this narrower genre and go beyond into the realm of the novel, and the first is certainly what Schlegel terms as Boccaccio's "Kunst des Erzählens". (44) If this talent is related to the "Novelle", then Schlegel would answer: "Die älteste Form für den ProsaRoman ein System von Novellen," or "Die systematische Form des Romans eine Kette von Novellen, die wie Theorema, Aporema, Problema auf einander folgt."(45) Yet the accent on "Kunst des Erzählens" leads to a further result that brings us into a closer correlation with the novel proper.

At first glance the "Novelle" is for Schlegel "eine Anekdote, eine noch unbekannte Geschichte, so erzählt, wie man sie in Gesellschaft erzählen würde, eine Geschichte, die an und für sich schon einzeln interessieren können muss [...] die streng genommen, nicht zur Geschichte gehört, und die Anlage zur Ironie schon in der Geburtsstunde mit auf die Welt bringt."(46) In this subjective mood resides the magic and divine beauty of the "Novelle". However, the native essence of this genre as an art of narration can be augmented, in that the narrator "bekannte Geschichten durch die Art, wie er sie erzählt und vielleicht umbildet, in neue zu verwandeln scheint." This leads to a subjective emergence of the author, and this to such a

degree that we become interested in his fate. "Man isoliere diese natürliche Eigen-
art der Novelle," Schlegel continues, "man gebe ihr die höchste Kraft und Ausbildung,
und so entsteht jene oben erwähnte Art derselben, die ich die allegorische nennen
möchte, und die wenigstens, mag man sie so oder anders bezeichnen wollen, sich
immer als Gipfel und die eigentliche Blüte der ganzen Gattung bewähren wird."(47)
Here we see a clear indication of what later is to become the poetic reflection of the
author within his work, so essential to Schlegel's theory of the novel. Accordingly,
he says with respect to Boccaccio and transgressing the distinctions between "Novelle" and novel: "Die wichtigsten Arbeiten dieses Dichters bleiben sonach seine
Romane."(48)

If Boccaccio has this indirect relation to Schlegel's concept of the novel, then
his true master in this poetic form was Cervantes, whom he calls "unter allen Ro-
mandichtern der tiefsinnigste, erfindungsreichste, künstlichste."(49) Schlegel goes
so far as to consider Cervantes' prose "die einzige moderne, die wir der Prosa eines
Tacitus, Demosthenes, oder Plato entgegenstellen können, eben weil sie so durchaus
modern wie jene antik und doch in ihrer Art ebenso kunstreich ausgebildet ist."(50)
But as has been noted before, the excellence of the romantic novel according to
Schlegel does not consist merely in prose, but also in the intermingling of various
styles, especially that of lyrics, and Cervantes is exemplary in his integration of the
lyrical, especially "in dem Witzigen, Farbigen, Musikalischen, wozu man noch das
Altertümliche, höchst Einfache, Naive, Strenge, Kindliche rechnen kann." By virtue
of this lyrical component, his prose is "ganz Symmetrie und Musik, keine andere
betrachtet die Verschiedenheiten des Stils so ganz wie Massen von Farbe und Licht,
keine ist in allgemeinen Ausdrücken der geselligen Bildung so frisch, so lebendig
und darstellend:

> Immer edel und immer zierlich bildet sie bald den schärfsten Scharf-
> sinn bis zur äussersten Spitze und verirrt sich bald in kindlich süsse
> Träumereien. Darum ist auch die spanische Prosa - versteht sich jene
> des Cervantes - dem Roman, der die Musik des Lebens phantasieren
> soll, und verwandten Kunstarten so eigentümlich angemessen wie die
> Prosa der Alten den Werken der Rhetorik und Historie.(51)

Schlegel also emphasizes the artistry and deliberation in the composition of
Cervantes' novelistic works, among which he stresses Galatea: "ein grosser, sehr
reich und künstlich zusammengesetzter musikalischer Schäferroman," "Don Quijote,
eines der allergründlichsten, tiefsten Produkte des Witzes und der Parodie" which
counts among the "vollendetste Meisterwerke der höheren romantischen Kunst in jeder
Hinsicht;" and Persiles, a work devoted to the higher religious feeling as Don Quixote
to wit and Galatea to love.(52) Schlegel was especially well qualified to analyze and
evaluate Cervantes so positively. His occupation with this author dates back to 1797,
when the Berlin publishing house Unger asked him translate the Don Quixote into
German, and Schlegel responded most affirmatively to this request, since as he put
it "die Uebersetzung klassischer Prosa und Romankunst schon sehr mein Augenmerk
sind und noch immer sein werden."(53) At this time he devoted much study to this
novel, the translation of which was finally abandoned because he reverted to the
classical authors, in whose works he again lived and breathed--and certainly also

because of the verses that had to be translated. (54) This project was then taken over and carried out by Ludwig Tieck in his illustrious romantic translation of Cervantes' novel: Leben und Taten des scharfsinnigen Edlen Don Quijote von La Mancha, Berlin 1799-1801"--four volumes of incomparable translation which accompanied Thomas Mann on his voyage to the new world after he was exiled from Germany and inspired him to his essay "Meerfahrt mit 'Don Quijote'."

Although the topic of this investigation is not a comparison of Thomas Mann with the Romantics, it is hardly possible to resist enumerating some observations made by Mann which are so close to the romantic understanding of Don Quixote. Mann notes the humoristic style of the work which again induces him to consider the humorous as "das Wesenselement des Epischen."(55) He recognizes that a "Volks- und Menschheitsbuch" eventually evolves from the modest concept of a gay open satire of which the poet might not have thought too highly initially. (56) Furthermore, Mann is amused by Cervantes' epic wit, but also realizes that his essence is "romantische Vexation, ironische Magie."(57) As the author of the Joseph-tetralogy, especially of that scene where Joseph, Jaakob's son, sits in the moonlight next to the well, so that the reader visualizes "die leibhaftige Gegenwart" of a person about whom millenia have drawn their images, Mann could not have failed to notice certain narrative parallels. He takes special delight when in the second part Don Quixote and his squire step out of the sphere of reality in which they have lived so far, namely, the novel, and enter the "potenzierte Wirklichkeit" of real life. Ironically, the narrated world of the printed page has a more realistic appearance than so-called "real life", causing Mann to comment:

Das sind Volten, recht nach E. T. A. Hoffmanns Sinn, wie man denn überhaupt wohl sieht, woher die Romantiker es haben. Sie waren nicht gerade die grössten Künstler, aber sie haben am geistreichsten nach- gedacht über die witzigen Tiefen und Spiegel-Unergründlichkeiten der Kunst und des Illusionären, und eben weil sie Künstler mit und über der Kunst waren, lag ihnen die ironische Auflösung der Form so gefähr- lich nahe. Es ist gut, sich bewusst zu halten, dass diese Gefahr mit jeder kunsthumoristischen Verwirklichungstechnik nahe beisammenwohnt. (58)

But perhaps even more interesting than these skeptical remarks about the romantic art of the illusionary is Mann's identification with this technique and the ensuing self-critical comment: "Ich will hoffen, dass der Humor solcher realisieren- den Gelegenheitsmacherei sich noch im ehrbar Kunstbewahrenden hält."(59) He perceives a parodistic tendency not too far from his own technique when he says: "Cervantes fällt aus der Rolle mit jenen Schäfergeschichten, als wollte er zeigen, dass er das, was die Zeit kann, auch noch kann, ja es sogar wie ein Meister be- herrscht." As the author of the Zauberberg , he recognizes the "symbolisch- menschliche Rang der Figur des Helden," and in the change of perspectives ("Wech- sel der Optik") on the part of the narrator between the ludicrous and the serious, he sees "eine weitgehende Solidarisierung des Autors mit seinem Helden, die Neigung, dessen geistigen Rang dem eigenen anzugleichen, ihn zum Mundstück eigener Ge- sinnungen und Meinungen zu machen [...]"(60) This solidarity between the author

and his hero finds expression in the invention of "lächerlich-kläglichste Demüti-
gungen für ihn und seine Hochherzigkeit, in komischen Erniedrigungsphantasien"--
humilities that Hans Castorp also has to suffer. In a typically Nietzschean twist,
Mann asks:

> Und doch liebt und ehrt ihn sein Dichter. Sieht sie nicht nach
> Kasteiung, nach Selbstverhöhnung und Selbstzüchtigung aus, all
> diese Grausamkeit? Ja, mir kommt vor, als gäbe hier einer seinen
> oft geschändeten Glauben an die Idee, an den Menschen und seine
> Veredelung dem Gelächter preis, und dieses bittere Sich-ins-
> Einvernehmen-Setzen mit der gemeinen Wirklichkeit sei eigentlich
> die Definition des Humors. (61)

If these observations on the artistry and levels of narration in Don Quixote
form a close contact with the romantic idea of the novel, then Mann coincides with
Schlegel in his historical derivation of the romantic novel from the "spätantiker
Roman". Just as this romantic critic referred to the early form of the romance
presented to us by Erwin Rohde, Thomas Mann noted:

> Nun weiss ich aber von Erwin Rohde und aus dem vorzüglichen Buch,
> das der Mythologe und Religionshistoriker Karl Kerényi in Budapest
> über den griechisch-orientalischen Roman geschrieben hat, dass die
> Fabulierer des späten Altertums solche Szenen ausserordentlich
> liebten." (62)

Friedrich Schlegel's brief remarks on the late hellenistic and Latin novels seemed
to reveal a new source of inspiration for the romantic concept of the novel, but
Thomas Mann's reference to Erwin Rohde and to the Jungian scholar Kerényi in-
tensifies these relationships. Another link joining Cervantes, the Romantics, and
Mann is Mann's recognition of Cervantes as the prototype of the artist, the
"artista" in the Italian meaning, comprising the artist and the artisan. Such a
writer accomplishes something concrete in contrast to the genius, the creative ego
of the late nineteenth century's cult of genius ridiculed by Hofmannsthal as "kranker
Adler". "Gewiss, das ist es," Mann says: "Die Künstler sind kranke Adler geworden durch den Verfeierlichungsprozess, den die Kunst weither durchgemacht." (63)
Schlegel held the same opinion of the "artista", even to the point of making it the
motif of his Gespräch über die Poesie. (64)

If on the basis of these varied sources and without poetic definitions as to
style and structure, one would try to condense Schlegel's concept of the novel to a
central underlying feature, this would most likely be the adventuresome and
fantastic narrative depiction of the marvelous. In fact, in his retrospective
description of 1812, he said about the novel:

> Immer strebt die Darstellung, so lang sie noch Darstellung bleibt
> und nicht bloss in ein Gedankenspiel der Laune, des Witzes und des
> Gefühls sich auflöst, auf irgendeine Weise, aus der beengenden

Wirklichkeit sich herauszuarbeiten und irgendeine Oeffnung, einen
Eingang zu gewinnen in ein Gebiet, wo die Phantasie sich freier bewegen kann; wären es auch nur Reiseabenteuer, Zweikämpfe, Ent-
führungen, eine Räuberbande oder die Ereignisse und Verhältnisse
einer fahrenden Schauspielergesellschaft. (65)

This is a presentation of the positive conditions for the production of the
novel. On the basis of our present experience of life, a negative condition could be
imagined under which this freedom of love, adventure, and the magical would be
suffocated and the romantic novel thus become an impossibility--some Hitler, some
Stalin, a "big brother" watching over you and making every imaginative and fantastic
drive impossible. Amazingly enough, Schlegel conceived of this eventuality, since
he had only to think of Fichte's "geschlossener Handelsstaat", a social and political
condition which would have denied Romanticism its very existence or at least considered it "polizeiwidrig". This interesting confrontation is set forth in Schlegel's
Vienna lectures on world literature:

Ich erinnere mich hierbei der Aeusserung eines berühmten Denkers,
welcher der Meinung war, dass bei einer durchaus vollkommen
Polizei, wenn der Handelsstaat völlig geschlossen und selbst der
Pass der Reisenden mit einer ausführlichen Biographie und einem treuen
Portraitgemälde versehen sein wird, ein Roman schlechtweg unmöglich
sein würde, weil alsdann gar nichts im wirklichen Leben vorkommen
könnte, was dazu irgend Veranlassung oder einen wahrscheinlichen Stoff
darbieten würde. (66)

II. "EIN ROMAN IST EIN ROMANTISCHES BUCH"

This significant result of these wide-ranging studies into the history of the novel, or "romance", is that Schlegel eventually assigned to the novel the most prominent place among all genres of modern literature. "Die Romane sind die Sokratischen Dialoge unserer Zeit," he says in Aphorism 26 of the Lyceum, having previously stated: "Drei herrschende Dichtarten: 1) Tragödie bei den Griechen, 2) Satire bei den Römern, 3) Roman bei den Modernen."(1) In his Gespräch über die Poesie he reduces these categories to two basic epochs of western literature: "Wie unsere Dichtkunst mit dem Roman, so fing die der Griechen mit dem Epos an und löste sich wieder darin auf."(2)

Here it should be noted that Schlegel distinguished two periods of European literature, Classicism and Romanticism, Antiquity and Modernity, and separated them to such an extent that he applied a different philosophy of history to each, as Lovejoy has already noticed.(3) Whereas Classicism exemplifies Herder's organic view of a cyclical, closed-circuit movement, the modern age is marked by Kant's ideal of an infinite progression towards a goal which can only be reached by way of approximation. From a more aesthetic vantage point, this subdivision of western literature essentially means that the classical genres are organic and natural, in that they grow, develop, and then die out, always remaining pure and untainted. In contrast, the modern genres are artificial and have no organic or natural basis.(4) They are indeed deliberate mixtures of the various forms developed by the ancient poets, the novel in its romantic formulation "Mischgedicht" presenting a perfect illustration. Building on this assumption, Schlegel can say: "Die griechische Natur-poesie ist das Epos, die moderne der Roman."(5) Yet the previous quotations indicate that he also liked to compress the essence of classical literature into tragedy. If Schlegel wavered in a predilection for either the epic or tragedy with regard to classical Antiquity, however, he did not vacillate with respect to the basic form of modern literature, at least not until 1800, and thought of the novel as comprising its essence. Thus just as Aristotle in his Poetics is revealed as the doctrinaire of classical literature in the forms of the epic and tragedy, Friedrich Schlegel is the theoretician of modern literature in the form of the novel. For him, everything truly modern in literature had a novelistic touch.

This idea was so provocative that Schlegel advocated abolishing the distinction between the historical category "romantic" and the genre specification of the novel: "Es muss ihnen nach meiner Ansicht einleuchtend sein, dass und warum ich fordere, alle Poesie solle romantisch sein; den Roman aber, insofern er eine besondre Gatting sein will, verabscheue."(6) Thus everything modern is of necessity "roman-artig". But what about the drama? What about lyric poetry? Here too, Schlegel provides an answer:

Dies abgerechnet, findet sonst so wenig ein Gegensatz zwischen dem Drama und dem Roman statt, dass vielmehr das Drama so gründlich und historisch wie es Shakespeare z. B. nimmt und behandelt, die wahre Grundlage des Romans ist. Sie behaupten zwar, der Roman habe am meisten Verwandtschaft mit der erzählenden ja mit der epischen Gattung. Dagegen erinnre ich nun erstlich, dass ein Lied ebenso gut romantisch sein kann als eine Geschichte. Ja ich kann mir einen

Roman kaum anders denken, als gemischt aus Erzählung Gesang
und andern Formen. Anders hat Cervantes nie gedichtet, und selbst
der sonst so prosaische Boccaccio schmückt seine Sammlung mit
einer Einfassung von Liedern. Gibt es einen Roman, in dem dies
nicht stattfindet und nicht stattfinden kann, so liegt es nur in der
Individualität des Werks, nicht im Charakter der Gattung; sondern
es ist schon eine Ausnahme von diesem. Doch das ist nur vor-
läufig. (7)

However, this equation of "romantisch" and "romanartig", of "romantische Poesie"
and "Romanpoesie", has to be taken with a grain of salt and is certainly too
succinct a formula for Schlegel's endeavors. The complexities of these terms
will be discussed in the next chapter. For the purpose of the present discussion,
one can perhaps accept this formula with one qualification. The equation of "romantisch" and "romanartig" is only valid if one keeps in mind that Schlegel had actually
two concepts of "romanartig", one in the broader sense and equal to "romantisch",
the other with a narrower meaning and referring to the novel as a genre.

The startling idea that Shakespeare's dramas, as essential expressions of
the modern spirit of literature, are actually "romanartig" gains in credibility if
one looks at other interpretations of Shakespeare by Schlegel. The following remark
can certainly be expected from his early period: "Das Maximum von politischem
Roman sind Shakspeare's historische Stücke alle zusammengenommen. Im Politischen
Roman der Geist der Nazion dargestellt. Ein Held, Eine Handlung demselben nicht
wesentlich." (8) Yet similar views can still be detected in the Vienna lectures on
literature of 1812, although he now prefers the concept "episches Gedicht" for
reasons to be explained later:

Die Stelle, wo er am meisten mit den übrigen Menschen zusammen-
hing, war das Gefühl für seine Nation, deren glorreiche Heldenzeit
in den Kriegen gegen Frankreich er aus den treuherzigen alten
Chroniken in eine Reihe dramatischer Gedichte übertrug, welche
durch das darin herrschende Ruhm- und Nationalgefühl sich dem
epischen Gedicht nähern. (9)

This image of Shakespeare as a novelist or "epischer Dichter" is again Schlegel's
focal point in his journal Deutsches Museum of 1812-1813: "Die Reihe der historischen Schauspiele [...] ist fast ein episches Gedicht zu nennen und überschreitet
auf jeden Fall, wie der Dichter es selbst hie und da fühlt und zugibt, die engen
Grenzen der Bühne." (10) These references to Shakespeare were chosen to exhibit
just how far Schlegel extended the dominion of the novel--for what could be
ostensibly more remote from it than the drama? Yet countless other aphorisms from
Schlegel's pen refer to other modern writers and modern genres, all viewed as being
"romanartig" just because they are modern. Not even the lyric verse of Petrarch is
excluded: "Petrarcha's Gedichte sind classische Fragmente eines Romans" (11)--not
such an eccentric notion, if one remembers that Goethe conceived of his early poems
as "Fragmente einer Biographie." In summary, Schlegel differentiated two phases

of European literature, one classical and culminating in either the epic or the tragedy, the other modern and romantic and permeated by a "romanhafter Charakter", a feature to be found in drama, lyric poetry, and all the other genres favored by the Moderns.

Schlegel was of course perfectly aware that not everything modern was "romanhaft". To be sure, already in the Middle Ages a new style of European literature blossomed bearing the seeds of Romanticism and thereby of the novel. There were the Provençal troubadours, the German minnesinger, and Dante's "dolce stil nuovo"; yet especially since the Renaissance, there was also Classicism, and even worse, Neoclassicism. As August Wilhelm Schlegel stated in his Vienna lectures on dramatic art and literature of 1808:

> [...] die Denkmäler alter Kunst wurden fleissig ausgegraben. Alles dies gab dem menschlichen Geist vielfache Anregungen und machte eine entscheidende Epoche in unserer Bildungsgeschichte [...] Aber es wurde auch sogleich mit dem Studium der Alten ein ertötender Missbrauch getrieben. Die Gelehrten, welche vorzüglich in dessen Besitz waren und sich durch eigene Werke auszuzeichnen nicht vermochten, schreiben den Alten ein unbedingtes Ansehen zu [...] Sie behaupten, nur von der Nachahmung der alten Schriftsteller sei wahres Heil für den menschlichen Geist zu hoffen; in den Werken der Neuern schätzten sie nur das, was denen der Alten ähnlich war oder zu sein schien. Alles übrige verwarfen sie als barbarische Ausartung. Ganz anders verhielt es sich mit den grossen Dichtern und Künstlern [...] Dante [...] erklärte den Virgil für seinen Lehrer, brachte aber ein Werk hervor, das unter allen, die sich nennen lassen, die von der Aeneide verschiedenste Gestaltung hat, und übertraf seinen vermeinten Meister sehr weit an Kraft, Wahrheit, Umfang und Tiefe [...] Da die Dichter meistens an der gelehrten Bildung Anteil nahmen, so entstand daraus ein Zwiespalt in ihnen zwischen der natürlichen Neigung und der eingebildeten Pflicht. Wo sie dieser opferten, wurden sie von den Gelehrten gelobt; insofern sie jener nachgingen, liebte sie das Volk. (12)

Looking at the modern world of literature as a whole then, one should distinguish two groups of writers: the followers of Aristotle and Horace, or the Neoclassicists; and the genuinely modern authors, who did not imitate the classical models, but abided by their own intuitions. Only this latter group could be considered to have a "romanhafter" character. Like his brother, but about a decade earlier, Friedrich Schlegel demarcated two types of literary Modernism, a sterile one in the neoclassical trend, and a truly modern one in the romantic vein: "Das Romantische bleibt ewig neu - das Moderne wechselt mit der Mode," he said in 1797. (13) This distinction between the merely modern, which deserves this attribute on the basis of a timetable, and the truly modern in the sense of originality, is most conspicuously expressed in the "Brief über den Roman" of 1800:

Ich habe ein bestimmtes Merkmal des Gegensatzes zwischen dem
Antiken und dem Romantischen aufgestellt. Indessen bitte ich Sie
doch, nun nicht sogleich anzunehmen, dass mir das Romantische und
das Moderne völlig gleich gelte. Ich denke es ist etwa ebenso verschieden, wie die Gemälde des Raffael und Correggio von den Kupfer-
stichen die jetzt Mode sind. Wollen Sie sich den Unterschied völlig
klar machen so lesen Sie gefälligst etwa die EMILIA GALOTTI die so
unaussprechlich modern und doch im geringsten nicht romantisch ist,
und erinnern sich dann an Shakespeare, in den ich das eigentliche
Zentrum, den Kern der romantischen Fantasie setzen möchte. (14)

Thus Romanticism and Modernism, "Roman" and the modern literary style, do not
completely coincide, but Romanticism and "romanhaft" apply only to certain progressive trailblazers of the modern age: "Da suche und finde ich das Romantische,
bei den ältern Modernen, bei Shakespeare, Cervantes, in der italienischen Poesie,
in jenem Zeitalter der Ritter, der Liebe und der Märchen, aus welchem die Sache
und das Wort selbst herstammt." (15) In order to emphasize the revolutionary
character of these authors in contrast to the Neoclassicists, Schlegel often preferred
the term "progressive Poesie" to Romanticism, a tendency particularly evident in
his aphorisms around 1797. Here he liked to oppose Classicism and Progression,
clearly an accentuation of the former dichotomy between Classicism and Romanticism:
"Die classischen Gedichtarten haben nur Einheit; die progressiven allein Ganzheit,"
or "classisch gleich fix, synthetisch. - Progressiv gleich bewegt, analytisch," and
most directly: "Classisch und Progressiv sind historische Ideen und kritische An-
schauungen.--Da kommen Kritik und Historie zusammen." (16) Progressive poetry
is based on and carries further the old romantic mandate: "Der romantische Imperativ
fordert die Mischung aller Dichtarten." (17) This mingling, however, is to be achieved
in the novel, and even if one chose a different genre, Schlegel would still call it
"romanartig"--just because of the mingling. Here the terms merge, and it becomes
clear why Schlegel called "romantische Poesie"--which is identical to "Romanpoesie"--
"progressive Universalpoesie".

Perhaps a similar distinction could be made by placing Schlegel's idea of
Classicism under closer scrutiny, a line of thought not to be pursued here, since
this investigation deals with the progressive poetry of the novel. Nevertheless, the
scope should be delineated for possible further research. Just as modern literature
falls into two categories, one chronological (Modernism), and the other typological
(Romanticism or progressive poetry), Schlegel seemed to view the classical age in
both the chronological sense as Antiquity and in the typological connotation, referring
to the most characteristic achievement of this epoch as Classicism. Antiquity then
would correspond to Modernism, and Classicism would find its parallel in Romanticism or Progression. So the historical dichotomy is accompanied by a typological
duality, that of perfection and unity on the one hand, and infinity and mingling on the
other. Although the typological antithesis of limitation and infinity, of "Einheit" and
"Fülle", of Classicism and Romanticism, rests on the historical division into
Antiquity and Modernity, it is by no means restricted to this. In other words, a
modern author is not antique by chronological definition, but he can be classical in
his accomplishment, just as Homer can have and is indeed imbued with romantic

features by Schlegel. Thus Schlegel can say: "Homer neigt sich zu Romantischem; vielleicht auch Vergil und Ovid," or "Vergil, Horaz, Ovid sind offenbar romantische Naturen."(18) But there is much more evidence for this transplantation of styles in his posthumous notebooks, not only in the direction of Antiquity towards Modernity, but also in the reverse progression. One can safely assume that this four-fold system of two historical and two typological categories formed the foundation of Schlegel's view of literary history, although through his unfortunate tendency to obscure matters for the sake of provocativeness, he often deliberately confused the two realms. Yet it is certainly clear that the two ages of European literature gain their marks of distinction not through mere representatives, but by pioneers. Just as the ancient Greek world attains classical achievement in Homer's epics or on the Attic stage, so does the modern world strive for its goal through the impetus of the Romantics in their endeavors for "Roman". (19)

Thus the enigmatic formula of the "Brief über den Roman", "Ein Roman ist ein romantisches Buch", discards its mysterious cloak and condenses Schlegel's complex system into a brief flash of brilliant formulation. After having reached this plateau, however, the real difficulty begins. The distinction between Modernism and Romanticism as conveying historical and typological realities having been made, the task now resides in examining more closely the difference between romantic and progressive poetry, two styles of modern literature that are intimately related, but nevertheless exhibit different nuances. Here again, Schlegel was not consistent in the application of his terms, but surveying all the relevant sources as a whole, one gains the impression that Romanticism is the style created by the pioneers of the modern age, the older Moderns, such as Shakespeare, Cervantes, the Italian poets, and authors of chivalric love and fairytales; whereas the Progressives are those who took up these modern features and carried them into the future in infinite variation of unexpected minglings. This does not, however, preclude the possibility of Schlegel's calling a Romantic a Progressive and vice versa. That he indeed thought of the romantic age as having come to a close is evidenced by his Paris lectures on European literature, where he presents Calderon as the last of the older Moderns, the last Romantic:

> Calderon ist als der letzte romantische Dichter anzusehen. Er lebte
> noch zu der Zeit, wo Corneille und Racine in Frankreich die roman-
> tische Poesie durch eine andere, eine der anti-klassischen nachge-
> bildete, völlig verdrängen - welche Tendenz sich allmählich über ganz
> Europa verbreitete und in allen Literaturen vorherrschend wurde. (20)

The Progressives are then those who in this age of predominant Neoclassicism cultivated the seeds of the Romantics. However, the differentiation of romantic and progressive as two styles is by no means consistent. Although it is worth mentioning that the two terms are not synonymous, one cannot fully demonstrate that Schlegel developed any clear tendency to mean different poems or different poets by them. There are certainly passages where he may seem to be moving that way when he contrasts for instance the two-fold conceptions of Hamlet and Don Quixote with that of Wilhelm Meisters Lehrjahre. (21) On the other hand, the 116th

Athenäumsfragment says that romantic poetry is a progressive universal poetry. This distinction is ultimately one between the historical realities of romantic poetry and its ideal tendency. Probably Schlegel has some hope that the ideal tendency would become more clearly manifest in his age than in the time of the historical romantic poets and thought that some of Goethe's work pointed that way. But these vague hopes were not fulfilled. For the most part, in Schlegel's usage romantic and progressive are different aspects or different nuances of the same poetry. (22)

Applied to the realm of the novel, Romantics are authors such as Cervantes who actually created the genre. The Progressives, characterized by "Streben nach dem Unendlichen", developed this poetic form in new combinations and thus cannot be completely circumscribed by definition:

> Die Geschichte der progressiven Poesie liesse sich erst dann voll-
> ständig a priori construiren, wenn sie vollendet wäre; bis jezt kann
> man nur Bestätigung der progressiven Idee in der Geschichte der
> modernen Poesie aufzeigen und Vermuthungen daraus folgern. (23)

Within romantic poetry the novel is the predominant genre, multifaceted, infinitely mingled, difficult to describe, but still definable. In progressive poetry, however, the novel is an ideal depicted in extravagant antitheses which can always be raised to a higher power--a perfect example of Kant's regulative idea, a goal to be reached only by approximation.

Yet even at this point we have still not come to the end of Schlegel's definitive theory of poetry, a concept by no means exhausted by a theory of the novel. Assuredly, the novel is the predominant genre of romantic literature and the ideal of progressive poetry, but it is only part of the final synthesis towards which Schlegel sought to direct the course of European literary history. More than a century before Gottfried Benn, Schlegel, as an architect of the ultimate goal of poetry, worked on the blueprint of what Benn was to call "das absolute Kunstwerk" and what Schlegel referred to as "absolute Poesie", the very climax of human achievement. At this time, Schlegel was an ardent admirer of Fichte's transcendental philosophy, which he considered as the pinnacle of theoretical and reflective accomplishment within the history of European thought. What Fichte had achieved in the realm of philosophy Schlegel wanted to attain in the domain of literature, if not by actual creation, then by mapping out its critical program. And to underscore this parallel, he coined a new term for this absolute poetry still to be created, namely, "transcendental poetry": "Die absolute Poesie--transcendentale oder speculative Poesie," or "Meine absolute Kritik für Classisches und Progressives so transcendental als Fichte's Wissenschaftslehre."(24) Thus transcendental poetry is not only based on progressive and romantic objectives, it is no longer limited to the novel, but transcends the achievements of the modern age and also tries to embrace the fruits of Classicism. "Harmonie des Antiken und Modernen scheint Geist meiner gesamten Poesie," Schlegel states, or "Die einzige pragmatische Kunstlehre für den Künstler ist die Lehre vom Classischen und Romantischen."(25) This synthesis has certainly been perceived before: "Die

Transcendentalpoesie scheint wie Ebbe und Fluth wellenförmig durch die Masse der modernen Poesie zu gehn."(26) For a certain period of time Schlegel believed Goethe to be the embodiment of this highest achievement of poetry, and he then considered Dante to be its representative: "Dantes Werk ist nichts als die gesamte Transcendentalpoesie," or "Dante [...] umfasst die ganze Transcendentalpoesie."(27) Shakespeare too is seen in this light. Yet none of these authors really gained the prize for having realized this new form, the essence of which seems to reside in the synthesis of two opposite artistic directions: condensation, concentration, interiorization--termed "Radizierung" by Schlegel--, and second, an encompassing of totality, external fullness, which he called "Potenzierung": "Die Transcendentalpoesie soll unendlich potenzirt und unendlich analysirt sein," or: "Das Wesen eines Werks ist gleichsam das Transcendentale, das absolut Innre, der condensirte und dann potenzirte Geist in Eins zusammen."(28) The terms "unendlich analysirt" and "condensirter Geist" in the above quotations stand for what usually and more consistently is called "Radizierung" in contrast to "Potenzierung" and is presented in infinite variation in the characteristic formula $\sqrt[0]{\frac{1}{0}} \frac{1}{0}$. The formula $\frac{1}{0}\sqrt[0]{\pi} \frac{1}{0}$ would then be the shortest expression of Schlegel's absolute ideal of poetry, and "Potenzierung" and "Radizierung" would designate what is otherwise known as "unendliche Einheit" and "unendliche Fülle".

Yet absolute or transcendental poetry is based on still another opposition, that of Realism and Idealism: "Die Transcendentalpoesie eingeteilt in die ideale und reale."(29) The main goal nevertheless remains the surmounting of all antinomies through a synthesis: "Die Transcendentalpoesie beginnt mit der absoluten Verschiedenheit des Idealen und Realen. Da ist Schiller also ein Anfänger der Transcendentalpoesie und nur halber Transcendentalpoesie, die mit der Identität enden muss."(30) But how is this reconciliation of ideality and reality to be understood? In Aphorism 42 of the Lyceum, Schlegel depicts the solution as being comparable to the manner of an ordinary Italian buffo, a type of transcendental buffoonery residing within the work yet surveying all from above:

> Es gibt alte und moderne Gedichte, die durchgängig im Ganzen und
> überall den göttlichen Hauch der Ironie atmen. Es lebt in ihnen eine
> wirklich transzendentale Buffonerie. Im Innern, die Stimmung,
> welche alles übersieht, und sich über alles Bedingte unendlich er-
> hebt, auch über eigne Kunst, Tugend, oder Genialität: im Aeussern,
> in der Ausführung die mimische Manier eines gewöhnlichen guten
> italiänischen Buffo.

Yet the most lucid and illuminating explanation of the means by which the synthesis of the real and the ideal is to be achieved is presented by Schlegel in the Athenäum. The fulfillment of the goal culminates in what he calls the poetry of poetry, the key to which lies in artistic reflection, the presence of the author in his work:

Es gibt eine Poesie, deren eins und alles das Verhältnis des Idealen
und des Realen ist, und die also nach der Analogie der philosophischen
Kunstsprache Transzendentalpoesie heissen müsste. Sie beginnt als
Satire mit der absoluten Verschiedenheit des Idealen und Realen,
schwebt als Elegie in der Mitte, und endigt als Idylle mit der absoluten Identität beider. So wie man aber wenig Wert auf eine Trans-
zendentalphilosophie legen würde, die nicht kritisch wäre, nicht auch
das Produzierende mit dem Produkt darstellte, und im System der
transzendentalen Gedanken zugleich eine Charakteristik des transzendentalen Denkens enthielte: so sollte wohl auch jene Poesie die in
modernen Dichtern nicht seltnen transzendentalen Materialien und Vor-
übungen zu einer poetischen Theorie des Dichtungsvermögens mit der
künstlerischen Reflexion und schönen Selbstbespiegelung, die sich im
Pindar, den lyrischen Fragmenten der Griechen, und der alten Elegie,
unter den Neueren aber in Goethe findet, vereinigen, und in jeder ihrer
Darstellungen sich selbst mit darstellen, und überall zugleich Poesie und
Poesie der Poesie sein. (31)

As this aphorism indicates, mere "transcendental buffoonery" in the sense
of an emergence of the author from his work is certainly not the only criterion for
transcendental poetry. This type involves a systematic preoccupation of the poem
with poetry in general as well as with its own poetic category that is exemplified
in the Divina Commedia. Inspirations for a discussion of this challenging term
can be found in an article by Raymond Immerwahr and in subsequent studies. (32)
On the whole, Schlegel seems to have thought of this goal of transcendental poetry
as a projection into the future, and in this assumption he is certainly right.
Transcendental poetry thus constitutes a surpassing of the ideal of the novel, not
in that this aim is entirely abandoned, but in that it is consumed in the ultimate
goal of absolute poetry. With respect to the topic of the novel proper, two levels in
Schlegel's discussion can be discerned: 1) the novel as a genre of romantic poetry,
that is, of Cervantes and the older Moderns, and 2) the novel as an ideal of
progressive poetry to be strived for in infinite variations. Despite all its termino-
logical complexities, this process of thought is not really so astonishing. Wouldn't
a learned critic seeking to demonstrate the possibilities of this genre start out by
characterizing past examples, present strivings, and future expectations?--wouldn't
he assume the attitude of a "rückwärts gekehrter Prophet"?

III. THE NOVEL AS A GENRE OF ROMANTIC POETRY: "MISCHGEDICHT"

True to his pattern, Schlegel formulated his concept of the novel most precisely after he had already detached himself from the issue and spoke in retrospect.
In his Paris lectures on European literature (1803), he gave a definition which can
be considered a condensation of all the experimental and fragmentary formulations
previously promulgated on the novel in his notebooks, his aphorisms in the
Athenäum, and in the "Brief über den Roman" (1800). Dealing with the literature
of modern and romantic times, Schlegel expresses an essential opinion on the novel:

Der Begriff des Romans, wie Boccaccio and Cervantes ihn aufstellen,
ist der eines romantischen Buches, einer romantischen Komposition,
wo alle Formen und Gattungen vermischt und verschlungen sind. Im
Roman ist die Hauptmasse Prosa, eine mannigfaltigere als je eine
Gattung der Alten sie aufstellt. Es gibt hier historische Partien,
rhetorische, dialogische, alle diese Stile wechseln und sind auf das
sinnreichste und künstlichste miteinander verwebt und verbunden.
Poesien jeder Art, lyrische, epische, Romanzen, didaktische, sind
durch das Ganze hingestreut und schmücken es in üppiger, bunter Fülle
und Mannigfaltigkeit auf das reichste und glänzendste aus. Der Roman
ist ein Gedicht von Gedichten, ein ganzes Gewebe von Gedichten. Es
ist klar, dass eine solche poetische Komposition, aus so mannigfalten
Bestandteilen und Formen gemischt, wo auch kein kurzes Mass die
äusseren Bedingungen beschränkt, eine viel künstlichere Verschlingung
von Poesie möglich macht als das Epos oder das Drama, da in jenen
wenigstens Einheit des Tons herrscht, in diesem aber, als für die
Anschauung bestimmt, alles leicht zusammengefasst und übersehen
werden muss. Das lyrische Gedicht kann seinem inneren Wesen nach
nur von sehr geringem Umfang sein und wäre daher das allerunstatt-
hafteste. Dem ursprünglich doch zur Lektüre und zum ruhigen besonne-
nen Nachsinnen bestimmten Roman ist die bunteste Verwicklung, Fülle
und Mannigfaltigkeit, die grosse Ausdehnung dem Charakter der
Gattung am meisten entsprechend. Auch ist hier, wo der Dichter sich
ganz seiner phantastischen Willkür und den Ergüssen seiner eigenen
Stimmung und den Spielen des Humors überlassen darf, wo er, durch
keine Einheit des Tons gebunden, mit Ernst und Scherz abwechselt,
Monotonie beinahe ganz unmöglich. (1)

Several elements are included in this definition, but the mingling of forms
and genres is most essential. To be sure, the main part of the novel consists of
prose, but this prose is much more varied than one had ever imagined, since
historical, rhetorical, and dialogue styles are used in infinite variation. Furthermore the novel incorporates manifold forms of lyric poetry, an interwoven fabric
of poems, and reveals itself as a composition which is a much more artistic intermingling than any other genre--epic, drama, or lyric poetry--all of which exhibit
a much greater unity of tone. This lays the foundation for the all-embracing character
and manifoldness of the novel, which is unified by the all-pervasive presence of the
author in his arbitrariness and humor, in his alternation of jest and seriousness,
which has always been understood by Schlegel, through the example of Socrates, as

a specific form of irony. Aside from these features of exterior universality and inner unity of composition, the novel is characterized in historical perspective as deriving from the prototypes of Boccaccio and Cervantes.

Before characterizing Cervantes' novels in particular, Schlegel emphasizes that the novel is the "ursprünglichste, eigentümlichste, vollkommenste Form der romantischen Poesie, die eben durch diese Vermischung aller Formen von der alten klassischen, wo die Gattungen ganz streng getrennt wurden, sich unterscheidet."(2) In other parts of these lectures the primary characteristic of the modern novel is regarded as the intermingling of prose and poems in contrast to the modern national epic exemplified by Camoes' Lusiaden, but the novel further distinguishes itself from this modern parallel to Homer by its being "viel zu spielend und scherzend."(3) This concept of the novel as an infinitely mingled poem finds its roots in the posthumous writings stemming from 1797, from which the aphorisms of the Lyceum and Athenäum are taken.

Aside from some scattered and sparse remarks in letters, Schlegel's critical interest in the genre of the novel can be traced back to the year 1796 and finds first expression in the context of his endeavor to establish fundamental types of philosophizing, such as mysticism, criticism, dogmatism, eclecticism, and so forth. Here we realize that in the first instance, the novel attracted him because of the all-embracing, universal character of the genre, which achieves its goal not so much through inner intensity, but rather by virtue of exterior totality and is thus associated with eclecticism. In the early notebooks of his intellectual diary, Philosophische Lehrjahre, Schlegel says: "Der Roman war von jeher das beste Organ der besten Eklektischen Philosophen der Modernen. Eklektische Philosophie im Wilhelm Meister. - Die Eklektische Philosophie = Lebensphilosophie."(4) His overriding concern for the novel, however, did not become manifest until the summer of 1797, when he supplanted the sub-division of European literature into Antiquity and Romanticism by the sharper dichotomy of Classicism and progressive poetry and conceived of the genre of the novel as the most characteristic form of the modern author in his progressive drive. This turning point occurred during Schlegel's decisive move from Jena to Berlin, in the course of which he stopped in Weissenfels to visit Novalis and began the notebook Gedanken. 1797 - Auf der Reise nach Berlin in Weissenfels.(5) This notebook abounds in antitheses depicting the classical and the progressive styles in the sense of limitation and self-transcendence, and with regard to the novel we read:

> Wie im classischen Gedichte, alle Menschen, Charaktere und Leidenschaften, kurz der Stoff classisch ist; so sollten alle Personen im Roman fortschreitend seyn; Maximum von Progressivität ist sein Ideal. - Meistens sehr unvollkommen.(6)

On the basis of his vast reading, Schlegel regarded the mingling of different elements and genres as the most general trait of the novel, and this to such a degree that the label "Mischgedicht" appeared to be an unnecessary tautology for its definition.(7) The novel transcends all genres, and its very essence is to combine all genres: "Der wahre Roman muss mit allen Gattungen der Naturpoesie und der gemischten

Kunstpoesie auch die reinste und vollständigste allumfassendste Gattung der Kunstpoesie verbinden; er muss Drama seyn."(8)

As in the initial quotation from these philosophical notebooks, the chief
virtue of the novel lies in its exterior totality, in the quantitative realm, and not
so much in its inner subtlety or quality. To apply Kant's terminology, the novel is
not so much pure poetry as it is practical poetry. In fact, Schlegel says: "Der Roman eine angewandte Poesie"(9) because it uses the other genres as ingredients for
its own creation. In the mingling and in the various degrees of universality and
intensity, however, differences within this genre can be detected: "Der Roman ist
bloss dem Grade und nicht der Art nach verschieden; jeder Roman ist eine Art für
sich. Hier ist das Rubriciren sehr illiberal."(10)

Although Schlegel considered rubrications as illiberal, he was nevertheless
strongly inclined to typify spiritual matters in 1797, and reference has already been
made to his attempts at classifying philosophy as being either mystical, sceptical,
dogmatic, eclectic, etc. Similarly, he tried to categorize the many novels he had
read by then into basic types. In other words, Schlegel sought to establish a typology
of the European novel on the basis of multifacted distinctions--national, stylistic,
thematic, or other peculiarities. In this context he observes: "Jakobi's Romane sind
von der abhandelden Art; Richter experimentirt bloss ohne darzustellen; er armirt
die Objekte und sezt sie in Contact," and he conceives of a negative and positive, a
mechanical and an organic novel:(11) "Im Cervantes und Meister ist positiver und
negativer reiner RomanStoff. - Idee eines mechanischen - chemischen - organischen
Romans. Der Meister der erste mechanische." But he also envisions national
qualifications, especially a German style: "Die originellsten Erscheinungen unter
den deutschen Romanen sind Ardinghello, Woldemar, Geisterseher, Werther; die
ersten gültigen Meister, Richter, und Tieck."(12) Of Tieck's novelistic peculiarities
Schlegel says: "Die Figurazion in Tiecks Romanen ist zugleich Novelle und Mährchen;
die Lizenzen von beiden,--"whereas Jacobi's Woldemar, later to be reviewed by
Schlegel, is seen as an anticipation of the organic novel: "Was noch zunächst ist der
ganz schwere philosophisch poetisch ethisch gesättigte organische Roman, ein höhe-
rer, besserer Jacobi."(13) Among the German representatives of the novel Goethe's
Wilhelm Meister was of course of prime importance for Schlegel at that time and
perhaps the second greatest source of inspiration after Don Quixote. Because of the
prominence of this subject, a special chapter will be devoted to it.

Schlegel established types of the novel not only according to gradations of
mingling and national characteristics, but also on the basis of certain tones, modes,
or styles. During this period of his critical career (1797-98), he cooperated with
Schleiermacher in carving out what Dilthey later called the system of "Geisteswis-
senschaften", a methodical search into "die geistige Welt", chiefly composed of
four autonomous spheres: religion, ethics, poetry, and philosophy.(14) In this line
of thought Schlegel characterized spiritual or intellectual phenomena, such as
philosophical systems and religious beliefs, according to whether they had a predominantly religious, ethical, poetic, or philosophical overtone. The novel too is
considered from this point of view, new types of the novel are developed, and thus
the novel becomes more sharply delineated. "Ist nicht alles, was wir jezt Roman

41

nennen, nur ethische Philosophie und ethische Poesie?" Schlegel asks and confronts the philosophical with the poetic novel: "Sonderbar dass der poetische Roman
rein systematisch der philosophische so fragmentarisch ist."(15) How the typology
of the ethical, philosophical, and poetic novel originated with Schlegel and that it
actually derives from the previous distinction of the ethical, philosophical, and poetic
styles is best expressed in the following aphorism:

> Wie muss Ethik Philosophie und Poesie versezt werden zu Roman? -
> Welche Philosophie ist Roman? - Alle die zugleich ethisch und
> poetisch ist. - Die Jacobische Philosophie macht den Woldemar so
> wenig zum bessern Roman, als die Kantische den Hippel. - Richter
> hat dagegen schon classisches Studium in seiner Gattung.(16)

The most succinct definition of the philosophical novel is certainly the following:
"Der philosophische Roman hat es mit dem Abstractum des menschlichen und mit
dessen eccentrischen Spitzen zu thun.--Die wahren eccentrischen Extreme sind die
göttlichen Momente im Leben."(17) Somewhat later this idea is specified: "Es ist
wohl eine Eigenschaft des philosophischen Romans, dass Menschen sich darin den
Engeln oder den Teufeln nähern."(18) To be sure, this type of novel is not identical
to philosophy, but remains entirely in the poetic realm. More precisely, it
constitutes a certain branch of poetry and a display of virtuosity, just as logic does
within the system of philosophy: "Logik das Correlat des Romans. Logik ist Kunst
der Philosophie. Roman ist gaya ciencia, Wissenschaft der Poesie."(19)

In this characterization, one might miss the religious novel, since four
branches of the spiritual world were established. This type is not lacking by omis-
sion, however. Although Schlegel now sees the novel as not yet approximating
religion, eventually the religious aura will not be limited to any specific type of
novel but could permeate them all. The novel is often seen as still developing, and
as mentioned earlier, even the projected new Bible is to emerge in the form of a
novel. Undoubtedly, the novel has many excellent qualities: it takes up various
genres in a whirlwind of mingling and is consequently no true genre in itself but
rather a parasitic genre; it excels by virtuosity and "gaya ciencia" but does not
yet reach the higher realm of religion. Schlegel even says: "Alle Freundschaft ist
heroisch und gehört also schon zur Religion, nicht mehr recht zum Roman," a
statement deriving from 1798. One year later, while working in Jena on his concept
of a new mythology, he remarked: "Roman in der Mitte zwischen der künstlerischen
und der religiösen Schrift" and continued: "Der Roman ist durchaus spielend, die
Mythologie ganz ernst."(20)

Although he did not use the term "type" himself, Schlegel tried to differentiate
basic types of the novel. That this was really his endeavor is indirectly evidenced
by the question: "Zweifel ob es von jeder Gattung unbestimmt viele Romane geben
kann, oder nur einen classischen?" and in the subsequent answer: "Vielleicht muss
es von allen Romanarten nur Einen, bestimmt viele, und unendliche viele geben."(21)
For what else is a type but a sub-division of which one, many, and infinitely many
can be representative? To be sure, this establishment of types of the novel is not an
end in itself. As one can expect from this author, such an undertaking is only the

preliminary step in the construction of the blueprint of a novel which supersedes all
historical examples in a hitherto unheard of mingling--a supernovel, as it were,
referred to as "absoluter Roman" by Schlegel. To elaborate this absolute novel is
indeed one significant goal in the Literary Notebooks from 1797 to 1799. Before this
topic can be presented, the search for further evidence on Schlegel's ideas about the
historical novel in the sense of "Mischgedicht" must be completed.

The concept of the novel as an infinitely mingled poem is also the starting
point in Fragmente zur Literatur und Poesie (1797), the early issue of which begins
with the remark:

> Die Meinung der Roman sei kein Gedicht, gründet sich auf den Satz:
> Alle Poesie soll metrisch sein. Von diesem Satz kann aber zum Behuf
> der Progressivität, aber auch nur für diese eine Ausnahme gemacht
> werden. - Der Roman ist noch ungleich gemischteres Mischgedicht
> als Idylle oder Satire, welche doch ein bestimmtes Gesetz der Mischung
> befolgen. - (22)

Here, Schlegel also points out more clearly what has to be mingled, namely the
idyllic, satirical, and progressive modes of poetry: "Ueberwiegt das Idyllische so
ists ein sentimentaler Roman, das Satirische so ists ein komischer, das Progressive
so ists ein philosophischer Roman." (23) All these particular accentuations should be
avoided, however, since they interfere with the main task of the novel, which is
mingling:

> Aber alle diese Extreme sind fehlerhaft weil dadurch das Wesen des
> Romans selbst nämlich die Mischung zerstört wird, eben darum schon.
> Es ist also dann gar kein Roman. Dies Uebergewicht ist gegen die po-
> litische Totalität. (24)

Regarding the historical origins and development of the novel, Schlegel comes
to a conclusion that summarizes the results of the previous chapter, namely, that
the novel originated in the epic of the Ancients, spread over the late hellenistic
romances and erotic writings, then reached the romantic world of medieval romances,
and finally, found full expression in Don Quixote. Schlegel segregates three stages of
this historical process:

> Stufen des Romans. 1) bei den Alten: Epos und Drama. Anfang des
> Mischgedichts in Prosa und mystische sentimentale Liebe, Erotika;
> 2) das absolut mystisch Wunderbare, das eigentlich Romantische;
> 3) Don Quixote. (25)

This evolution concerns of course only the novel proper. In the broader sense, as
can be anticipated, Dante's Divina Commedia is regarded as a novel, and Shakespeare's
tragedies are mixtures of classical tragedy and the novel. (26) What was just called
the parasitic character of the novel finds evidence in No. 120: "Wenn es Dichtarten
geben soll, und auch nicht, so muss Eine Dichtart alle übrigen vereinigen." This

bestows external comprehensiveness upon the novel: "Im Roman ist unbeschränkte Ganzheit, d. h. beschränkte Unganzheit, Streben nach jener."(27) However, what about the unity of such a work? Schlegel was clearly aware that unity is a necessary quality of every work and not only of the poem.(28) It appears to be that the unity of the novel is achieved through the presence of the author within the work, through his all-pervading individuality: "Die meisten Romane sind nur Compendien der Individualität." According to another observation Schlegel maintains: "Der Roman tendenzirt zur Parekbase, welche fortgesezt etwas humoristisches hat. - "(29) The term "parabasis" derives from the function of the chorus in the Greek tragedy and more precisely designates the emergence of the chorus from action in its addresses and comments to the audience. Schlegel regarded this phenomenon as an anticipation of the novelist's appearance within his own work, a stepping out of his realm, which he also found in a later form of the theater, in the histrionic style of the clown in the Italian commedia dell' arte and called "transcendental buffoonerie."(30)

These ideas underly the aphorisms of the Lyceum, where Schlegel characterizes the novel Faublas because of its social wit and serenity as the champagne of this genre and furthermore stresses the role of the individuality of the author in Aphorism 89, but even better in Aphorism 78: "Mancher der vortrefflichsten Romane ist ein Kompendium, eine Enzyklopädie des ganzen geistigen Lebens eines genialischen Individuums." In the aphorisms of the Athenäum, the psychological aspect of an analysis of unnatural lusts, horrifying torture, insulting infamy, and disgusting impotence in the areas of sensual and intellectual realism is brought into connection with the novel--an idea which can already be found in the Notebooks.(31) Here it becomes obvious that Diderot, especially his Religieuse, is thought of in this context. Tieck's works are presented as some of the finest examples of the modern novel, especially his William Lovell.(32) The merit of this novel is seen in its depicting and elaborating an entirely new character. Such praise seems to relate this work to the type of the philosophical or psychological novel, but here its failure is also detected. Since the character is "unglücklicherweise poetisch", a conflict arises between the poetic and philosophical emphases: "Das ganze Buch ist ein Kampf der Prosa und der Poesie, wo die Prosa mit Füssen getreten wird und die Poesie über sich selbst den Hals bricht." In other words, the poetic or fantastic element does not really come through and stands in danger of being misunderstood as merely flat sentimentality. Only his Sternbald achieves a happy balance of philosophical seriousness, artistic religiosity, and fantastic poetry, the latter element characterized, interestingly enough, as arabesque:

> Aber der Sternbald vereinigt den Ernst und Schwung des Lovell mit
> der künstlerischen Religiosität des Klosterbruders und mit allem
> was in den poetischen Arabesken, die er aus alten Märchen gebildet,
> im ganzen genommen das Schönste ist: die fantastische Fülle und
> Leichtigkeit, der Sinn für Ironie, und besonders die absichtliche
> Verschiedenheit und Einheit des Kolorits. Auch hier ist alles klar
> und transparent, und der romantische Geist scheint angenehm über
> sich selbst zu fantasieren.(33)

In these aphorisms Schlegel also envisions his theme of "absoluter Roman", and in this regard one could first refer to the famous Fragment No. 116 quoted in the introduction. Upon closer consideration, the ideas expressed there are not so much concerned with the novel in the narrow sense of the genre of "Mischgedicht", but rather with "Romanpoesie" in the broader connotation, embracing works such as Dante's Divina Commedia, Shakespeare's dramas, and Petrarch's lyrics. Most precisely, however, this revolutionary topic is taken up in the often overlooked Aphorism No. 252, which condenses Schlegel's concept of poetics, his "Philosophie der Poesie" and culminates in a philosophy of the novel. Here the critic admits that he has something in mind that has never been visualized before. Referring first to his poetics in general, Schlegel says:

> Sie selbst würde zwischen Vereinigung und Trennung der Philosophie
> und der Poesie, der Praxis und der Poesie, der Poesie überhaupt und
> der Gattungen und Arten schweben, und mit der völligen Vereinigung
> enden. Ihr Anfang gäbe die Prinzipien der reinen Poetik, ihre Mitte die
> Theorie der besonderen eigentümlich modernen Dichtarten, der didak-
> tischen, der musikalischen, der rhetorischen im höhern Sinn u.s.w.
> Eine Philosophie des Romans, deren erste Grundlinien Platos politi-
> sche Kunstlehre enthält, wäre der Schlussstein. Flüchtigen Dilettanten
> ohne Enthusiasmus, und ohne Belesenheit in den besten Dichtern aller
> Art freilich müsste eine solche Poetik vorkommen, wie einem Kinde,
> das bildern wollte, ein trigonometisches Buch.

The content of this philosophy of the novel, which will appear to the inexperienced reader as a text on trigonometry would to a child, will form the subject of the next chapters. To sum up, the inquiry into Schlegel's historical inspirations, the Gespräch über die Poesie should be taken as a foundation. The first section, "Epochen der Dichtkunst" already provides an interesting insight, since it derives Cervantes' practice of the novel from Heliodor, (34) but the third part, "Brief über den Roman" provides the most material for Schlegel's philosophy of the novel. To be sure, the importance of this portion is by no means exhausted by its providing historical information. Raymond Immerwahr has already shown how this "letter" is structured and what its essential components are, (35) but the passages on the history of the European novel summarize what has been the object of research in this chapter.

IV. BRIEF UEBER DEN ROMAN

This famous but difficult piece of Schlegel's criticism will be discussed solely from the perspective of the history of the novel, and other aspects, such as structure, personages, and irony will be disregarded. Indeed, this letter can be interpreted as an arabesque, not only in the derogatory sense of "sickly wit", but in the higher meaning of "wahre Arabesken". The concluding exclamation "das wären wahre Arabesken!" is really an understatement and should actually be applied to the letter as a whole, of course not in the subjunctive connotation, but in the indicative form. In other words, the theory of the novel which Schlegel plans as a future project in the middle of the treatise and imbues with the attribute of possible arabesques is actually presented in the letter istelf. One should not be surprised, however, that his observations on the novel consist primarily in historical examples. "Historice est philosophandum" was Schlegel's device. (1) He claimed to be disgusted by any theory which was not historical and said in the "Epochen der Literatur" of the Gespräch: "Die Theorie der Kunst ist ihre Geschichte."(2)

In fact, a broad and fascinating history of the novel is implicit in the "Brief" and can be deduced from it. In order to make this history visible, one only has to break apart the sophisticated structure of the work, which can best be depicted by the image of many boxes within boxes. Abiding by this image, one can say that Schlegel deliberately disarranged the historical facts by putting them into these boxes and thereby bringing them out of chronological order. So one only has to take the facts out of the boxes and set them up in a chronological row to grasp Schlegel's theory of the novel, which is truly a history of the novel. This will be my contribution to the lively discussion of this piece of criticism. (3)

The interpretation of the "Brief über den Roman" has been intentionally complicated by the author through an interesting confusion of terminology. In the second half of the work Schlegel states, as has been noted before, "Ein Roman ist ein romantisches Buch," ironically combining the broader concept of "das Romantische" or "Romanpoesie" with the narrower term for the genre of the novel. To emphasize this fusion Schlegel uses a special technique in the passages immediately surrounding this statement. From the broad point of view, the two concepts, "romantisch" and "Roman" (romanhaft) are identical, as presented in the thesis of Chapter 2. It would nevertheless be provocative if "romantisch" were substituted for "Roman", especially if in the previous sentence the impression has been given that "Roman" is to be taken in the narrow sense of the genre. This is exactly what Schlegel does, for instance, when he confronts "Roman" with "Schauspiel" and continues: "Das Schauspiel soll auch romantisch sein," or when he contrasts "Roman" and "Lied", but then comments: "Dagegen erinnere ich nun erstlich, dass ein Lied ebenso gut romantisch sein kann," and furthermore goes on to say: "Ja ich kann mir einen Roman kaum anders denken, als gemischt aus Erzählung, Gesang und andern Formen."(4) This constant exchange of "romantisch" and "Roman" makes sense only if one considers "romanhaft" and "romantisch" as being equal. However, it would be a mistake to assume that in this "Brief" Schlegel dealt with "Romanpoesie" only in the wide sense of "romantische Poesie". He certainly occupied himself with the genre of the novel in the strict meaning, which emerges quite distinctly from the general background of romantic poetry. He even develops a universal history of the epic similar to Lukács' "Geschichte der grossen Epik".

In order to avoid any confusion about the subtle play of words in the "Brief" and our interpretation of it, especially with regard to the equation of "romantisch" and "romanartig", one should always keep in mind that the more consistent of these two terms is "romantisch", whereas "romanartig" shows either a restricted or a broad meaning. In other words, these terms cannot always be equated, and one has to ask oneself in every instance where "Roman" and "romanartig" occur, whether Schlegel uses the terms in the narrow or broad sense. As is known, critics have not agreed on the interpretation of these concepts. For some, "Roman" and "romanartig" equal "romantisch", other interpreters see a difference, in that "romantisch" always has both qualitative and historical connotations.(5) It refers to the literature of the romantic age and its qualities evoked in the reader. I think this dilemma can be overcome by accepting a dual, namely, wide and narrow content of "Roman" and "romanartig".

If one established the chronology of the great epic, the first period is that of the classical epic, which differs from modern literature by virtue of several characteristics. The epic's classical style is opposed to the modern because it does not permit that "die Einflüsse der eignen Stimmung im geringsten sichtbar werden; geschweige denn, dass er (the author) sich seinem Humor so überlassen, so mit ihm spielen dürfte, wie es in den vortrefflichsten Romanen geschieht."(6) Whereas the modern novel is based on the subjectivity and individuality of the author to the extent of often being no more than "ein mehr oder minder verhülltes Selbstbekenntnis des Verfassers, der Ertrag seiner Erfahrung, die Quintessenz seiner Eigentümlichkeit,"(7) the classical style is more objective. Classical poetry furthermore derives from mythology and pointedly avoids truly historical content: "Die alte Poesie schliesst sich durchgängig an die Mythologie an, und vermeidet sogar den eigentlichen historischen Stoff [...] die romantische Poesie hingegen ruht ganz auf historischem Grunde, weit mehr als man es weiss und glaubt."(8) The classical and the modern forms of the epic also differ in their underlying concepts of poetic unity, which in the romantic period is not limited to the unity of narration. On the contrary, this unity is constantly broken and transcended by the narrator:

> Der dramatische Zusammenhang der Geschichte macht den Roman
> im Gegenteil noch keineswegs zum Ganzen, zum Werk, wenn er es
> nicht durch die Beziehung der ganzen Komposition auf eine höhere
> Einheit, als jene Einheit des Buchstabens, über die er sich oft
> wegsetzt und wegsetzen darf, durch das Band der Ideen, durch
> einen geistigen Zentralpunkt wird.(9)

Thus as in his early study on Greek poetry, Schlegel distinguished two basic types of European literature, objective and subjective, harmonious and interesting, classical and romantic. However, in contrast to the early work much more emphasis is given here to the modern period and even to contemporary authors.

The romantic epoch is represented for Schlegel by "jene Grossen", (10) but who are these authors? In one instance, Ariosto, Cervantes, and Shakespeare are mentioned; in another, Petrarch and Tasso are referred to; then the name of Boccaccio turns up; and finally, "jene Grossen" are identified as those older Moderns in the well-known statement:

Da suche und finde ich das Romantische, bei den ältern Modernen,
bei Shakespeare, Cervantes, in der italiänischen Poesie, in jenem
Zeitalter der Ritter, der Liebe und der Märchen, aus welchem die
Sache und das Wort selbst herstammt. (11)

This historical denomination of Romanticism is nothing new. What is of
importance in this text is that Schlegel discusses the specific qualities through which
"jene Grossen" excel and summarizes them in four categories--the fantastic,
sentimental, the musical, and the picturesque. Most fundamental among these
categories of the romantic style are the first two, which are intimately interrelated, as is evidenced in the statement: "Denn nach meiner Ansicht und nach meinem
Sprachgebrauch ist eben das romantisch, was uns einen sentimentalen Stoff in einer
fantastischen Form darstellt." (12) The grand style of the Romantics thus rests on a
perfect union and integration of the sentimental and the fantastic. Sentimentality is of
course not to be understood in the deteriorated modern sense of the lacrymose, but
rather in the original meaning of "spirit of love". The interaction of the two forces
is so strong and vital that this enigma of love can only be grasped by fantasy and
expressed as a riddle:

Nur die Fantasie kann das Rätsel dieser Liebe fassen und als Rätsel
darstellen; und dieses Rätselhafte ist die Quelle von dem Fantastischen in der Form aller poetischen Darstellung. Die Fantasie strebt
aus allen Kräften sich zu äussern, aber das Göttliche kann sich in
der Sphäre der Natur nur indirekt mitteilen und äussern. Daher bleibt
von dem, was ursprünglich Fantasie war, in der Welt der Erscheinungen
nur das zurück was wir Witz nennen. (13)

The predominance of the one or the other force in this fusion gives the romantic style
variety. Thus Petrarch and Tasso have a tendency for the sentimental, whereas
Ariosto is more fantastic. Similar relationships can be observed in the mingling of
the two other categories of the romantic style: "Tasso ist mehr musikalisch und das
Pittoreske im Ariost ist gewiss nicht das schlechteste." (14) But the musical and the
picturesque are only secondary qualities, which derive from art forms extraneous
to literature, namely painting and music. They can furthermore be traced from the
primary qualities, in that the picturesque and painting are expressions of the fantastic,
and music is related to the sentimental to such an extent, "dass ichs ohne Scheu
wagen möchte, sie eine sentimentale Kunst zu nennen." (15) At any rate, this is the
romantic style in its grand expression, achieved only by the great authors and falling
apart immediately thereafter.

The ensuing period of deterioration is termed "kränklich" (16) and leads to a
predominance of the sentimental without its fantastic cloak. As is known from the
remark about Tieck's Lovell, such a fashion corrupts the sentimental and gives it
an infamous meaning, "wo man fast alles unter dieser Benennung versteht, was auf
eine platte Weise rührend und tränenreich ist, und voll von jenen familiären Edel-
mutsgefühlen, in deren Bewusstsein Menschen ohne Charakter sich so unaussprechlich glücklich und gross fühlen." (17) The declining process continues and brings
about the extinction of the fantastic. Whereas during the romantic age, fantasy

shimmered in brilliant wit, this later period exhibits only a "buntes Allerlei von
kränklichem Witz", and is altogether an unromantic and unfantastic age, producing
as literature a pile of "schmutzige Bände", "verworrene, ungebildete Redensarten",
"schlechte Bücher".(18) If one asks to which period Schlegel refers here, the answer is: "von Fielding bis zu Lafontaine", that is, the literature of the eighteenth
century up to his own time.(19)

Now in this unromantic age marked by the extinction or malady of the
imagination, there are certain authors who are of course also "sick"--what else
could be expected under such sickly conditions?(20) They cannot hold a candle to
the great ones, in Schlegel's opinion. Their productions are grotesque, not ideally
beautiful, "keine hohe Dichtung, sondern nur eine 'Arabeske'."(21) However, they
can be excused for their shortcomings because whatever has developed under such
sickly circumstances cannot be anything but sickly itself. Aside from these failings
their works still reveal originality of fantasy and thus might help us on the way "den
göttlichen Witz, die Fantasie eines Ariost, Cervantes, Shakespeare verstehn zu
lernen [...] (22) Schlegel believes that even in an unromantic age, "Naturpoesie",
the natural force of poetry, is strong enough to break through in at least some authors.
Yet who are these authors?

Schlegel mentions Laurence Sterne and emphasizes his humor, "eine geist-
reiche Form" which inspires a delight similar to what we experience when observing
the witty "Spielgemälde" called arabesques.(23) He praises Diderot's _Fataliste_ because of its "Fülle des Witzes" which is free of sentimental ingredients, reasonably
planned, and executed with a firm hand. Again, the term "arabesque" comes to light:

> Ich darf es ohne Uebertreibung ein Kunstwerk nennen. Freilich ist
> es keine hohe Dichtung, sondern nur eine - Arabeske. Aber eben
> darum hat es in meinen Augen keine geringen Ansprüche; denn ich
> halte die Arabeske für eine ganz bestimmte und wesentliche Form
> oder Aeusserungsart der Poesie.(24)

The humor of Swift along with that of Sterne is a manifestation of "Naturpoesie"
within this sickly and unromantic age, but the laurels go to Jean Paul, who although
following in Sterne's wake, is placed above the British model:

> [...] und stelle Richtern also auch darum über Sterne, weil seine
> Fantasie weit kränklicher, also weit wunderlicher und fantastischer
> ist. Lesen Sie nur überhaupt den Sterne einmal wieder. Es ist lange
> her, dass Sie ihn nicht gelesen haben, und ich denke er wird Ihnen
> etwas anders vorkommen wie damals. Vergleichen Sie dann immer
> unsern Deutschen mit ihm. Er hat wirklich mehr Witz, wenigstens
> für den, der ihn witzig nimmt: denn er selbst könnte sich darin leicht
> Unrecht tun. Und durch diesen Vorzug erhebt sich selbst seine
> Sentimentalität in der Erscheinung über die Sphäre der engländischen
> Empfindsamkeit.(25)

In these authors, the arabesque is still a "Naturprodukt", but they lay the foundations for its becoming a "Kunstwerk" and being raised to its true potentiality. (26)

From this more conciliatory pose towards contemporary literature, Schlegel can make concessions to and see positive features even in the "sogenannte Romane" which do not conform to his theory, and here among others, the formerly rejected Fielding is re-examined. The so-called sentimental novel in the vein of Richardson is acknowledged, amazingly enough, because of its potentialities for novelistic realism:

> Alle sogenannten Romane, auf die meine Idee von romantischer Form freilich gar nicht anwendbar ist, schätze ich dennoch ganz genau nach der Masse von eigner Anschauung und dargestelltem Leben, die sie enthalten; und in dieser Hinsicht mögen denn selbst die Nachfolger des Richardson, so sehr sie auf der falschen Bahn wandeln, willkommen sein. Wir lernen aus einer Cecilia Beverley wenigstens, wie man zu der Zeit, da das eben Mode war, sich in London ennuyierte, auch wie eine britische Dame vor Delikatesse endlich zu Boden stürzt und sich blutrünstig fällt; das Fluchen, die Squires und der Wakefield gibt uns einen tiefen Blick in die Weltansicht eines Landpredigers; ja dieser Roman wäre vielleicht, wenn Olivia ihre verlorne Unschuld am Ende wieder fände, der beste unter allen engländischen Romanen. (27)

However, these novels are not realistic enough for Schlegel, they do not live up to his expectations in this direction: "Aber wie sparsam und tropfenweise wird einem in allen diesen Büchern das wenige Reelle zugezählt!" (28) This realistic trend is much more effectively pursued in the genres of "Reisebeschreibung, Briefsammlung, und Selbstgeschichte," which for him constitute, especially if read in a romantic mood, "ein besserer Roman als der beste von jenen." The autobiography is highly esteemed because of the possibilities it allows for the arabesque, in that here a movement from the naive into the arabesque can take place, and as examples Schlegel mentions Rousseau's Confessions as "ein höchst vortrefflicher Roman" and Gibbon's memoirs as a "komischer Roman". (29)

As one now realizes, the "Brief" contains a comprehensive history of the novel, not in the sense of a chronological enumeration of everything novelistic, but of a digested, a critically evaluated history--in Hegel's terms "begriffene Geschichte". Schlegel established the canon of the novel and carried out the judicious distinguishing task of the critic. After having depicted the historical background of the epic genre in general and presented the emergence of the novelistic prototype as "Mischgedicht", the "Brief" examined contemporary authors with regard to potentialities for the future. This historical portrait is filled with remarks about and insights into essential components of the novel, such as the individuality of the author, the special unity underlying this genre, the play of irony, the role of humor, the contrast of form and content, the alternation from naivitée to deliberation, as well as the part of reality, "das Reelle": "die Masse von eigner Anschauung und dargestelltem Leben."

In a word, through this history Schlegel presents his theory of the novel; this "Brief über den Roman" actually is his theory of the novel according to the motto: "Die Theorie der Kunst ist ihre Geschichte." This, however, would have been difficult to detect, had he presented the history in chronological order; in the present structure of intended confusion and intermingling, his theory is still hardly noticeable. Thus the spice of irony must be tasted when towards the end the author postpones the elaboration of his theory for some future date and exclaims: "Wenn solche Beispiele ans Licht träten, dann würde ich Mut bekommen zu einer <u>Theorie des Romans</u>, die im ursprünglichen Sinne des Wortes eine Theorie wäre." For what else has he portrayed but a theory which is immediately thereafter defined as: "eine geistige Anschauung des Gegenstandes mit ruhigem, heitern ganzen Gemüt, wie es sich ziemt, das bedeutende Spiel göttlicher Bilder in festlicher Freude zu schauen." (30) In this passage Schlegel also claims: "Eine solche Theorie des Romans würde selbst ein Roman sein müssen" and thus points to an idea of a novel of the novel. This brief essay is certainly not a novel, and the above hypothesis might be shattered, but if the demand for a "Roman" is limited to artistic structure, then this short piece would fulfill the requirement. Yet there is even stronger evidence. Discussing this planned theory of the novel in a novel on the novel, Schlegel continues: "Das wären Arabesken." As Raymond Immerwahr has already demonstrated, this "Brief" is indeed the most faultless example of what Schlegel understood by the arabesque. In this context, it is worth mentioning that the concept of a novel of the novel is also applicable to a novel Friedrich Schlegel actually wrote, <u>Lucinde</u>. Indeed, recent interpretations of <u>Lucinde</u> point out the highly artistic structure of the little work in the sense of a "Roman des Romans."(31) However, the frequent assumption that Schlegel wrote this "Brief über den Roman" in order to justify his <u>Lucinde</u> is too far-reaching a conclusion,(32) especially if one considers the broad historical terrain that is covered in his essay.

V. THE TYPOLOGY OF THE NOVEL

The phrase "blosse Arabeske" and the expectation of "wahre Arabesken" in the "Brief über den Roman" seem to indicate that the present stage of the "unfantastic era" can be overcome. As far as the novel was concerned, Schlegel had not merely futile hopes, but worked concretely as a critic on something greater in this genre than had ever existed before: the absolute novel. This would seem to be a daring undertaking, but appears even more ambitious if one takes into consideration that the construction of this novel is only part of an overriding effort to bring poetry to its apex, to prepare the absolute work of art. This enormous undertaking is equated to God and presented as the combination of the absolute maximum of the novel plus the absolute maximum of poetic philosophy plus the absolute maximum of poetic poetry and in other notations termed transcendental poetry: "Die absolute Poesie = transcendentale oder speculative Poesie."(1) How is this to be understood? Is it to be taken as a mere quantitative combination, a tallying, the evolution from learned criticism to creative poetry? Are actual expectations to be combined with these hypothetical ideas?

There is certainly enough evidence in the literary notebooks to answer these questions in the positive. Upon closer scrutiny a different impression arises, which can perhaps be best expressed by Kant's formula of a regulative idea in the sense of an infinite process of striving without ever attaining the goal, or in the language of Jaspers' existentialistic interpretation of Kant, a borderline concept, a "Grenzbegriff der Erfahrung".(2) This thought process presents itself here, in the realm of literature and criticism, as the interesting attempt to elucidate the creative drive and the literary task by raising the poetic ideal to the highest power, by confronting possible achievements in the real world with an unreachable goal and thereby bringing the idea of poetry into clearer focus. In this context it is revealing to note that Schlegel circumscribed his objective as "das unmögliche Ideal der Poesie".(3)

This interpretation gains support if one looks at other aphorisms. Such a reaching out for something unheard of without the assumption that it will ever be achieved is regarded as the essence of the modern mind. As Schlegel already comprehended in the early essay on Greek poetry, since no absolute is possible in our world, modern man's search for it continues on:

> Die moderne Poesie geht entweder auf absolute Fantasie - oder auf absolute Lust - absoluten Schmerz - absolute Mimik (Shakspeare) - absolutes Pathos - absolute Form (Shakspeare). Absoluten Enthusiasm - absolute Kunst - absolute Wissenschaft pp., überhaupt das Absolute. Absolutes Wunderbares.(4)

For this tendency Schlegel uses the term approximation in conceiving of the absolute novel as something "dem sich jeder andre approximiren soll" and labels "absolute Poesie und absoluter Roman" as "wahre Ideale". He discovers a cyclical tendency in literary history leading up to the highest and then beginning again at the bottom.(5)

In a later entry in his notebooks, Schlegel specifies how his aphorisms on the novel have to be read and understood, namely, chronologically, and interpreted as "experimentirende Fragmente".(6) Indeed, this is the most fruitful way to proceed, since they are shifting in their terminology and confusing in their fantastic associations.

This critic is certainly constantly on the move; however, by following his ideas in chronological order, one realizes a certain line of thought in the establishment of the absolute novel.

The term "absolute novel" appears for the first time in No. 363 of the Literary Notebooks: "Der absolute Roman muss wie Homer ein Inbegriff der ganzen Zeitbildung sein." Yet previously, the same idea appeared in the denomination of "vollkommner Roman" or as an example of complete mingling, (7) characterized in No. 274 as an amalgamation of absolute ethics, absolute philosophy, and absolute politics. The absolute character of the novel is furthermore expressed in the statement: "Alle Werke sind nur Studien und alle Werke sollen Romane sein," a thought that finds its explanation by the ensuing entry: "Studium heisse das Werk wodurch nur der Künstler weiterkommt; Werk wodurch die Kunst selbst desgleichen. - "(8) Schlegel's critical endeavor, however, resides not only in setting up a new ideal of the novel, but also in rejecting failures, imperfect and finite realizations of this genre according to his critical motif:

> Das Pragmatische in der Kunstlehre ist die Rangordnung der Dicht-
> arten und die daraus hergeleitete Angabe neuer Kunstarten, oder
> vielmehr Kunstindividuen (Bestimmung der reinen Abarten und Un-
> arten).(9)

This negative task of separating the "Abarten und Unarten" consists in a characterization of types of the novel which do not fulfill the ultimately envisioned goal and belong to the "Prolegomena des Romans".(10) In other words, Schlegel seeks to isolate types of the novel which manifest its incompletion and imperfection:

Vom unvollkommnen Roman gibst grade <u>vier</u> Arten.(11)

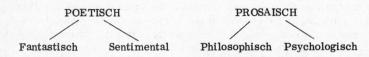

POETISCH   PROSAISCH

Fantastisch   Sentimental   Philosophisch Psychologisch

We therefore have four basic types of the novel as it has heretofore existed, two in the poetic realm, the fantastic and sentimental novels; and two in prosaic expression, the philosophical and the psychological novels. These are four fundamental forms in Schlegel's discussion in 1797, later to be supplanted by other typologies, but essential and initial to his dealing with the subject:

> Fantastischer Roman, Sentimentaler Roman, psychologischer Roman
> und philosophischer Roman die vier einzig möglichen Kunstromane.
> Jeder Roman der nicht dazu gehört ist ein NaturRoman.(12)

First one has to find out what he understood by these classifications.

The philosophical and psychological novels go hand in hand because they are predominantly in prose. Hans Eichner pointed out that according to No. 384, they find their prototypes in Diderot's <u>Religieuse</u> which is psychological, and <u>Jacques le</u>

fataliste, which is philosophical.(13) But there is certainly much more evidence for an illustration of these types in the notebooks. The psychological novel incites the imagination according to No. 358:

> Die Schönheit des psychologischen Romans oder vielmehr seine Grösse besteht in einer unerschütterlichen Kälte. Er muss die Einbildung nur heiss machen, das Herz gar nicht beschäftigen, die Sinne auch nicht. Er nimmt den Stoff von Shakspeare und die Form von den Modernen.

In these prophetic views, Schlegel goes so far as to postulate the psychological novel as being absolutely psychological, a quality so distinct that this novel's objective could not be presented in a treatise.(14) In another aphorism, he says: "Im psychologischen Roman ein Held und eine Heldin, und alle andern Charaktere in gehöriger Abstufung. - Im psychologischen Roman alles was die Erwartung spannen, immer höher spannen und endlich befriedigen kann."(15) The psychological novel has to present "alles ausgeführt, begründet, entwickelt," whereas the philosophical novel offers "alles kühn toccirt, hingeworfen genialisch (wie Blitz und Sturm) - fast Caricatur - Alles extrem und eccentrisch."(16)

To give another of these contrasts:

> Im psychologischen Roman die vornehme Würde und Gleichmässigkeit der römischen Historie, die dichterische Ausfüllung und Rundung der Griechen. - Im philosophischen Roman die Schwere und gedrängte Fülle, das Schneidende der Griechischen Rhetorik, das Schmeissende der römischen Rhetorik.(17)

The philosophical novel appears to arise out of a more serene, urbane, humorous, and ironical mood. It embraces a philosophy of wit and the already familiar technique of parabasis which together with the styles of the mimic and the urbane creates what is called humor.(18) Socrates was undoubtedly Schlegel's model for the philosopher! This becomes even more evident if one looks at further notations on the philosophical novel, such as: "Philosophischer Roman ein Buch, welches der Correctheit auf jeder Seite Nasenstüber giebt," or: "Für den philosophischen Roman müsste man die deutsche Sprache durchaus zotisiren," and finally, "Im philosophischen Roman alle möglichen Extreme; eine alte Frau ist schon ein gutes Extrem."(19)

Because of its philosophical and intellectual nature one might be inclined to relate this type to the critical novel, which is differentiated shortly thereafter, and they are indeed interconnected: "Kritischer Roman und philosophischer Roman haben eine Diagonaltendenz."(20) With regard to the critical novel, the "Roman des Romans" of the "Brief über den Roman" also comes to mind: "Philosophie des Romans im Roman selbst," or: "Im philosophischen Roman eine philosophische Ansicht des Romans und eine Romantische Ansicht der Philosophie."(21) It is not sure, however, if the critical novel is not simply a variation of the psychological novel, a supposition which would find evidence in Nos. 706 and 853.

The two other types of this initial scheme, the fantastic and sentimental novels, are united by their poetic quality and are much more difficult to distinguish: "Fantastisches und Sentimentales im poetischen Roman nicht zertrennlich; entweder eines herrscht und beides verschmilzt sich, oder beides ist gleich und verschmilzt sich nicht."(22) Indeed, they will soon be taken up under the category of the poetic novel and then integrated along with the ethical and philosophical novel into the new typology of philosophical, poetic, and ethical novels--already known to us from Philosophische Lehrjahre.(23) "Wir haben philosophische Romane (Jakobi), poetische (Goethe)," Schlegel says in Aphorism 571. Eichner discovered that the model for the fantastic novel was Tasso's Orlando furioso and the ideal of the sentimental type was his Gerusalemme liberata, (24) but the notebooks abound in material for exemplifying these two styles:

> Romeo und Hamlet sind beide = Sentimentaler Roman + philosophischer
> Roman, aber im Hamlet präpondirt philosophischer Roman, im Romeo
> der Sentimentale Roman. - In Sturm und Sommernachtstraum herrscht
> das Fantastische.(25)

Further illustrations for these modes can be found in Petrarch, Pulci, Cervantes, and Guarini; but the fantastic is also exemplified by the genre of the fairytale as we find it in Tieck and Goethe: "Darin hat Tieck recht, dass in den Volksmährchen oft absolute Fantasie ist," or: "In Goethe's Mährchen ist indifferente absolute Fantasie auf die vollkommenste Weise."(26)

These four types of novels are often brought together in Schlegel's writings:

> Absolute philosophische Romane und absolute psychologische Romane
> lassen sich unendlich viele machen; aber Sentimentales Romanzo
> braucht man nur eines zu machen und auch nur Ein Fantastisches
> Romanzo. Man liebt eigentlich nur einmal und man erreicht den Gipfel
> der Wollust nur einmal.(27)

But this underlying scheme will soon change or will rather be enriched by the discovery of new types of the novel. The rhetorical novel seems to be the manifestation of an effective practical style within this genre(28) and by distinguishing itself from the poetic concerns in the mode of the fantastic and the sentimental, comes closer to the philosophical type. The former segregation of psychological and philosophical novels from the fantastic and sentimental novels can then be reduced to an opposition of rhetorical and poetic or rhetorical and mystical novels.(29) In the realm of the poetic novel, initially subdivided into the fantastic and the sentimental, Schlegel introduced an important addition by way of the mimic, which is to be understood as the biographical novel.(30) The new tri-partition of the poetic novel is illustrated by the three parts of Dante's Divina Commedia: "Mimischer Roman überwiegt in Dante's Hölle, Sentimentaler Roman im Fegefeuer, Fantastischer Roman im Himmel." On the basis of Shakespeare these three styles appear as the following: "In einigen Stücken von Shakspeare dominirt Fantasie (Sommernachtstraum), in andern Sentimentalität (Romeo), Mimik (Komödien), Politik (in den historischen Stücken)."(31)

All these species of the novel, distinguishing themselves by a "spezifische Einheit", are to be combined in the absolute novel, which has "alle möglichen Einheiten."(32) But before this can be dealt with, further enrichments of the initial typology should be encountered. In his Aphorism No. 744 Schlegel mentions twelve novels, all of which cannot be characterized here. Most exciting is certainly his recognition of the type of the <u>historical</u> novel first introduced in connection with the <u>political</u> novel:

> Urbanität ist nicht im Politischen Roman und im Historischen Roman
> sondern im Mimischen Roman und im rhetorischen Roman nöthig. -
> Liesse sich nicht auch ein prophetischer Politischer Roman, das Ideal
> der Nazion in die Zukunft verlegt denken? Das Maximum von Politi-
> schem Roman sind Shakspeare's historische Stücke alle zusammenge-
> nommen. Im Politischen Roman der Geist der Nazion dargestellt. Ein
> Held, Eine Handlung demselben nicht wesentlich.(33)

Viewed from the initial blueprint, the historical novel obviously has to be ranged within the category of the critical-philosophical-prose novels, but it is certainly more interesting that from the point of view of content, Schlegel considers "Legende die Urform des Historischen Romans."(34) This type of the novel is best depicted in No. 1251, where it is related to Horace: "Der organische Historische Roman strebt nach einem Ideal von absoluter Natur und Zeitalter. – (Auch Horatius strebt in seiner Poesie nach einem solchen politischen historischen Ideal)."

The historical novel will soon have to make way for the <u>ethical</u> novel, but does not seem to be identical to it if one looks at some traits of this new type:

> Im ethischen Roman die höchste Cohäsion, Fluss weder Lücken noch
> Sprung; Gespräche, Träume, Briefe, Erinnerung. Schöne Geschwätzig-
> keit. - <u>Confessions</u> gehören zu Romantischen Romanen. - Liessen sich
> nicht schönere ethische Geheimnisse geben?(35)

Obviously, the ethical novel excels not so much in its comprehension of an age, but rather in an individual mood of harmony, cohesion, and is thus almost reminiscent of the "objective" poetry of the Ancients. In fact Schlegel says: "Für die ethischen Romane ist auch Sophokles Vorbild; ernste hohe Schönheit die über den Reiz und über das Entzücken selbst erhaben ist."(36)

With this recognition of the ethical novel, the typology of the philosophical, poetic, and ethical novels has been reached, a typology familiar through <u>Philosophi-sche Lehrjahre</u>, and here one comes to the end of Schlegel's typological schematiz-ing. These three types form the basis for his further characterizations. In No. 1341 one reads: "Die musikalische Wiederholung des Interesses an der eignen Person findet wohl nur im philosophischen und poetischen Roman Statt, nicht im ethischen Roman." In No. 1352 he states: "Im poetischen Roman ein unendlich Ethisches, im philosophischen Roman ein analysiertes Ethisches; im ethischen Roman beides." To be sure, he still mentions the organic novel, calling forth the sub-division into the organic, chemical, and mechanical of the <u>Philosophische Lehrjahre</u>,(37) but

from then on, he typifies novels more and more according to national characteristics.

The entry No. 1353 sheds light on the <u>German</u> novel, and No. 1456 wittily
summarizes its essence: "Die Sünde und die Kunst sind die Pole des Deutschen
Romans." Other aphorisms depict the English novel:

> Auch die Engländischen poetischen Romane gehn alle auf ein absolutes
> Maximum von Rührung; Goethe hat diese Waare am besten gefertigt;
> seine Manufactur die einfachste und feinste; aber vielleicht sollte sie
> in Entzücken verwandelt werden. - In fast allen Romanen viel Ballast
> ausser im Meister und im Don Quixote. (38)

Within the national scope of the <u>French</u> novel, Diderot attracted Schlegel's fascination,
as is shown in the following aphorism: "Jacques von Diderot ist nicht so wohl ein
Roman als eine Persifflage dagegen. Der Herr im Jacques ist vortrefflich null.
Diderot behandelt die Neugier wie eine ganz ausgelassene und in der Religieuse wie
eine sehr intriguante Coquette." (39) The epic poetry of the Iberian Peninsula is still
centered in Cervantes for Schlegel, (40) but gains new interest through Camões, not
a novelist, but an epic poet in the Homeric vein. This selection reveals Schlegel's
beginning departure from the novel as the supreme genre. The following fragment can
serve as a summary of the multifaceted investigations Schlegel undertook into the
nature and the various shapes of the novel:

> Immer war es ein adliches Religiöses Aesthetisches gebildetes
> Leben, aus dem der Roman entsprang und wohin er wieder wollte. Er
> geht also in sich selbst zurück. - Die Engländischen Romane sind ein
> System für sich, die französischen und die deutschen bilden nur ein
> Ganzes. (41)

VI. THE NOVEL AS AN IDEAL OF PROGRESSIVE POETRY: "ABSOLUTER ROMAN" AND THE ABANDONMENT OF THE NOVEL

The overriding goal of these typologies is to construct the absolute novel as the specific form of progressive literature. "Progressives Gedicht ist der Roman," Schlegel says. (1) The term absolute seems to imply that there can only be one novel on this level of perfection and that this novel is a synthesis of all incomplete ones:

> Absoluter Roman = psychologischer Roman + philosophischer Roman + Fantastischer Roman + Sentimentaler Roman + absolute Mimik + absolut SentimentalFantastisches + absolutes poetisches Drama rhetorisches Drama + Prophetie. (2)

On the other hand, Schlegel is not entirely sure as to whether there should be only one or a plurality of "absoluter Roman", since it is conceivable that one of the many ingredients of which this novel is composed could predominate and color the entire work: "Es giebt vom absoluten Roman sehr viele Arten, je nach dem dieser oder jener Bestandtheil präponderirt." (3) At any rate, this genre is an amalgamation: "Im absoluten Roman muss alles verschmolzen werden, und was nicht verschmolzen werden kann, muss wegbleiben." It is a "Maximum von Mischung", a "gebildetes künstliches Chaos", even a synthesis of Classicism and Romanticism, in that the style of the absolute novel should be progressive, but its content classical. Furthermore, the absolute novel is a fusion of philosophy and poetry, of art and science, of prosaic and poetic elements: "Der Roman ist Poesie in Verbindung mit Wissenschaft, daher mit Kunst; daher die Prosa und die Poesie der Poesie." (4)

Whereas these observations deal with the structure of the absolute novel, other remarks delineate its content and relationship to reality. First of all, this ideal novel combines the presentation of the age with the depiction of the individuality of the artist:

> Der absolute Roman muss Darstellung des Zeitalters sein wie das classische Epos. - Absoluter Roman = absolute Historische Poesie + absolute politische Poesie + absolute Individualpoesie = universelle Bildungslehre, poetische Lebenskunstlehre, Darstellung des Zeitalters, Inbegriff des Künstlers. (5)

Thus this novel strives to synthesize two absolute postulates: "Roman überhaupt die Vereinigung zweier Absoluten, der absoluten Individualität und der absoluten Universalität." (6) Subjectivity has to be made objective, and it would be an error to assume that the novel constituted a subjective poetic form. (7) Indeed, this genre has a realistic tendency which is essential to its very nature: "Der Roman muss sich nothwendig auf einen bestimmten Zeitpunkt beziehen: dieser Realismus ist in seinem Wesen gegründet." (8) The novel is not absorbed by infinity, but rather tries to step out of it: "Der Roman strebt nicht nach dem Unendlichen, sondern aus dem Unendlichen heraus." (9) In other words, it uses the previously mentioned techniques of "Potenzierung" and "Radizierung": "Willkührliches Zusammenziehn und Entfalten im Vortrag des Romans; diese Elasticität der Darstellung (im Cervantes) ist sehr episch." (10) In this, the absolute novel is "unbedingt", but in a completely natural way similar to that of musical composition: "Die Methode des Romans ist die der Instrumentalmusik. Im Roman dürfen selbst die Charaktere so willkürlich behandelt werden, wie die Musik ihr Thema behandelt."(11) This naturalness can also be imagined in the sense of not permitting alterations and then appears to be in line with necessity. Schlegel even comments: "Einen Roman muss man eigentlich gar nicht ändern, nicht corrigiren können," and in this light, the novel gains the aura of a "Religiöse Schrift".(12)

Thus in the idea of the absolute novel, this genre has been raised to its highest power. However, just by relating the novel to the concept of a religious writing, doubts and feelings of reluctance arise in Friedrich Schlegel with regard to the novelistic genre so highly esteemed until then. There are only a few aphorisms in which the novel is envisioned as carrying the religious message, the predominant theme in Schlegel's thought since the summer of 1798 and later to be consumed by the idea of a new mythology. To the degree that the religion of the new mythology grows in importance, the novel slips from its high and eminent place within Schlegel's poetics until it is finally abandoned. This tendency has already been detected in his philosophical notebooks but finds its parallel in the literary aphorisms of 1798 to 1800.

In the enumeration of the poetic forms of Romanticism in Aphorism No. 1622, the novel glimmers rather inconspicuously: "Die jetzigen (Romantischen) Natur Formen sind Confessionen - Reisebeschreibungen - Volkssagen - und orientlische Mährchen. (Briefsammlungen - Familiengemählde - KunstlerRomane)." A few aphorisms mirror a reflection of the old enthusiasm for the novel as an art form, and one of them still considers it as an absolute creation: "Der Roman ist offenbar absolutes System, ein Buch im höchsten Sinne."(13) But an ensuing entry reduces this to a mere ambition "dass jeder Roman ein absolutes Buch sein will."(14) From now on Schlegel progressively abandons the novel, which is soon ranged among "falsche Poesie" and furthermore, belittled in the comment: "Confessions, Arabesken und dass Frauen Romane schreiben, ist der ganze Gewinn vom sogenannten Roman des Zeitalters."(15) Shortly thereafter, it is regarded as expressing what has already been the essence of poetry in the past and no longer as a creation of something new: "Vom Roman kann man nur fodern was das Wesen der Poesie ist, Naiv - Grotesk - Fantastisch - Sentimental."(16) As characteristics of the novel, Schlegel lists: "1) Vermischung des Dramatischen, Epischen, Lyrischen. 2) Entgegensetzung gegen das Didaktische. 3) Rückkehr zur Mythologie und selbst zur classischen Mythologie," but it is precisely this return to mythology that dethrones the novel.(17) Another component that frees itself from the novel and attains its own recognition to the detriment of the novel is the fairytale: "Das Wesentliche im Roman ist die chaotische Form - Arabeske, Mährchen."(18) If here the fairytale is still integrated within the novel, Schlegel is nevertheless about to make it independent and raise its value.(19) Another genre encroaching upon the novel's domain is lyric poetry, as can clearly be seen in the aphorisms "Zur Poesie 1800".(20) "Die Poesie muss jetzt und will jetzt durch Encyclopädie und durch Religion reformirt und centrirt werden," Schlegel says, and the idea of the encyclopedia becomes another substitute for the heretofore favored form.(21) A classification of realistic and poetic genres established in the same year does not even mention the novel: "Sage, Mährchen, Novelle gehn auf das wirkliche Leben; Arabeske, Schäfergedicht, Legende sind alle nur poetische Poesie - Darstellung der Kunst, der Poesie, künstlerischer Menschen und des poetischen Lebens."(22) Another genre emerging on its own from the totality of the novel is the "Novelle".(23) Then once again the novel is included among the elementary forms of mythological poetry: "Roman, Epos, Elegie, Fantasie, Vision - sind die Elemente zur Form der mythologischen Poesie."(24) Although in No. 2028 the term "absoluter Roman" shows up and is considered along with the absolute epic as "die höchsten Arten", this fragment is obviously an entry taken over from an earlier writing.(25) In the later parts of the notebooks, Schlegel concentrates altogether on lyric poetry and was strongly inspired therein by Jakob Böhme's emphasis on the irrational side of human nature. This is given credence in the notation:

> Die Grundquellen der Poesie sind Zorn und Wollust und zwar die
> einzigen. Scherz und Ironie müssen von jenen durchdrungen sein,
> um wahre Poesie zu werden. Jenes sind die Elemente des Lebens.
> Bildung rein zur Kunst und diesem entgegengesetzt - herrscht im
> zweiten Grade der Poesie. - Zorn und Wollust die Pole, Witz die
> Indifferenz.(26)

Böhme will soon be elevated to a position within the triumvirate of the romantic age by Schlegel: "Dante, Böhme und Shakspeare machen ein Dreieck, zusammen der moderne Homer."(27)

This increasing scepticism towards the novel found expression also in print in the last volume of the Athenäum. Critics have noticed that in the Gespräch über die Poesie, which together with Novalis' Hymnen an die Nacht forms the aesthetic apex of this last issue, a detachment from this esteemed genre is evident.(28) Here of course they are not referring to the "Brief über den Roman", which summarizes the early Schlegel's opinion about the novel, but to the second section of the Gespräch, "Rede über die Mythologie". This speech indeed brings up something new in its demand for a spiritual center of the European soul, a new religious basis also in the realm of literary production. "Ich gehe gleich zum Ziel," Schlegel stated definitively,(29) "es fehlt, behaupte ich, unsrer Poesie an einem Mittelpunkt, wie es die Mythologie für die Alten war, und alles Wesentliche, worin die moderne Dichtkunst der antiken nachsteht, lässt sich in die Worte zusammenfassen: Wir haben keine Mythologie." Alfred Schlagdenhauffen, for instance, realizes a break between the poetic doctrine of the letter on the novel and this inspired talk on mythology and is of the opinion that from now on, the goal is no longer the novel, but symbolic poetry.(30) Indeed, in his Ideen, another section of the third volume of the Athenäum, Schlegel treats the novel with a certain disrespect and in the only notation referring to this genre, states that it is not religious enough for the present task of poetry:

> Nur durch Religion wird aus Logik Philosophie, nur daher kommt
> alles was diese mehr ist als Wissenschaft. Und statt einer ewig vollen
> unendlichen Poesie werden wir ohne sie nur Romane haben, oder die
> Spielerei, die man jetzt schöne Kunst nennt.(31)

This awakening negative attitude towards the novel can also be traced in the philosophical notebooks of Philosophische Lehrjahre, and it has been demonstrated that already in the summer of 1798, after the members of the romantic school had united in Dresden and the theme of religion was coming into the foreground, the novel ceased to be the prime genre of poetry. (32) In the latter section of the Philosophische Lehrjahre, one comes across an aphorism such as this: "Am einfachsten wäre es wohl, durch einen Roman das Romantische zu verkündigen; aber jezt nicht mehr zureichend."(33) During the period of his Paris lectures of 1803-1804, however, occupying himself again with the history of this genre, Schlegel comes to some more positive evaluations and can then say: "Vielleicht soll es nur einen Styl geben, mit Nuancen (also unendlich viele) - ausser im Roman, wo Purismus Variation und höchste Kunst des Styls gefodert wird."(34)

Whereas in the philosophical lectures of the Cologne period (1804-1806), the novel is not even mentioned, the most cogent critique of this genre can be found in the unpublished lectures Ueber deutsche Sprache und Literatur, Cologne, 1807, and the criticsm gains in value when one realizes that this course of lectures is perhaps the most significant document of Schlegel's poetics. (35) The novel is first discussed in the context of the romantic style, the essence of which is still viewed as "mingling", but now chiefly in the Shakespearean sense of an amalgamation of tragic and comic elements. Thus the modern drama is an essential expression of the romantic style. It should be noted that these Cologne lectures were delivered one year before August Wilhelm Schlegel in his Geschichte der dramatischen Kunst und Literatur presented Calderon and Shakespeare as the culmination of romantic writing. (36) In Friedrich Schlegel's lectures too the mingling is no longer reserved for the novel, and he claims: "Jede Art von Werk kann romantisch sein."(37) Yet the achievement of romantic mingling is by no means the highest goal in these lectures. As in his early treatise on Greek poetry of 1795-97, Schlegel here again conceives of the synthesis of Romanticism and Classicism as being the ultimate, and he demands from the modern poets an "Erhebung zur Klassik". (38)

After having discussed the romantic style as a mingling of the fantastic and the sentimental tone, (39) Schlegel examines the genre more closely, again mentioning the late hellenistic novels, but relegating them to a position of unimportance. (40) The novel cannot be characterized because it is unfinished, incomplete, although manifold. Only Boccaccio and Cervantes are regarded as representatives of this genre, but all in all, the novel demonstrates a decline of poetry. (41) Although Boccaccio excels in some features, which have been derived from the Ancients, his main characteristic is ordinary conversational language, "wertlose Nachahmung der Alten."(42) Cervantes receives a better evaluation because he was more inventive, and his talent is even conveyed by the term originality, "Erfindung":

> Was nun aber besonders an dem Roman zu bemerken und das Vorzüglichste, Ausgezeichnetste und Erstliche, ist die Erfindung. Dies ist auch, was Cervantes als das hauptsächlichste Verdienst ansieht, und worin er den höchsten Wert seiner Werke setzt. Hieraus entspringt ein bestimmter Begriff und Charakter für die ganze Gattung. Der Roman ist eigentlich die Poesie der Erfindung. (43)

However, what seems to be a virtue must actually be traced back to a failing, since this initially praised talent for invention is only a substitute for a lack of poetic mythology and can only be justified in cases where such a mythology cannot be detected. (44) According to Schlegel, one might question why a poet should display such a "Verschwendung von so viel Kraft und eigener Erfindung" instead of abiding by the old mythology "um das eine Gedicht zu vollenden." This criticism applies even to the highly regarded Cervantes, and Schlegel asks whether it would not have been a greater gain for poetry, had Cervantes re-formed the old "Ritterbücher" instead of displaying his talent for invention. (45)

To be sure, Schlegel does not deny Cervantes his due praise: "In diesem Bestreben liegt etwas Grosses," but it is rather disappointing to realize that he compares the greatness of this endeavor to nothing more than the achievement of Greek comedy:

> Das Drama der Neueren hatte nicht sowohl Gelegenheit, sich wie die alte Komödie zu bilden, aber der Roman kann freilich die Stelle derselben vertreten. So haben das <u>Decamerone</u> des Boccaz und <u>Don Quixote</u> viel Aehnlichkeit mit der alten Komödie - mit dem Unterschied, dass freilich ein so grosses, umfassendes Werk wie letzteres nach ganz anderen Regeln und Gesetzen entworfen und anders zu beurteilen ist als eine Komödie. (46)

In comparison to the novel and perhaps to any other genre in the epic realm, the fairytale has aroused Schlegel's critical predilection:

> In dem Märchen ist aber das Wunderbare das notwendige Element hiermit. Das heisst, insofern das Wunderbare hier die Hauptsache, tritt auch eine grössere Fülle des Wunderbaren ein als in der Mythologie. In keiner alten Mythologie ist es in so starken Massen vorhanden, wie im Märchen. Hier herrscht wie im Roman die grösste Willkürlichkeit, es ist auch Poesie der Erfindung.

Indeed, there are two offspring of the novel that are of great consequence for Schlegel, the "Novelle" and the "Märchen". (47) Yet it is the fairytale that wins first prize:

> Einfachheit und Treue an der Ueberlieferung. Das Märchen aber bietet als diejenige Form, welche die wunderbarste, willkürlichste Darstellung erlaubt, und nicht allein fähig ist, das Fabelhafteste aufzunehmen, sondern auch entgegengesetzte Sphären von wunderbaren Dingen, hat wegen der grossen Willkürlichkeit hierzu am besten die Hand. Weil nun also gewisse Werke, die durchaus zur Vervollkommnung der Poesie gehören, nur in dieser Gattung ausführbar sind, scheint seine Notwendigkeit begründet.

The novella, the fairytale, and the novel signify the attempt to achieve a poetry of poetry. For this endeavor, one can name several quite extraordinarily poetic fairytales, according to Schlegel, but in the genre of the novel he finds only a few truly

outstanding works, "neben sehr vielen unbedeutenden und Missgeburten."(48)
Later on in these lectures, the novel is envisioned in more general fashion, but
the result is rather poor.(49) The novel might be able to lead back to a poetic
life, and that is all; it certainly cannot form the basis for poetry. The novel appears
rather as an introduction to poetry:

> [...] als Zurückführung zu dem poetischen Leben, zur Poesie, als Versuche,
> das Zeitalter wieder zur Poesie einzuführen; und so muss man also
> wohl die neuern ausgezeichnetsten deutschen Romane wie Sternbald und
> Meister betrachten, (die man aus einer zufälligen Beziehung auf die
> Kunst auch Kunstromane genannt hat, wiewohl die Kunstansicht im
> Meister bei aller Objektivität und Schönheit poetischer Darstellung doch
> einen prosaischen Kern hat). Eine eigene neue Poesie begründen, kann
> der Roman gar nicht.

To be precise, the novel is too subjective, too individualistic.(50) Novalis'
Heinrich von Ofterdingen is still esteemed as a good novel because of many episodes
which are related to the fairytale, and so is Wilhelm Meister, in which Schlegel
finds many dispersed novellas.(51) Yet on the whole, the result is that modern poetry
takes a back seat to the older forms.(52)

Having delivered these lectures in Cologne, Schlegel went to Vienna and
Hungary and on this journey carried along a notebook bearing the title "Gedanken"
(1808-09) chiefly devoted to political themes, but also containing many aesthetic
observations.(53) If in the Cologne lectures, the fairytale and the novella enjoy
prominence, this text reflects a greater emphasis on lyric poetry, an accent already
noted in the last issue of the Athenäum and also evidenced in the Cologne lectures.
Lyric poetry, more specifically the "Lied", clearly supplants the novel. In an early
notation, Schlegel states: "Einteilung der Poesie nicht in episch-lyrisch-dramatisch,
sondern in Lied-Gedicht und Schauspiel. - Gedicht ist das gemischte, didaktische-
romantische. Lied das Höchste der reinen Poesie."(54) Somewhat later, he goes so
far as to say: "Wo keine lyrische Poesie ist, da ist gar keine," whereas the novel's
true value is seen only in fairytales and legends: "Der Roman in Versen ausschlies-
send den alten Märchen und Legenden bestimmt."(55)

There is especially one form of the novel rejected by Schlegel, namely, the
"Künstlerroman", depicted as a false genre: "Noch eine andre und eigne Form des
Romans wäre aber die Verbindung desselben mit dem Platonischen Dialog: (ist
eine falsche Gattung) dahin zielt offenbar der sogenannte KünstlerRoman"(56) Indeed,
the entire form of the novel now appears as mere imitation. Furthermore, the novel
is a sympton of degeneration, still to be utilized, but in the form of "Künstlerroman",
it is a false tendency.(57) Poetry must be progressive, and only lyric poetry can
depict the future, not solely in the sense of what is to come, but in the sense of
eternity:

> Epische - die Vergangeheit
> Dramatische (mythisch) - (Zukunft) keine Zeit
> Roman - Gegenwart
> Lyrische - Ewigkeit? Zukunft?(58)

What had formerly been viewed as the highest creative task is now assigned to lyric poetry: "in der lyrischen Poesie der lebendige Gott."(59) Poetry may lower itself to drama, but should maintain a strict isolation and separation from the common novel. (60) National life can be presented in the drama, but epic poetry finds its best expression in "Gedichten" and can perhaps be sub-classified into mundane and spiritual poetry dealing with God and nature.(61) "Lieder", however, comprise genuine poetry:

> Lieder sind die eigentliche Poesie, Schauspiele dann das nächste
> wenigstens zu duldende. Gedichte zum Lesen - dahin alles übrige
> auch der Roman; wenn es kein Gedicht in welcher Form es sei, so
> ist es gar nichts.(62)

Four years later, Schlegel delivered his Vienna lectures on Geschichte der alten und neuen Literatur (1812), considered as his most accomplished work in literary criticism. Here the novel is presented as a "verfehlte Gattung".(63) Cervantes' novel, in spite of its "hohe innre Vortrefflichkeit" is regarded as a fateful "gefährliches und irreleitendes Beispiel der Nachahmung,"(64) since it spurred on the genre of the modern novel. Why does Schlegel object to this genre? The answer is provided at the beginning of the twelfth lecture:

> In allen diesen Versuchen, die prosaische Wirklichkeit durch Witz
> und Abenteuer, oder durch Geist und Gefühlserregung zu einer
> Gattung der Dichtkunst zu erheben, sehen wir die Verfasser immer
> auf irgend eine Weise eine poetische Ferne suchen; sei es nun in
> dem Künstlerleben des südlichen Italiens, wie oft in den deutschen
> Romanen, oder in den amerikanischen Wäldern und Wildnissen,
> was vielfältig bei den Ausländern versucht worden. Ja, wenn auch
> die Begebenheit ganz im Lande spielt, immer strebt die Darstellung
> so lange sie noch Darstellung bleibt, und nicht bloss in ein Ge-
> dankenspiel der Laune, des Witzes und des Gefühls sich auflöst,
> auf irgend eine Weise aus der beengenden Wirklichkeit sich heraus-
> zuarbeiten, und irgend eine Oeffnung, einen Eingang zu gewinnen
> in ein Gebiet, wo die Fantasie sich freier bewegen kann.(65)

In other words, he objects to the novel's escape from reality, but one should not expect Schlegel's ideal to be a naturalistic depiction of reality. He thinks rather of a poetic transformation of reality, a symbolic vision, as has been mentioned in my introduction.(66) From this point of view, he can maintain a higher opinion of Richardson, or of the English novel as a whole, than of the French novel in the style of Voltaire and Diderot.(67) But the novel in its more general and extroverted form certainly does not fulfill Schlegel's expectations of poetry at this point, an expectation to be met by lyric poetry.

Thus the theme Friedrich Schlegel and the modern novel ends with a dis-appointment, although during one period of his career, he raised the novel to a higher demand and esteem than had any other critic. In the beginning of this study, he was compared to Aristotle in the sense that just as Aristotle was the theoretician of classical poetics, more particularly, the epic and tragedy, Schlegel was the prophet of modern poetics with regard to the novel. This assertion must now be specified. To the same degree that the novel is gradually abandoned, or ceases to occupy Schlegel's main aesthetic interest, symbolic poetry--more precisely, lyrics-- gains in stature, a mine of thought that has not yet been explored by criticism.

PART TWO

NOVALIS

I. NOVALIS CRITICISM IN THE LIGHT OF NEW INSIGHTS

At the end of July, 1798, Friedrich Schlegel wrote from Dresden to his friend and correspondent Friedrich von Hardenberg: "Ich muss Dir nur hiemit declarieren, dass ich gesonnen bin, auch über den Mittelpunkt Deiner Philosophie [...] mit Dir in Correspondenz zu sein."(1) This central motif of Novalis' philosophical thought so succinctly referred to by Schlegel here is a topic of elusive quality, not only because Novalis was anything but a systematic thinker, but also because most critical study devoted to this romantic author has focused upon his imaginative creative works. Critics have drawn on the more abstract theoretical statements mainly to underscore a particular interpretation of a poetic work with the authority of the poet's own pronouncement. One need only recall to mind the famous dictum that the world must be romanticized and its many occurrences in critical literature to illustrate this point.(2) Furthermore, such references have chiefly been limited to the more familiar fragments published in the Athenäum, whereas the bulk of his direct expression of personal philosophical views has remained a somewhat mysterious entity. Only recently have critics attempted to penetrate the cloak of obscurity and confusion surrounding the thousands of fragments which record Novalis' ideas on poetry, the poet, philosophy, life, politics, etc., and few have succeeded in drawing conclusions as to what exactly seems to constitute the "Mittelpunkt" of his philosophy.(3)

There is good reason to believe that this central idea in Novalis' thought is what he and Friedrich Schlegel termed "Transzendentalpoesie", that rhythmic process of Fichtean thought which they imbued with a poetic view of the world. Novalis developed a concept of emergence out of the self alternating with a return back into the self which reflected the dialectical relationship of inner reality with the external world. Indeed, by studying nature we are directed inwardly towards the core of our being, and conversely, by examining the self, we are led back to nature again.(4) Thus Novalis believes that this process allows us to perceive nature or the external world as something human and thus analogous to ourselves:

> Sie zeigt, dass wir alles nur so verstehn können und sollen, wie wir
> uns selbst und unsre Geliebten, uns und euch verstehn. Wir er-
> blicken uns im System, als Glied - mithin in auf und absteigender
> Linie, vom Unendlich kleinen bis zum Unendlich Grossen - Menschen
> von unendlichen Variationen. Wir verstehn natürlich alles Fremde
> nur durch Selbstfremdmachung--Selbstveränderung--Selbstbeobachtung.
> Jezt sehn wir die wahren Bande der Verknüpfung von Subject und
> Object - sehn, dass es auch eine Aussenwelt in uns giebt, die mit
> unserm Innern in einer analogen Verbindung, wie die Aussenwelt
> ausser uns mit unserm Aeussern und jene und diese so verbunden
> sind, wie unser Innres und Aeussres.(5)

He continues by remarking that so-called transcendental philosophy, the connection between object and perception, now appears in a totally different light. Novalis thus assumes an identity between subject and object, an organic relationship: "Die innre Welt is gleichsam mehr Mein, als die Aeussre [...] Was ausser mir ist, ist gerade in mir, ist mein - und umgekehrt."(6) This poetic perception of the world marks the transcendental poet, the transcendental individual par excellence,(7) and the dialectical relationship between the inner and the outer realms, the poet and nature, forms the essence of Novalis' "grosse, alles verändernde Idee"(8) he mentions in letters and fragments and even relates to his beloved Sophia:

> Indem ich glaube, dass Söffchen um mich ist, und erscheinen kann, und diesem Glauben gemäss handle, so ist sie auch um mich - und erscheint mir endlich gewiss - gerade da, wo ich nicht vermuthe - In mir, als meine Seele vielleicht etc. [...] und gerade dadurch wahrhaft ausser mir - denn das Wahrhaft Aeussre kann nur durch mich - in mir, auf mich wirken -(9)

This dialectical process is also depicted by Novalis in terms of "Romantisieren" and "Logarithmisieren", whereby romanticizing is the elevation of the commonplace to the realm of the extraordinary, the distant and mysterious: "Ferne Philosophie klingt wie Poesie - weil jeder Ruf in die Ferne Vocal wird [...] So wird alles in der Entfernung Pöesie - Poëm. Actio in distans. Ferne Berge, ferne Menschen, ferne Begebenheiten etc. alles wird romantisch, quod idem est - daher ergiebt sich unsre Urpoëtische Natur."(10) The inverted process of logarithmization involves the reduction of the ideal to the real, the strange to the familiar, and both together constitute "Wechselerhöhung und Erniedrigung".(11)

Rudolf Haym's fundamental discussion of Novalis touches upon his political and philosophical thought, but in the main, it centers in the impact of personal experiences on his imaginative work and emphasizes Novalis' emotional aspect, fantasy having little bearing on intellect. He even characterizes the difference between Friedrich Schlegel and his friend Novalis as a polarity of rationality and fantasy: [...] "sie sind nur darin gänzlich verschieden, dass jener zur Verfestigung seiner Unbedingtheiten kein anderes Mittel als den pointierenden Verstand hat, während dieser die Erzeugnisse seiner Schwärmerei im Herzen trägt und sie glänzend mit den Fäden seiner Phantasie umspinnt."(12) Korff too presents Novalis almost exclusiv-ly as a subjective nature, stressing his magic idealism as the process by which he attempted to subjectivize the entire objective world, to overcome the empirical through the absolute. Indeed, Korff believes that for Novalis the source of all truth is the subject: "Da die Quelle aller Wahrheit das Subjekt ist, ist die Aufgabe aller Erkenntnis die Subjektivierung des Objektiven, und eben das ist in diesem Stadium 'Romantik'." When he refers to Novalis in the context of "Geist", it is not with reference to his intellectual or rational powers, but to his belief in the "Wunder- und Zauberkraft des Geistes."(13)

Oskar Walzel does discuss Novalis' intellectual views, relating them to the thought of Kant, Fichte, and Hemsterhuis, but he is so limited by space that his discussion must of necessity be superficial and misleading, insofar as he concludes simply that Novalis eventually returned from philosophy to poetry.(14)

René Wellek tends to stress the unrealistic, dreamlike quality of Novalis' ideal of poetry in his concentrated presentation, and he relegates Novalis' critical thought to the level of "mere aphoristic statements of opinions," which according to Wellek, are completely lacking in originality and are totally dependent on Schelling.(15)

Some critics have delved further into Novalis' theoretical works and seem to be aware of the incorrect view of this author as a mere representative of fantasy, imagination, and emotion, to the utter neglect of his high regard for the utilization of man's rational faculties in the creative process. Kurt May's analysis of <u>Heinrich von Ofterdingen</u> and <u>Wilhelm Meister</u> points out the obvious distinctions which have caused critics to place these two novels in direct opposition as the "romantic" versus the "classical" types, but the analysis of the "Meister" and "anti-Meister" concludes in a questioning of the entire stylistic typology as postulated by Fritz Strich, and May disputes the value and feasibility of placing styles in mutually exclusive categories. (16) He further demonstrates how Novalis' <u>Ofterdingen</u>, heretofore regarded as an open-ended fairytalelike excursion into the infinite without definite form or plan is actually the product of a carefully structured organization of chapters that do not flow eternally into one another with arbitrary beginnings and endings, but are rather independent units that can stand alone. This is no longer the poet of the blue flower of Romanticism, the voice of irrational emotion and unbounded freedom of the fantasy. May concludes with a rather startling idea, namely, that Novalis is not the representative of what is usually envisioned by Romanticism: "Von Novalis aus [...] scheint jedenfalls die Romantik in ihrem Ursprung der Klassik nicht wie Gegensatz dem Satz zu widersprechen, sondern erscheint als Versuch zur Steigerung der Klassik in einem höheren Ausgleich, einer Synthese zwischen ihr und einem Gegensatz, der für sich gar nicht realisiert ist. Oder ist das nun Romantik nicht mehr? Doch diese Problematik wächst wirklich 'ins Unendliche'." (17)

Wilhelm Dilthey was perhaps the first to be aware of the possible importance of a thorough study of Novalis' theoretical writings for a new interpretation of his imaginative works, if not for the entire period referred to as the "romantic" age: "Wie konnte auf die Dichtung Goethes und Schillers dieser jähe Absturz, diese ganze andersartige Entwicklung, diese schrankenlose Herrschaft der Subjektivität, der Phantasie, der Hingabe an die Natur, ja fesselloser Willkür folgen?" he asks, and concludes with the comment that it would indeed be an accomplishment "wenn einer oder der andere, auf Grund dieser Darstellung, einmal zu Novalis griffe, in der Voraussetzung, dass seine Fragmente vielleicht doch nicht so völlig willkürlich und zusammenhanglos, sein Ofterdingen nicht so grenzenlos verschwommen seien, als es den bisherigen Kritikern Hardenbergs erschienen ist." (18)

A glance at the latest major undertaking in the Novalis research, namely, the new Novalis edition edited by Richard Samuel, will reveal just how intent some modern critics are upon changing the one-sided image Novalis has been saddled with as an eternally ecstatic youth with his head in the clouds and no contact with reality at all. In the third volume <u>Das philosophische Werk II</u>, one is presented with not only his scientific studies of the Freiburg period, but also his technical writings pertaining to his worldly profession in the salt mines, among which are his "Aufzeichnungen zum Berg- und Hüttenwesen", "Practische Einfälle und Ideen", "Geologische Aufzeichnungen", "Aus einem Salinenprotokoll", and "Arbeitspläne und Büchernotizen". (19)

The ensuing chapters will constitute a further venture into the lesser known territory of Novalis's theoretical ideas and will shift the focus to Novalis as a serious critical thinker, thereby elaborating further the "Mittelpunkt" of his thought by realigning the unbalanced perspective of much of past criticism. Such an endeavor seems best undertaken by means of a systematic and chronological consideration of the countless fragments containing essential information as to Novalis' ever-expanding view of the nature and function of poetry, its character and task--what poetry has been in the past and what it is to become in the future.

Novalis' high regard for poetry as the crowning glory of mankind has often been discussed by critics, and indeed, his reference to the art of poetry as "göttliches Feuer", his emphasis on poetry as the civilizing force in its power to tame raw nature, to humanize, his evaluation of the poet to a position above ordinary men, and his vision of poetry as that gift which enables man to rise above himself--all attest to Novalis' view of poetry as man's highest achievement. Yet poetry for Novalis is not only a product of the imagination, the result of a flight of fantasy away from the real world, but rather a noble art involving almost all human capacities, the emotional and the intellectual, the spiritual and the rational, the imaginative and the philosophical: in short, the qualities of the human heart, mind, and soul. (20) These are the two poles of the human spirit and composition that Novalis sought to integrate into a powerful creative force to accomplish the synthesis of the finite with the infinite, to reconcile individual man to the vastness of the universe through the art of poetry. (21)

In truth, poetry is the "ächt absolute Reelle" for Novalis: "Dies ist der Kern meiner Philosophie. Je poëtischer, je wahrer." (22) It is noteworthy, however, that this well-known statement includes not merely a praise of poetry to the highest degree, but also gives concrete evidence to Novalis' desire to formulate the poetic urges he experienced into a distinct philosophy. In other words, he wished to give some order to vague notions about creativity, and although his youth was characterized by qualities of fantasy and tremendous enthusiasm for the undefined aspects of life, for "Empfindungen und Gefühle", he was capable of enough self-criticism to visualize the dangers in such a lopsided approach to life and poetry. In a letter to Professor Reinhold in Jena of October 5, 1791, the young student Hardenberg still wrote in effusive tones of enthrallment:

> Tausend Szenen schweben um meinen innern Sinn, denen die Fantasie
> und die Errinnerung Leben verleiht, die in magischesten Beleuchtung,
> in romantischen Massen eine zehnfach verstärkte Wirkung thun [...]
> Alles verschmilzt in das unnennbare und untheilbare Ganze einer
> lieblichen Dämmrung, wo nur die äussersten Umrisse, die schönsten
> Contoure noch sichtbar sind und schon allmälich in den Nebel der
> Vergangenheit zerrinnen. Aber den Zauber der Aussicht, wer vermag
> den zu beschreiben, da ihn die Seele mit Mühe fasst. (23)

Yet even here, Novalis recognized that unbounded fantasy can actually cloak the very reality he attempted to fathom: "Ich sehe mich in allen den lächerlichen, sonderbaren, abentheuerlichen und unnatürlichen Masken, mit welchen mich eine herrenlose Fantasie und die Grille des Augenblicks bekleidete und bedaure nur die geduldigen Freunde des pfadlosen Irrlings." (24) In a later letter to his father, who obviously wished a more orderly, disciplined life for his son, the Leipzig student assured him that experience and education, "Bildung", would certainly serve to mitigate his immoderate nature:

[...] Die Erfahrung wird ihre Hand an meine Bildung legen und in
ihrem hellen Lichte wird manche romantische Jugendidee ver-
schwinden und nur der stillen, zarten Wahrheit dem einleuchtenden
Sinne des Sittlichguten, Schönen und Bleibenden den Plaz überlassen.
Mein Sinn wird Charakter, meine Erkenntnisse werden Grundsätze
meine Fantasie wird Empfindung, meine Leidenschaftlichkeit, wol-
tätige Wärme, meine Ahndungen werden Wahrheit, meine Einfalt
Einfachheit, meine Anlage wird Verstand, meine Ideen werden
Vernunft. (25)

The expectation of military service with its subordination and disciplined way of
life had its positive aspects for Novalis as he continued in the same letter: "Hier
wird meine Fantasie das Kindische, Jugendliche verlieren, was ihr anhängt, und
gezwungen seyn, sich nach den festen Regeln eines Systems zu richten. Der Romantische Schwung wird in dem alltäglichen, sehr unromantischen Gange meines Lebens
viel von seinem schädlichen Einfluss auf meine Handlungen verlieren [...] (26)

Thus Novalis' later dictum as expressed to August Wilhelm Schlegel on
February 24, 1798, "die Wissenschaften müssen alle poëtisirt werden" does not
deny the value of the scientific branches of knowledge, but indicates a desire to
reconcile philosophy with art, the intellectual with the emotional realms, the past
with the present and the future. (27) In Novalis' view of cultural history, the true
artist does not originate first, but comes about in a stage of culture that follows
that of the scholastic thinker and the raw, intuitive poet--thus this true artist is
also a product of growth, of synthesis. (28) There is indeed a synthetic aura, if
not distinct drive, about Novalis' critical thinking, and a pervasive feeling that poetry
should not be regarded as one pole of life to be set in opposition to rationality, but
rather the glorious product of an amalgamation of seemingly antagonistic forces. We
shall even see, in contradiction to Korff, that the subject is not to dominate the object,
but rather to enter into a beneficial interaction with the outer world. (29) Philosophy,
art, and religion are to merge into an entity in the service of the state and mankind.
History, philosophy, and poetry together mutually complement and complete one
another, as Novalis explains in his Hemsterhuis-Studien in the fall of 1797:

Geschichte - Philosophie - und Poësie - Die Erste schafft an - die
2te ordnet und erklärt - Die Dritte hebt jedes Einzelne durch ausgesuchte Kontrastirung mit dem übrigen Ganzen und wenn die Philosophie durch Bildung des äussern Ganzen, oder durch die Gesetz-
gebung, die vollkommene Poësie möglich macht, so ist gleichsam
die Poësie der Zweck derselben, durch den sie erst Bedeutung und
anmuthiges Leben erhält - denn die Poësie bildet die schöne Gesellschaft, oder das innere Ganze - die Weltfamilie--die schöne Haus-
haltung des Universi - Wie die Philosophie durch System und Staat
die Kräfte des Individuums mit den Kräften des Weltalls und der übrigen
Menschheit paart, und verstärckt - das Ganze zum Organ des Individuums, und das Individuum zum Organ des Ganzen macht - So die
Poësie [...]

Thus it is within the realm of both philosophy and poetry to unite the individual with the universe: "Durch die Poësie wird die höchste Sympathie und Coactivitaet - die innigste, herrlichste Gemeinschaft wircklich. Durch die Philosophie - möglich."(30)

In order to bring the manifold aphorisms by Novalis into order, the following chapters will deal with the various aspects of his concept of poetry. The second chapter is devoted to Novalis' view of poetry as a universal force involving all mankind, but also as the particular expression of "Dichtung" created by the poet. The third chapter revolves about the poet and his craft, that particular union of imagination and practical ability that results in a work of art. Novalis' goal involves not only the fusion of imaginative and intellectual qualities within the work of art, but also the distinct synthesis of poetry and philosophy, an endeavor which forms the subject of chapter five. These general concepts of the nature and task of poetry do not, however, remain in the realm of speculation for Novalis, since he envisioned the realization of the goals he outlined within the genre of the novel. The novel <u>Heinrich von Ofterdingen</u> indeed consumed his thoughts and energy during the last years of his life, and its construction was based on these poetic ideals.(31)

II. "POESIE" AS THE HIGHEST EXPRESSION OF HUMAN ACHIEVEMENT:
INTELLECT AND IMAGINATION

If one were to ask just what Novalis meant by "Poesie", one would have to embrace the universal aspects of poetry in its entirety, its definition as the soul and force of life, nature, and man, the power that raises man above his own level and links him to the infinite. Yet poetry for Novalis also includes the more restricted and professional interpretation of "Dichtung", namely, that particular art that lies within the domain of the artist of language, the individual whose ambition and task is to poetize life through verbal expression.

Poetry as defined in the broader meaning is a topic that engaged Novalis' thought throughout his brief life, and he ascribed to this force the most noble and powerful characteristics, the spark of the infinite and the absolute in the finite world. In an essay of his youth "Von der Begeisterung", written under the pseudonym of Friedrich Waller and exhibiting the clear influence of Herder, Novalis describes the first poetic impulse of man, the original attempt at verbal expression of the inner poetic urge fired up by enthusiasm. His description conveys the image of a universal and primordial drive, primitive at first in its manifestation, but developing into a cultivated art of a religious and poetic nature.

The Orient, the homeland "der Menschheit, Sprache, Dichtkunst und daher auch der Begeisterung," was the fertile atmosphere out of which this "göttliches Feuer" originated. From his earliest writings, poetry embodied Novalis' ideas of man's most original and existential mode of expression, a universal force existing within primitive man even before he was equipped with the verbal tools to give it shape. (1)

In his philosophical studies of 1795-96, Novalis emphasized the civilizing power of poetry in a fragment that compares the poetry of modern man to the chorus of Greek drama, both being "Handlungsweise der schönen, rhythmischen Seele-- begleitende Stimme unsers bildenden Selbst--überall leise Spur des Fingers der Humanitaet." Poetry is the force of enlightenment, rhythm, and art, and is viewed by Novalis as victory over raw nature, a humanizing element of life. (2) Poetry is described as a unifying power for both the Gods and man in a later fragment among the "Vermischte Bemerkungen", since the fable encompasses the history of the "urbildliche Welt"--antiquity, present times, and the future. "Die Menschenwelt ist das gemeinschaftliche Organ der Götter. Poësie vereinigt sie, wie uns."(3) The famous fragment of 1798 referring to the fairytale in particular also conveys Novalis' picture of poetry as an all-encompassing power that joins the individual to the vastness of the universe which here has the mythical dimensions of a "Feen- welt", of a homeland having no distinct location or boundaries:

Es liegt nur an der Schwäche unsrer Organe und der Selbstberührung, dass wir uns nicht in einer Feenwelt erblicken. Alle Mährchen sind nur Träume von jener heymatlichen Welt, die überall und nirgends ist. Die höhern Mächte in uns, die einst als Genien unsern Willen voll- bringen werden, sind jezt Musen, die uns auf dieser mühseligen Lauf- bahn mit süssen Erinnerungen erquicken. (4)

Thus Novalis' "Poesie" would seem to have some similarity to Schopenhauer's will or Fichte's ego in its mode of existence, for like these, poetry exists both as a universal entity and as the higher powers within us. It is a supra-individual force of cosmic proportions finding expression, however, only through individuals.

Continuing in the vein of thought relating to poetry as a civilizing, humanizing element among men, Novalis simply states in a collection of aphorisms dashed down during the month of February, 1798, that poetry is the basis of society, just as virtue is the basis of the state. The religious tinge of this definition of poetry is emphasized when he goes on to explain that virtue and poetry together form religion. Furthermore, poetry mixes everything together for its great purpose among purposes, the "Erhebung des Menschen über sich selbst."(5) Fragment No. 46 states: "Die Poesie lösst fremdes Daseyn in Eignem auf," and here again poetry seems to have a religious or mythical function, for what else does religion or myth do but bring the unknown closer to us by transforming "fremdes Daseyn" into something familiar and understandable?(6) Indeed, the connection between poetry and religion is noted in another fragment of February, 1798, in the collection entitled "Poëticismen", in which Novalis draws upon the experience of antiquity for a parallel: "Bey den Alten war die Religion schon gewissermassen das, was sie bey uns werden soll - practische Poesie."(7)

The later notes referring to poetry in this light seem to converge in the idea of poetry as a latent or potential power to be utilized and brought to fruition through man's own efforts. It is a force that when unleashed and fully developed, serves to heighten and intensify human life:

Alle Poesie unterbricht den gewöhnlichen Zustand, das gemeine Leben, fast wie der Schlummer, um uns zu erneuern - und so unser Lebensge- fühl immer rege zu erhalten.(8)

In a collection of "Anekdoten" stemming from May and June of 1798, Novalis again highlights the synthetic aspect of poetry: "Was wir Glauben an Versöhnung nennen, ist nichts als Zuversicht einer vollendeten poetischen Weisheit in den Schicksalen unsers Lebens," a life that one should poetize and allow to be poetized according to one's inclination.(9) In the early autumn of 1798 (Aug. - Sept.), Novalis comes to the conclusion that the only true entity is poetry. "Die Poesie ist das ächt absolute Reelle. Dies ist der Kern meiner Philosophie. Je poëtischer, je wahrer."(10) Having made this dictum so central to his philosophy of life, it is easy to see why Novalis then urged all men to realize poetry within their own lives: "Man muss eine poëtische Welt um sich her bilden und in der Poesie leben," he wrote to Caroline Schlegel on the 21st of January, 1799, in a letter expressing concern about his progress as a poet, his problem of retaining the poetic spirit while immersed in the demands of everyday, bourgeois life.(11) So it is understandable "warum am Ende alles Poesie wird," as he writes in 1799-1800, for this "Poesie" is not a distinctly new state, but rather a condition that is all-embracing, that integrates history, religion, morals, the practical and the aesthetic realms of life. This sentiment, however, expresses the _wish_ for the full realization of poetry in the world, rather than its achievement.(12)

In all of these definitions and descriptions, we see that poetry has a unifying and conciliatory nature, for it is the element that links man to the universe, that enables him to rise above his own human level to that of the gods, that relates the unknown to the known. Thus, our initial thesis that Novalis' concept of poetry is not one-sided, but rather represents an attempt to depict a unity of disparate forces, an entity having a synthesizing function, seems to have gained concrete evidence.

Turning to those aphorisms that describe the art of poetizing, the practice of "Dichtung" in the narrower sense, we see the same line of thought as we have traced in the discussion of poetry as a universal force and then as a prerequisite dimension of the poet. Here again, a shift of emphasis can be detected, a shift from the view of poetry as a function and expression of the purely emotional component of the poet's make-up, to the more balanced concept of poetry as an art requiring manifold talents encompassing the emotional and the rational, the subjective and the objective aspects of creative ability. Indeed, it is within this category of poetry that one sees the most pronounced attempt to depict "Dichtung" as a broad, combinatory creative power, an amalgamation of various subordinate arts that does not content itself with either mere imitation of nature or with idle and imaginatory speculations. This endeavor and corresponding attitude towards poetry, however, is an outgrowth of Novalis' increasing maturity and critical distance, and is thus not evident in his earliest writings.

Novalis' youthful affinity for the lighter, gayer type of poetry, reminiscent of Goethe's Leipzig verses, is expressed in his abundant praise of the anacreontic style with its grace and naivitée, its simplicity and spontaneity. In an early essay "Ueber Anakreon und seine Dichtungsart" dating back to 1788-1790, he concludes his exuberant glorification of this pleasant poetry with a clear statement in favor of the momentary poetic outpouring as opposed to the creation of a more reasoned, well-constructed product: "Ein anakreontisches Lied ist das Werck eines Augenblicks nicht der kalten Ueberlegung. Es ist ein Impromtü."(13) It is clear that Novalis' early thoughts on poetic art were sympathetic towards "natural" poetry and critical of the sophisticated wit promulgated by the Germans and much appreciated by the French, and obviously the concept of poetry as encompassing both nature and wit, simplicity and sophistication, as a synthesizing force, had not yet occurred to the young Romantic:

Wenn sanftes Vergnügen und reizende Grazie eine eigne Dichtungsart haben so ists gewiss die zärtliche Anakreontische. Wie angenehm sind nicht seine Dichtungen! Wie lachend seine Schilderungen! Wie reizend seine Bilder und wie belebt! Les ich ihn, so scheint er mir nicht Dichter, nein! der wollüstigste, liebenswürdigste, verführerische Grieche. Ich bin mit ihm bey Tische, ich folge ihm und seiner Geliebten in eine Laube, heilig der Liebe, ich folg ihm in seinen reizenden Tändeleyen und er macht mich eben so froh, eben so von Wonne trunken als sich; ich empfinde ihm nach. Diese reizende Naivität, Wahrheit und Natur sind die grössesten Reize der lyrischen Stücke Anakreons und sie werden dadurch für uns nach so vielen Jahrhunderten, da die Sitten (sich) so sehr geändert haben, noch interessant und angenehm. (14)

This early emphasis on the close relationship between poetry and nature is to remain with Novalis, but it develops from this rather naturalistic point of view to a more symbolic one, the emphasis moving from mere imitation of nature to the incorporation of its organic qualities within poetry. In other words, poetry resembles nature insofar as it too is a living, growing, organic and vital force. Indeed, the most primitive and all-pervasive form of poetry, the fable, contains various stages of growth in an organic historical vein: "Die Fabellehre enthält die Geschichte der urbildlichen Welt--Sie begreift Vorzeit, Gegenwart und Zukunft."(15) In 1797-98 Novalis describes language as having several dimensions, "entweder-- mechanisch--atomistisch--oder dynamisch," but the truly poetic language is like nature itself: "Die ächt poetische Sprache soll aber organisch Lebendig seyn. Wie oft fühlt man die Armuth an Worten--um mehrere Ideen mit Einem Schlage zu treffen."(16) As has been noted earlier, Novalis does not regard poetry as being divorced from reflective thought, he is no advocate of "l'art pour l'art", but rather adheres to the view that an _idea_ must be at the center of a poetic work of art.

A following fragment from the same collection of "Vermischte Bemerkungen" of 1797-98 gives further evidence for Novalis' increasing distance from his former emotion-based ideal of poetry, yet he does not deny the value of some degree of intoxication and ecstatic rapture within literary production: "Halb berauscht kann ein Kunstwerck seyn--Im ganzen Rausche zerfliesst das Kunstwerck - ." Continuing the thought, Novalis reveals the reason behind such a pronouncement, emphasizing the relationship between nature and poetry. Man is neither animal nor plant, and thus his life cannot and should not be completely analogous to these forms of organic life in nature. It follows that his poetic endeavors should reflect the human component that separates man from other organisms, and in his denoting this element as free- dom, Novalis exhibits his dependence upon the idealistic vein of philosophical thought:

Aus dem Menschen wird ein Thier - Der Karacter des Thiers ist dythyrambisch. Das Thier ist ein übersättigtes Leben - die Pflanze ein mangelhaftes Leben. Der Mensch ein freyes Leben.(17)

It is undoubtedly this freedom of man that allows him to maintain his sover- eignty above extremes. The subsequent groups of aphorisms in Novalis' philosophical notes fall under the headings "Poesie" and "Poeticismen", date back to the month of February, 1798, and continue on into May of the same year. They deal more directly with the phenomenon of poetry and give greater and more detailed elaboration of the elements that comprise poetry, whether this be in the shape of a drama, lyric ode, or novel.(18) Aphorism No. 44 depicts the contents of a drama as an essentially organic composition, but the end result and purpose of this natural, organic develop- ment is idealistic rather than naturalistic. This is not natural cyclical growth in the sense of an eternal recurrence of everything, but rather culminates in "einem Läuterungs, Reduktionsprocess"(19). These thoughts underscore Novalis' deter- mination to achieve a balanced type of poetry, for a "vollständiges Drama" would trace and depict both the rising and the falling phases of action, the growth and decline of an organic figure. In other words, Novalis' concept of poetry is living and dynamic, rather than static, and it must somehow fulfill an ideal or attain a goal in its depiction. It is poetry with a purpose, as is also stressed in a rather disjointed aphorism of February-May, 1798, which concludes in a clear reference to romantic and didactic poetry:

> Heftiger Karacter, ruhiger Ausdruck. Je höher wir stehn, desto mehr
> gefällt uns alles - behagt uns jede Action - wir machen dann alles mit
> Vergnügen - höchste Ruhe und Bedürfnis - Verhältnisslosigkeit - stete
> Bereitwilligkeit in jedes Verhältnis zu treten - und sich darnach zu
> stimmen [...] Aeussre, und innere Poesie. Poesie im Ganzen - Poesie
> im Einzelnen, z. B. ad 1. Hermann und Dorothea - z. B. 2. Louise.
> Jenes vielleicht romantische, dies descriptive Poesie
> romantische didaktische Poesie(20)

Yet these comments also support the thesis that Novalis sought to create a poetry which was equipoised between subjectivity and objectivity, universality and individuality. Even the balance between the vehement intensity of the character and the calmness of the expression extolled fits into this pattern. The manifoldness of "Poesie" is given further emphasis in a comparison between the various branches of the arts and the individual genres within poetry in the "Denkaufgaben" of May and June of 1798. Here we see again an equation of variety and unity:

> Plastik, Musik und Poesie verhalten sich wie Epos, Lyra und Drama.
> Es sind unzertrennliche Elemente, die in jedem freyen Kunstwesen
> zusammen, und nur nach Beschaffenheit, in verschiednen Verhältnissen
> geeinigt sind.(21)

Later in his "Anekdoten" Novalis simply states the complete identity of these three forms of art, thus granting an all-encompassing dimension to poetry: "Musik-Plastik, und Poesie sind Synonymen."(22) In a further note he remarks: "Durch-dringung von Plastik und Musik - nicht blos Vermittelung", an obvious reference to what poetry should be.(23) The same approach and tendency towards inclusivity is evidenced in another short and crisp equation: "Körper - Seele und Geist sind die Elemente der Welt - wie Epos, Lyra und Drama die des Gedichts."(24) Thus we see that poetry embraces for Novalis not only the musical and plastic arts, but also the three genres; just as the body is incomplete without both soul and intellect, so is a poetic work of art imperfect if it neglects one element in its composition. It is perhaps this variety and yet totality in Novalis' definition of poetry that allows him to think of entitling it with the same name given by Friedrich Schlegel, namely, "progressive Universalpoesie". It is true, Novalis does not expressly refer to any of his excursions on poetry as being elaborations of this title, but it seems to be significant that this striking phrase is included among his listings of "Titel der Fragmente" enumerated during July and August of 1798 and follows, interestingly enough, the proposed title "Von der Definition der Poesie".(25)

Two further aphorisms of July/August 1798 give additional evidence for Novalis' rejection of a type of "pure" poetry having no basis in an idea, for both indicate the close relationship between the poet's individuality and his product. The first claims: "Aechte Kunstwercke müssen persönlich seyn," and the second states that language, far from being the essence and sole content of poetry, is only a function of a tool, a means to an end within a poetic creation. (26) A poem does not consist purely of language, sounds, etc., but conveys the idea of its creator: "Sprache im eigentlichen Sinn ist, Function eines Werckzeugs als solchen. Jedes Werckzeug drückt, prägt die Idee seines Dirigenten, aus." (27) Another concise and more original formulation of the same idea is given in the "Allgemeine Brouillon" of 1798/99: "Worte sind acustische Configurationen der Gedanken." (28)

Yet poetry is not a distinctly rational exhibition of an idea, but rather an associative configuration and has an organization similar to that of a dream; further-more, like the make-up of a dream, poetry too is essentially free:

> Der Traum ist oft bedeutend und prophetisch, weil er eine Naturseelen-wirckung ist - und also auf Associationsordnung beruht. Er ist wie die Poësie bedeutend - aber auch darum unregelmässig bedeutend - durchaus frey. (29)

The fragments of the later years, 1799-1800, referring to poetry in more specific terms, reveal the influence of Böhme, if one considers the increasing usage of the word "Gemüt" and the importance attached to it as well as the stress on the symbolic nature of poetry, its character as an outward and tangible representation of an inner and intangible sphere. Here too Novalis considers words as a medium for the expression of poetry and does not grant them the aesthetic independence and necessity as would the new critic! Poetry is seen in these years as depiction of the "Gemüt", but "Gemüt" is a rather comprehensive term--even the key to the riddles of the universe for Jakob Böhme:

> Poësie ist Darstellung des Gemüths - der innern Welt in ihrer Gesamt-heit. Schon ihr Medium, die Worte, deuten es an, denn sie sind ja die äussre Offenbarung jenes innern Kraftreichs [...] (30)

A parallel to nature is drawn in the fashion Hardenberg recommends for this depiction of the "Gemüt" in poetry, since such presentation "muss, wie die Darstellung der Natur, selbstthätig, eigenthümlich allgemein, verknüpfend und schöpferisch seyn." What "eigenthümlich allgemein" could possibly mean in concrete terms is a difficult question, but the antithetical nature of the phrase, the juxtaposition of what would seem to be almost mutually exclusive connotations, only points to Novalis' insistence upon giving due consideration to both aspects, the particular and the general, to be conveyed by poetry. (31) He continues the fragment by taking up his former anti-naturalistic position, granting some similarity between the realism of poetry and nature, but denying identity; for depiction of nature, like that of "Gemüt", should not be realistic--it should be idealistic. Poetry should exhibit its subject matter, "nicht wie es ist, sondern wie es seyn könnte und seyn muss." (32)

Another example of Novalis' drive for maintaining the inclusivity of poetry, often at the expense of clarity in his formulations is given in Fragment No. 695 of the same late collection: "So muss auch die Poësie schlechthin bloss verständig, künstlich, erdichtet-Fantastisch! etc. seyn."--only understandable and yet fantastic--

quite a tall order! (33) Yet this is no more than what Novalis himself attempted to achieve within his own poetic creations, to varying degrees of success. (34)

Finally, Novalis delves into more concrete expressions of what he thinks poetry should encompass and what type of characterizations should be incorporated in "ein Gedicht". To be sure, these more specific explanations do not reveal an attitude differing from what has already been presented here, but re-emphasize poetics as a combinatory art embracing the elements of related arts:

> Die Poetik liesse sich freylich als eine Combination untergeordneter Künste betrachten, z. B. der Metrik, der Sprachkenntniss, der Kunst, uneigentlich zu reden, witzig und scharfsinnig zu seyn; Werden diese Künste gut verbunden und mit Geschmack angewandt, so wird man das Produkt Gedicht nennen müssen. (35)

With regard to characterization, poetry should neglect neither the requirement of generality, nor that of peculiarity; it should be both specifically determined and yet free, transparent and yet mysterious--a tremendous integration of seemingly paradoxical elements. But Novalis admits to the difficulty of the task:

> Aechte, poëtische Charactere sind schwierig genug zu erfinden und auszuführen. Es sind gleichsam verschiedne Stimmen und Instrumente. Sie müssen allgemein, und doch eigenthümlich, bestimmt und doch frey, klar und doch geheimnissvoll seyn. (36)

Yet if it is difficult to imagine such characters, where shall their models be found? If one looks to real life for their images, that too presents a problem, as Novalis continues, since very few people are actually characters. Indeed, they are as rare as good actors, and many people simply lack the natural talent to be characters. So it lies within the task of the poet to search out models for his characterizations very carefully if he turns to reality for inspiration: "Man muss wohl die Gewohnheitsmenschen, die Alltäglichen, von den Characteren unterscheiden." (37)

In this vein of explicit opinion as to how to go about producing good literature, Novalis gave his brother Karl advice after he had read a manuscript Karl had sent to him for comments in Weissenfels, probably during April of 1800. Again the accent is on originality and conciseness in language, and on allegorical, rather than imitational depiction of nature. "Freund, ich habe theils corrigirt, theils blos angestrichen," Novalis begins, and he then tries to mitigate his criticism by remarking that his brother's own "poëtisches Gefühl" will certainly tell him what is offensive in his work. Specifically, he suggests:

> In Gedichten vermeide Wortklang.
> In der Prosa werde voller, gedrängter.
> In der Komposition, wie in den Gedanken.
> In den Gedanken originell, wunderlich, neu.
> In der Composition wie in den Gedanken.
> Ja keine Nachahmung der Natur. Die Poësie ist durchaus das Gegentheil.

Höchstens kann die Nachahmung der Natur, der Wircklichkeit nur
allegorisch, oder im Gegensatz, oder des tragischen und lustigen
Effects wegen hin und wieder gebraucht werden.
Alles muss poëtisch seyn. (38)

When all is said and done, however, Novalis' comments on his concept of
"Dichtung" remain in the realm of possibility and are not very precise or definitive.
Perhaps this is the result of his own insecurity as to how to effect the high ideal he
imagines and reflects upon. Indeed, a very late fragment mirrors this problem;
poetry like any significant phenomenon, undoubtedly is greater and more elusive
than any definition or circumscription could possibly indicate:

Worinn eigentlich das Wesen der Poësie bestehe, lässt sich schlechthin nicht bestimmen. Es ist unendlich zusammengesezt und doch
einfach. Schön, romantisch, harmonisch sind nur Theilausdrücke des
Poëtischen. (39)

III. THE POET AND HIS CRAFT: IDEALITY AND REALITY

In a letter to Friedrich Schlegel dated December 26, 1797, Novalis comments on his recent introduction to Schelling, whose Ideen had attracted his attention. Although Schelling does not seem to fit into the context of a poet, Novalis regarded him from the point of view of poetic as well as philosophical qualities: "Er hat mir sehr gefallen--ächte Universaltendenz in ihm--wahre Strahlenkraft--von Einem Punct in die Unendlichkeit hinaus. Er scheint viel poëtischen Sinn zu haben."(1) Just what does Novalis mean by "poetischer Sinn", and what is the significance of moving from one point out into infinity for the artistic person? A rather carefully constructed statement to be found among the "Vermischte Bemerkungen" dating from 1797 to 1798 sheds some light on this question, for here he elaborates upon the great style of depiction so much admired in Goethe:

> Selbstentäusserung ist die Quelle aller Erniedrigung, sowie im Gegen-
> theil der Grund aller ächten Erhebung. Der erste Schritt wird Blick
> nach innen, absondernde Beschauung unseres Selbst - Wer hier stehn
> bleibt geräth nur halb. Der 2te Schritt muss wircksamer Blick nach
> aussen - selbstthätige, gehaltne Beobachtung der Aussenwelt seyn.(2)

These two steps would seem to parallel the phrase referring to the progression from one point to infinity, for it involves the artist's contemplation of his singular being and his subsequent reflection upon the endless material provided by the outer world. He continues:

> Der Mensch wird nie, als Darsteller, etwas Vorzügliches leisten, der
> nichts weiter darstellen mag, als seine Erfahrungen, seine Lieblings-
> gegenstände, der es nicht über sich gewinnen kann, auch einen ganz
> fremden, ihm ganz uninteressanten Gegenstand, mit Fleiss zu studiren
> und mit Musse darzustellen.

This ability to go beyond the boundaries of one's own individual and familiar realm, to study strange objects in a world alienated from the ordinary person, and to view them with perception as valuable subjects for depiction, this talent seems to constitute "poetischer Sinn" for Novalis. The poetic individual looks at himself and his experiences in the light of the outer world with which he is confronted, and he possesses a drive towards universality in his attempt to embrace all in his craft: "Der Darsteller muss alles darstellen können und wollen. Dadurch entsteht der grosse Styl der Darstellung, den man, mit Recht an Göthe, so sehr bewundert."(3) The particular traits that determine the poetic spirit and separate the poet from other men are not only quantitative in nature, however, but also qualitative. It is not only the wide scope of interest and inclusivity of subject matter that characterizes the poet and gives him a unique stamp, but also the distinctive manner in which he perceives and absorbs that which he observes. In the section "Neue Fragmente" of his "Fragmenten Studien XI" dating from 1798, Novalis delineates the particular poetic sense as a primarily intellectual or spiritual one and describes the poet as one who sees the world, both objective and subjective components, from a perspective quite different from that of the ordinary man:

> Wie der Mahler mit ganz andern Augen als der gemeine Mensch die
> sichtbaren Gegenstände sieht - so erfährt auch der Dichter die Be-
> gebenheiten der äussren und innern Welt auf eine sehr verschiedne
> Weise vom gewöhnlichen Menschen. Nirgends aber ist es auffallender,
> dass es nur der Geist ist, der die Gegenstände, die Veränderungen
> des Stoffs poëtisirt [...] (4)

Yet every individual is gifted with some creative abilities and might be capable
of bringing forth an artistic production, when not in actuality, then at least in
potentiality, according to Novalis. His strong emphasis on practical considerations
that have bearing on creative endeavors is astounding, especially if one considers
Novalis as the naive "Romantic", but this realistic bent is perhaps a consequence of
his activities in the salt mines, an area of practical pursuits, where tools and work-
able approaches were of primary necessity. A vivid illustration is given in the "Vermischte Bemerkungen" of 1797-98:

> Werckzeuge armiren den Menschen. Man kann wohl sagen, der
> Mensch versteht eine Welt hervorzubringen - es mangelt ihm nur
> am gehörigen Apparat - an der verhältnismässigen Armatur seiner
> Sinneswerckzeuge. Der Anfang ist da.(5)

He continues with an example of a naval architect, in whose idea the principle of a
war ship is couched, but it is only through "Menschenhaufen und gehörige Werck-
zeuge und Materialen" that this idea may be actualized. This entire process, or
the realization of the original idea in a concrete product, is achieved through the
builder's absorption, amalgamation, and organization of these various ingredients
that are propelled into action "- indem er durch alles dieses sich gleichsam zu
einer ungeheuern Maschiene macht.":

> So erforderte die Idee eines Augenblicks oft ungeheure Organe -
> ungeheure Massen von Materien, und der Mensch ist also, wo nicht
> actu, doch Poetentia, Schöpfer.(6)

From this example, it is clear that Novalis regarded the art of poetry as a
craft, and the poet cannot rely on pure imagination, flights of fantasy, or even
brilliant flashes of insight or wit alone. To these natural talents must be added the
practical ones of diligence, organization, useful tools, and keen perception. In other
words, poetry is not only the spirit which inspires the poet, the ether which surrounds
and uplifts him, but it is also a skill which can be cultivated and made to blossom.(7)
To be sure, this skill is one of the intellect, and the tools are more apt to be those
of language and musical rhythm rather than the chisel or the paint brush. And although Novalis has said that every man is "Schöpfer" at least in the realm of possibility,
it is clear that he was cognizant of the very small percentage of men who utilized
their potentialities and developed their talents to the degree of the true artist. The
feature of universality is again stressed in a short aphorism of the "Neue Fragmenten-
sammlungen" of 1798 where Novalis states: "Der ächte Dichter ist allwissend - er
ist eine wirckliche Welt im Kleinen."(8) Furthermore, the one who has attained

the level of aesthetic artistry towers above his contemporaries: "Der Künstler steht auf dem Menschen, wie die Statue auf dem Piedestal."(9)

The special way of looking at the world that characterizes the poet does not, however, make him superior to objective reality. Like ordinary men, he too is dependent upon his environment, and because of his deep sensitivity and perception, he is perhaps even more subject to exterior conditions than others. Consequently, the historical age in which one lives has great influence upon the flowering of poetry, and intermingled with his lofty praise of the artist as a superior creature, Novalis expressed his scepticism when regarding the cultivation of poets in his own era. The poet may exist in eternity through his work, but the poet as an individual lives in a particular place in a particular time:

> Alles, was un umgiebt, die täglichen Vorfälle, die gewöhnlichen Ver-
> hältnisse, die Gewohnheiten unserer Lebensart, haben einen ununter-
> brochnen, eben darum umbemerckbaren, aber höchst wichtigen
> Einfluss auf uns. So heilsam und zweckdienlich dieser Kreislauf uns
> ist, insofern wir Genossen einer bestimmten Zeit, Glieder einer spe-
> cifischen Corporation sind, so hindert uns doch derselbe an einer
> höhern Entwicklung unsrer Natur. Divinatorische, magische ächtpoë-
> tische Menschen können unter Verhältnissen, wie die Unsrigen sind,
> nicht entstehn. (10)

This pessimism with regard to the stimulation of poetic achievement in his time is a logical outgrowth of Novalis' picture of the poet and his qualities and his assessment of his own "unpoetic" age. In a later fragment from the same collection of "Poësie" he takes up his earlier and ever-predominant theme of the artist's intellectual preception, his ability to view and integrate foreign objects, to observe and make what he sees his own. It thus follows that he will be either elevated and inspired or subdued and depressed by what his environment has to offer.

> Dieses Vermögen eine fremde Individualitaet wahrhaft in sich zu
> erwecken - nicht blos durch eine oberflächliche Nachahmung zu
> täuschen - ist noch gänzlich unbekannt - und beruht auf einer höchst
> wunderbaren Penetration und geistigen Mimik. Der Künstler macht
> sich zu allem, was er sieht und seyn will. (11)

Novalis continues in this same vein of thought in May of 1798 and elaborates upon the artist's ability to draw from life:

> Alles muss Lebensmittel werden. Kunst, aus allem Leben zu ziehn.
> Alles zu beleben ist der Zweck des Lebens. Lust ist Leben. Unlust
> ist Mittel zur Lust, wie Tod Mittel zum Leben. (12)

Thus the artist's task is a heightening of man's task in general. He does to an extra-ordinary degree that which everyone seeks to do with his life, namely, to impart meaning to it through joy, sorrow--even death, and to extract every possible value from it. This in itself is an art for Novalis: "Mensch werden ist eine Kunst."(13)

THE POET AND HIS CRAFT: IDEALITY AND REALITY

In tracing the development of Novalis' thoughts on the artist, one becomes aware of his desire to include both poles of the artistic personality--the traits that bind him to all men and those that serve to separate him from the masses, his human qualities on the one hand, and his particularly genial ones, on the other hand. Therefore the very progression of his ideas in this alternating fashion reveals the intensity of this artistic problem for Novalis himself--the balancing and integration of both aspects, the generally human and the specifically aesthetic, the realms of the artist as a man and as a creator, his finite and his infinite nature.

Having devoted some aphorisms to what the artist maintains in common with ordinary men, Novalis in his subsequent group of notes concentrates on the distinguishing traits, the peculiarities and superior gifts that elevate him above the common folk. "Der Künstler ist durchaus transcendental" he states in Aphorism No. 40 of "Poesie", and in No. 42 he grants him generative and healing powers: "Poesie ist die grosse Kunst der Construction der transscendentalen Gesundheit. Der Poet ist also der transscendentale Arzt."(14) This hardly resembles the typical critical view of the "romantic" poet or ideal thereof--the sickly, decadent creature on the verge of madness who cannot even renew his own spirits, to say nothing of serving as physician to others. The poet seems to be the link between man and the infinite; he serves in the mediating position of ministrating to finite man's infinite desires, of serving his transcendental nature. It is perhaps for this reason and because of his unique position among and yet above ordinary mortals, that Novalis imbues him with mystical or religious powers: "Nur ein Künstler kann den Sinn des Lebens errathen" he writes in May, 1798, (15) and in June/July of the same year, his image of the poet enlarges to include magical dimensions: "Der Zauberer ist Poet. Der Profet ist zum Zauberer, wie der Mann von Geschmack zum Dichter."(16) In this context, it is interesting to note some of Novalis' comments on other authors, particularly Lessing, whom he admired to a degree, but whose exclusively rational attitude and lack of magical qualities he criticized. These comments also stem from the month of February, 1798:

> Lessings Prosa fehlts oft an hieroglyphischen Zusatz. Lessing sah
> zu scharf und verlor darüber das Gefühl des undeutlichen Ganzen,
> die magische Anschauung der Gegenstände zusammen in mannichfacher
> Erleuchtung und Verdunckelung.(17)

His criticism is again directed against one-sidedness, the emphasis on rationality and clear-sightedness, with the resultant loss of perspective of the whole, which for Novalis always includes the invisible, less tangible realm. The lack of wide scope and exclusive attention to the "realistic" side of life is what made Voltaire repulsive to Novalis:

> Voltaire ist einer der grössesten Minuspoëten, die je lebten. Sein
> Candide ist seine Odyssee. Schade um ihn, dass seine Welt ein
> Pariser Boudoir war. Mit weniger persönlicher und nationaler
> Eitelkeit wär er noch weit mehr gewesen.(18)

THE POET AND HIS CRAFT: IDEALITY AND REALITY

Another group of fragments center in the qualities more central to the poet's craft, his approach to his work. Although he has formerly stressed the artist's broad scope (the prerequisite of universality), Novalis now turns to the necessity for selectivity and precision--the poetic telescope pointing to the stars becomes the poetic microscope for studying minute specimens. In this realm of exactness, the poet's judgment is of primary significance, his ability to separate the grain from the chaff, and he who fails this test bears the brunt of Novalis' scorn.

> Der Stümper weiss in keiner Kunst, wovon die Rede ist - er ahmt
> affenmässig nach - und hat keinen Sinn für das Wesentliche der Kunst.
> Der ächte Mahler etc. weiss das Mahlerische und Unmahlerische
> überall wohl zu unterscheiden. So ist es mit dem Dichter, dem
> Romancier, dem Reisebeschreiber. Der Chronikenschreiber ist der
> Stümper in der Geschichte--er will alles geben und giebt nichts. So
> durchaus. Jede Kunst hat ihre Individuelle Sfäre - wer diese nicht
> genau kennt und Sinn für dieselbe hat - wird nie Künstler. (19)

Such a statement serves to balance and clarify Novalis' previous claim that the artist should be able to depict everything or that he transforms himself into everything he sees and seeks to be. (20) It is not naturalism or photographic inclusivity for which Novalis pleas, for although the poet should not close his eyes to alien objects for depiction and should consider all the facets of life as possible subject matter, his very skill and poetic genius will of its own accord proceed in a selective manner. He will not dismiss anything à priori, but neither will he merely record every image his eye's retina conveys to his memory. The naturalistic artist would seem to fall prey to the fate of the chronicler who aspires to so much and accomplishes so little. In this thought, we again see Novalis' attempt to keep his views within moderation, to avoid extremes.

In the "Allgemeine Brouillon" of 1798-99, Novalis augments his discussion of the poet's sphere and the exact study of life to which he must devote his energies:

> Das Leben ist etwas, wie Farben, Töne und Kraft. Der Romantiker
> studirt das Leben, wie der Mahler, Musiker und Mechaniker Farbe,
> Ton und Kraft. Sorgfältiges Studium des Lebens macht den Romantiker,
> wie sorgfältiges Studium von Farbe, Gestaltung, Ton und Kraft den
> Mahler, Musiker und Mechaniker. (21)

It is again interesting to note the emphasis on poetry as a skilled craft--the Romantic, painter, and musician are placed on the same plane with the mechanic. Certainly the repetition and juxtaposition of "Musiker und Mechaniker" underscore Novalis' wish to regard the poet as artist and artisan. Yet the poet does not pursue a purely scientific investigation of life, but goes beyond empiricism. Thus, "Der Poët versteht die Natur besser wie der wissenschaftliche Kopf." (22) The parallel between the poetic and the scientific approaches is given a new twist in the fragments of the last years, 1799-1800, fragments in which Novalis' concern with placing poetry between the realms of science and religion, with designating poetry as the art requiring both perception and reflection, seeing and thinking, the tangible and the intangible becomes paramount.

> Dichtkunst ist wohl nur - willkührlicher, thätiger, produktiver Gebrauch unsrer Organe - und vielleicht wäre Denken selbst nicht viel etwas anders - und Denken und Dichten also einerley. Denn im Denken wenden ja die Sinne den Reichtum ihrer Eindrücke zu einer neuen Art von Eindrücken an - und was daraus entsteht, nennen wir Gedanken. (23)

Thus in poetry, there is an interrelationship and interaction between sense impressions, thinking, and the resultant formation of new impressions. Mere receptivity to new impressions or exuberant flights of fantasy will not equip the poet sufficiently to meet his task. Careful and quiet meditation are also required; indeed, without this second step, fantasy alone will die:

> Durch unaufhörliches freyes Nachdenken muss man sich begeistern. Hat man gar keine Zeit zum Ueberschauen, zum freien Meditiren, zum ruhigen Durchlaufen und Betrachten in verschiednen Stimmungen, so schläft selbst die fruchtbarste Fantasie ein, und die innre Mannigfaltigkeit hört auf. Für die Dichter ist nichts nützlicher, als eine flüchtige Betrachtung der vielen Weltgegenstände und ihrer Eigenschaften sowie der mancherley Wissenschaften.

A personal note underlines the closeness of this two-fold approach to Novalis' own poetic procedure: "Ich lese jezt zu wenig und meditire zu wenig." (24)

As if to contradict the widely accepted notion that the Romantics sought to transform words into music or a picture, Novalis takes the reverse position and claims that the poet's only concern is with concepts: "Der Dichter hat bloss mit Begriffen zu thun. Schilderungen etc. borgt er nur als BegriffsZeichen. Er gibt poëtische Musik und Mahlerey - diese wird oft mit Poësie verwechselt, z. B. von Tieck, auch wohl von Göthe."(25) Therefore "Poesie", although often a component of music or painting, is never to be regarded as a substitution for such; it is rather an art in itself.

The last fragments of 1799-1800 are primarily devoted to the "Sinn für Poësie" which the poet must by nature possess. (26) A clear leaning towards the mystical and religious aspects of the poet's character becomes quite evident in these later notations, and Novalis' thoughts on the subject turn to poetry as symbolism. The poet has the capacity to imbue words with symbolic meaning, to recognize and incorporate within his work "den redenden Geist aller Dinge und Handlungen."(27) He comprehends the inner significance of objects and actions and frees the spirit within nature to make it available to ordinary mortals. He is an interpreter, a translator, a link between man and nature--he is indeed a special kind of priest. Therefore, although poetry makes use of language and words, it is "von Rede - (Sprach)Kunst himmelweit verschieden." In the final analysis, poetry is indescribable:

Es giebt einen speziellen Sinn für Poësie - eine poëtische Stimmung
in uns. Die Poësie ist durchaus personell und darum unbeschreiblich
und indefinissabel. Wer es nicht unmittelbar weiss und fühlt, was
Poësie ist, dem lässt sich kein Begrif davon beybringen. Poësie ist
Poësie.(28)

Aphorism No. 443 presents the most comprehensive picture of Novalis' last
meditations on the poet and his talents. The phrase describing the poet as "wahrhaft
sinnberaubt", the symbolic nature of poetry, as well as the emphasis on the duality of
life, the invisible and visible worlds, is clearly reminiscent of Plato. But with Novalis,
it is the poet, not the philosopher, who serves as the mediator between the two
realms; he is the mystical prophet who sees the invisible and is able to depict the un-
portrayable. He is the intermediary between subject and object, "Gemüt und Welt":

Der Sinn für Poësie hat viel mit dem Sinn für Mystizism gemein. Er
ist der Sinn für das Eigenthümliche, Personelle, Unbekannte, Ge-
heimnissvolle, zu Offenbarende, das Nothwendigzufällige. Er stellt das
Undarstellbare dar. Er sieht das Unsichtbare, fühlt das Unfühlbare
etc. Kritik der Poësie ist Unding. Schwer schon ist zu entscheiden,
doch einzig mögliche Entscheidung, ob etwas Poësie sey oder nicht.
Der Dichter ist wahrhaft sinnberaubt--dafür kommt alles in ihm vor.
Er stellt im eigentlichsten Sinn Subjekt-Objekt vor - Gemüt und Welt.
Daher die Unendlichkeit eines guten Gedichts, die Ewigkeit. Der Sinn
für Poësie hat nahe Verwandtschaft mit dem Sinn der Weissagung und
dem religiösen, dem Sehersinn überhaupt. Der Dichter ordnet, vereinigt,
wählt, erfindet - und es ist ihm selbst unbegreiflich, warum gerade so
und nicht anders.(29)

There is much worthy of commentary in this statement, but in truth, these
expressions of Novalis' high regard for poetry and explanation of its noble function
merely sum up what has already been presented here of his thought in great detail.
Only one facet of this image remains to be examined, namely, the mystical component.
It has been claimed that Novalis turned from his studies of Goethe to Jakob Böhme
in February of 1800 and was deeply moved, even experiencing "eine innere Er-
schütterung" by what he read of the German mystic.(30) The placing of Böhme's
name into what was once Goethe's foremost and eminent position gives witness to
this inner reaction, for in a fragment Novalis refers to Goethe as the "Böhme von
Weimar".(31) The fragments of 1799-1800 contain a reference to a treatise on Jakob
Böhme which had presumably found its way into Novalis' hands, and he continued
here: "Seinen Wert als Dichter. Ueber dichterische Ansichten der Natur überhaupt."(32)
On the 23d of February, Novalis described what he saw in the great mystic, namely,

[...] den gewaltigen Frühling mit seinen quellenden, treibenden
bildenden und mischenden Kräften, die von innen heraus die Welt
gebären [...]

and he continues with specific reference to his own work:

> Um so besser ist es, dass die Lehrlinge ruhn - die jezt auf eine ganz
> andre Art erscheinen sollen - Es soll ein ächt sinnbildlicher, Natur-
> roman werden. Erst muss Heinrich fertig seyn - Eins nach dem Andern,
> sonst wird nichts fertig. (33)

It would seem that Böhme was certainly influential in directing Novalis' endeavors in poetic creativity towards a more symbolic approach, and although Novalis'
earlier aphorisms refer to poetry as a mediating art, an indication of the infinite in
finite form, these later fragments are more definitive, more self-confident, so to speak
and they are the first notes to refer directly to poetry as a <u>symbolic</u> art. (34)

Novalis' enthusiasm for Böhme's ideas again evidences his own penchant for
dualistic thought, and an understanding of Böhme's world view gives insight into the
romantic author's recognition of the poet as the mid-point between polar opposites.
For both Novalis and Böhme the existence of opposites in the universe does not preclude productive action; indeed, they are the stimuli and necessary prerequisites for
dynamism. According to Böhme, without evil there would be no good; according to
Novalis, without the existence of both world and eternity, there would be no poetry
(or rather no need for it). Böhme writes:

> Es ist in der Natur immer eines wider das andre gesetzt, dass eines
> des andern Feind sei, und doch nicht zu dem Ende, dass sich's feinde;
> sondern dass eines das andre im Streite bewege und in sich offenbare,
> auf dass das Mysterium Magnum in Schiedlichkeiten eingehe. (35)

It was perhaps the vividness and convincing aspect of Böhme's great symbol of the
"Zinnteller" as the mirror of the sun, the man-made reflecting device that is absolutely necessary for the sun to be able to prove its very existence, that made Novalis
view in symbolism poetry's most effective mode of expression. Böhme's symbolic
view of nature found a receptive audience in Novalis. Furthermore, the mystic's
central positioning of "Gemüt" in his system and his regard of "Gemüt" as the key
to all the puzzles of the universe undoubtedly struck a familiar chord in the romantic
poet. Böhme wrote of this quality: "Des Menschen Gemüt ist ein Gegenbild der ewigen
Kraft Gottes, [...]" ein Bild oder Gegenwurf göttlicher Wissenschaft [...]" (36)
Novalis' claim that the poet represents both subject and object, "Gemüt und Welt",
and carries these opposites within his own person seems to be a variation of Böhme's
view of man as the microcosmos:

> Ein jeder Geist forschet nur in seine eigene Tiefe und dasjenige,
> darinnen er sich entzündet: [...] So siehe dich nur selber an, was du
> bist, und siehe die äussere Welt an mit ihrem Regiment, was die ist: so
> wirst du finden, dass du mit deinem äusseren Geiste und Wesen die
> äussere Welt bist. Du bist eine kleine Welt aus der grossen, dein äusse-
> res Licht ist ein Chaos der Sonne und des Gestirnes, sonst könntest du
> nicht vom Sonnenlicht sehen. (37)

Finally, the religious aura and basis of Böhme's writings and the preference for expressing religious feelings and the Godhead solely in symbolic terms might explain the increasingly religious tone and call for symbolic poetry in Novalis' later notations.

Returning to Novalis, we shall conclude our discussion of his image of the poet and the qualities he must possess with two extensive passages from his last collection of fragments of 1799/1800 and addenda. In the first description of what the poet should be able to achieve, his versatility and flexibility is stressed:

Der Dichter muss die Fähigkeit haben, sich andre Gedanken vorzustellen, auch Gedanken in allen Arten der Folge und in den mannichfaltigsten Ausdrücken darzustellen. Wie ein Tonkünstler verschiedne Töne und Instrumente in seinem Innern sich vergegenwärtigen, sie vor sich bewegen lassen und sie auf mancherley Weise verbinden kann, so dass er gleichsam der Lebensgeist dieser Klänge und Melodieen wird [...] so muss der Dichter den redenden Geist aller Dinge und Handlungen in seinen unterschiedlichen Trachten sich vorzubilden, und alle Gattungen von Spracharbeiten zu fertigen und mit besondern, eigenthümlichem Sinn zu beseelen vermögend seyn. Gespräche, Briefe, Reden, Erzählungen, Beschreibungen, leidenschaftliche Aeusserungen, mit allen möglichen Gegenständen angefüllt, unter mancherley Umständen und von tausend verschiednen Menschen muss er erfinden und in angemessnen Worten aufs Papier bringen können. Er muss im Stande seyn über alles auf eine unterhaltende und bedeutsame Weise zu sprechen, und das Sprechen oder Schreiben muss ihn selbst zum Schreiben und Sprechen begeistern. (38)

The last fragment of significant interest to our topic depicts the poet as the sovereign virtuoso in command of the particular and the general, nature and "Gemüt", as long as he strives to form variety into unity, to amalgamate all the available materials into a totality. And how does he do this? through his intellect, freedom and poetic execution:

Des Dichters Reich sei die Welt, in den Fokus seiner Zeit gedrängt. Sein Plan und seine Ausführung sei dichterisch, das ist, dichterische Natur. Er kann alles brauchen, er muss es nur mit Geist amalgamiren, er muss ein Ganzes daraus machen. Das Allgemeine wie das Besondere muss er darstellen - alle Darstellung ist im Entgegengesetzten und seine Freiheit im Verbinden macht ihn unumschränkt. Alle dichterische Natur ist Natur. Ihr gebühren alle Eigenschaften der letzteren. So individuell sie ist, so allgemein interessant doch. Was helfen uns Beschreibungen, die Geist und Herz kalt lassen, leblose Beschreibungen der leblosen Natur - sie müssen wenigstens symbolisch sein wie die Natur selber, wenn sie auch dein Gemüthszustandsspiel hervorbringen sollen. Entweder muss die Natur Ideenträger oder das Gemüth Naturträger seyn. Dieses Gesetz muss im Ganzen und im Einzelnen wirksam sein. Egoist darf der Dichter durchaus nicht erscheinen. Er muss sich

selbst Erscheinung sein. Er ist der Vorstellungsprophet der Natur,
so wie der Philosoph der Naturprophet der Vorstellung [...] Der
Dichter bleibt ewig wahr. Er beharrt im Kreislauf der Natur [...]
Alle Darstellung des Dichters muss symbolisch oder rührend sein
[...] (39)

Finally, a look into <u>Heinrich von Ofterdingen</u> with respect to Klingsohr's
assertions about the poet will serve to round out the picture presented here. His
advice to Heinrich has engaged much interest among critics, and although many
have in the past regarded Klingsohr's objective approach to poetry as a stance in
antithesis to Novalis' beliefs, even as a portrayal of Goethe, newer interpreters
view Klingsohr's statements as being compatible with Novalis' own ideas. (40)
Seen from the perspective of an over-all profile of his aphorisms, this affinity is
not only plausible, but obvious. Klingsohr's first warnings to Heinrich that the
poet's craft is a strict one, that he must do more than rely on pure fantasy and
receptivity to images, and that skill in observation and meditation are essential--
all are reminiscent of Novalis' aphoristic statements. The duality of the poet's
character, his "offenes Gemüt" and "Gewandheit im Nachdenken und Betrachten"
are nothing but variations of Novalis' incorporation of "Gemüt und Welt" within
the poet, the emotional and rational components of his totality. Poetry is an art to
be cultivated and perfected--this is not only the voice of Klingsohr, but also that
of Novalis. (41) One also sees in this statement Novalis' fear of the domination of
the poet's imaginative powers to the detriment of his philosophical ones, a concern
expressed in his earliest letters and motivating his continuous efforts to strike a
balance. It is true that a magical aura surrounds the poet, for "In der Nähe des
Dichters bricht die Poesie überall aus. Das Land der Poesie, das romantische
Morgenland, hat Euch mit seiner süssen Wehmut begrüsst," but the other weight of
the balance is with moderation and precision in depiction. (42) When Heinrich asks
whether an object can be too extravagant for poetry, Klingsohr replies:

Allerdings. Nur kann man im Grunde nicht sagen, für die Poesie,
sondern nur für unsere irdischen Mittel und Werkzeuge. Wenn es
schon für einen einzelnen Dichter nur ein eigentümliches Gebiet
gibt, innerhalb dessen er bleiben muss, um nicht alle Haltung und den
Atem zu verlieren: so gibt es auch für die ganze Summe menschlicher
Kräfte eine bestimmte Grenze der Darstellbarkeit, über welche hinaus
die Darstellung die Nötige Dichtigkeit und Gestaltung nicht behalten
kann, und in ein leeres täuschendes Unding sich verliert. (43)

One need only recall to mind our discussion of Novalis' view of poetry as a craft not
unlike that of the mechanic, an art dependent on proper tools of language, to draw
parallels. And are the following heedings not an echo of the youthful Hardenberg's
own fears about his excessive fantasy as expressed in the letter to Professor
Reinhold on October 5, 1791?

> Besonders als Lehrling kann man nicht genug sich vor diesen Aus-
> schweifungen hüten, da eine lebhafte Phantasie nur gar zu gern nach
> den Grenzen sich begibt, und übermütig das Unsinnliche, Ueber-
> mässige zu ergreifen und auszusprechen sucht. (44)

It is true that in the unity/variety continuum of poetry Klingsohr's emphasis seems
to be chiefly upon the unity factor and that given the wide choice of subject matter
available in the world, he prefers to stay within familiar regions:

> Der ältere Dichter steigt nicht höher, als er es gerade nötig hat,
> um seinen mannigfaltigen Vorrat in eine leichtfassliche Ordnung zu
> stellen, und hütet sich wohl, die Mannigfaltigkeit zu verlassen, die
> ihm Stoff genug und auch die nötigen Vergleichungspunkte darbietet
> [...] Die beste Poesie liegt uns ganz nahe, und ein gewöhnlicher
> Gegenstand ist nicht selten ihr liebster Stoff. Für den Dichter ist die
> Poesie an beschränkte Werkzeuge gebunden und eben dadurch wird
> sie zur Kunst. (45)

This elaboration would seem to contradict Novalis' claim in the "Vermischte Bemerkungen" that a poet "muss alles darstellen können und wollen," and that he must
not restrict himself to personal experiences and common subjects; but perhaps this
discrepancy can be explained in terms of Novalis' own maturation. Although the
"Vermischte Bemerkungen" date only three years prior to Klingsohr's characterization
in Heinrich von Ofterdingen, Novalis has purposely depicted Klingsohr as an older,
very experienced poet, whose judgment would naturally be somewhat conservative. (46)
Could it be that Novalis foresaw his own development as approaching the standpoint
of reasonable orderliness so praised by Klingsohr? A glance at his own plans for
further depictions would seem to uphold this theory, for in the main, they involve
topics lying close at hand. (47) It would also seem that Hardenberg's last love, Julie,
turned his sights from the enthusiasm for the infinite aroused by his "heavenly
betrothed" and youthful beloved Sophia to the more practical questions of planned
marital life on earth, right down to the household finances! In his "Geschichten an
Julie", he concludes a group of rather mundane reflections with the phrase "Poesie
des Lebens", indicating his tendency, at least during this phase of his life, to grant
poetic values to quite ordinary things:

> Was ich gelesen habe. Reflexionen über die Menschen - den Weltlauf
> - die politischen Geschichten - unsre künftige Einrichtung - meinen
> Wunderglauben an Sie. Ihre Gewohnheiten. Fränzschen, Caroline
> etc. Die Liebe in jedem Zeitalter. Einteilung des Tags - über die
> Geschäfte - der Morgen, der Abend - der Kreis einer Frau - ihre
> Beschäftigungen. Kleine Kriege zwischen Mann und Frau. Kinder.
> Poesie des Lebens.
> (Ersparnisse in der Kochkunst - an Butter, Eiern. Gebrauch des
> Oels.) (48)

93

Thus one can see that even this still young Novalis of 1800 might indeed have agreed with Klingsohr's dictum: "Der Stoff ist nicht der Zweck der Kunst, aber die Aus-führung ist es [...] Daher kann man sagen, dass die Poesie ganz auf Erfahrung be-ruht."(49) Finally, Klingsohr's belief in the innate poetic drive within every man coincides with Novalis' fragment: "[...] und der Mensch ist also, wo nicht actu, doch Poetentia, Schöpfer." Klingsohr, Heinrich's mentor expresses it in this fashion:

> Es ist recht übel [...] dass die Poesie einen besonderen Namen hat,
> und die Dichter eine besondere Zunft ausmachen. Es ist gar nichts
> Besonderes. Es ist die eigentümliche Handlungsweise des mensch-
> lichen Geistes. Dichtet und trachtet nicht jeder Mensch in jeder
> Minute?(50)

Thus Novalis' poet is an individual of many talents and pursuits. He has the imagina-tion necessary to gaze into eternity, the intellect required to grasp its essence, and the practical skill with which to transform it into a product palatable to ordinary mortals; he is capable of riding into flights of fantasy on the wings of poetic enthusiasm, but he has the good sense to brake his speed and come back to earth when the heights of infinity make him giddy and threaten loss of contact with earthly reality. He stands above mankind, but seeks to communicate with men; he observes everything in the world for possible subject matter, but then selects that which is most suitable to his art. In short, he has the "poetischer Sinn" which reconciles opposites and unifies the Gods and man: "Die Menschenwelt ist das gemeinschaftliche Organ der Götter. Poesie vereinigt sie, wie uns."(51)

An artist who is able to combine the talents of critical reflection and artistic depiction, thinker and creator, is for Novalis the complete human being, the "ächte Gelehrte", "der vollständig gebildete Mensch--der allem, was er berührt und thut eine wissenschaftliche, idealische, synkritistische Form giebt."(52) Furthermore, everything that he does, says, suffers, and hears must be an artistic, technical, and scholarly product.

> Er spricht in Epigrammen, er agirt in einem Schauspiel, er ist Dia-
> logist, er trägt Abhandlungen und Wissenschaften vor - er erzählt
> Anecdoten, Geschichte, Märchen, Romane, er empfindet poëtisch;
> wenn er zeichnet, so zeichnet er, als Künstler, so, als Musiker: Sein
> Leben ist ein Roman - so sieht und hört er alles - so liesst er.(53)

Thomas Mann was later to develop this concept in his critical writings and defines it as a school of European intellectuals which merges art and perception, "den Begriff des Künstlers mit dem des Erkennenden."(54) Here the border separating art from criticism has become less distinct than ever before, and one finds critics of artistic temperament as well as poets with a distinctly critical intellect and style. This type of artist wants to perceive and depict, and Mann notes that the pain necessarily accompanying this dual endeavor bestows upon his life "die sittliche Weihe".(55)

94

THE POET AND HIS CRAFT: IDEALITY AND REALITY

Novalis was very much aware of the unfinished state of his own critical opinions and considered his philosophical writings as a collection of fragments requiring further improvement and organization. The fragmentary character of his work has provided difficulties for critics and students, but Novalis freely admitted to his shortcomings and foresaw a future literature when one would read nothing but "schöne Komposition - als die literarischen Kunstwerke." (56) Not having reached this "schöne Zeit", however, Novalis regarded his own critical writings to be at times incorrect, insignificant, or inappropriate:

Das Umklammerte ist ganz problematischer Wahrheit - so nicht zu brauchen. - Von dem Uebrigen ist nur weniges reif zum Drucke - z. B. als Fragment. Das Meiste ist noch roh. Sehr - sehr vieles gehört zu Einer grossen höchstwichtigen Idee. Ich glaube nicht, dass etwas Unbedeutendes unter dem Undurchstrichnen ist. Das Angestrichne wollt ich in eine Sammlung von neuen Fragmenten aufnehmen und dazu ausarbeiten. Das Andre sollte bis zu einer weitläufigeren Ausführung warten. Durch Fortschreiten wird so vieles entbehrlich - so manches erscheint in einem andern Lichte - so dass ich vor der Ausführung der grossen, alles verändernden Idee, nicht gern etwas Einzelnes ausgearbeitet hätte. (57)

Thus the bulk of Novalis' fragments appeared to him to be merely ragged thoughts or inceptions of an interesting mental sequence, whereas others seemed to be players' chips of transitory value. Some, however, have the stamp of his innermost conviction, (58) and in sifting through this wealth of aesthetic theory, philosophical speculation, and personal commentary, the reader is often rewarded by just such gems. They are fragments in the sense of a microcosm mirroring the universe of an individual's thought, a succinct and compressed expression of a central idea.

IV. THE SYNTHESIS OF POETRY AND PHILOSOPHY

Although the discussions of poetry in the universal sense, as a prerequisite characteristic of the artist, and in the distinct meaning of "Dichtung" have so far been limited to a presentation of how Novalis envisioned poetry in the past and in his own time, there have yet been indications of a view to the future. Indeed, the mere postulating of an ideal has as a necessary correlate the realization that all has not been achieved, that there is a future goal to be realized. It is to this side of poetry, its prescriptive aspect, that we now turn our investigation. If one looks to Novalis for the answer to the question as to what poetry should achieve in the future and wherein lies the task of the poet, two distinct but interrelated spheres of interest have bearing on the subject. The first concerns Hardenberg's never-ending preoccupation with philosophical thought, his intense efforts to comprehend the minds of philosophers such as Fichte, Schelling, and Hemsterhuis, and to integrate rational trains, if not systems of thought within his own poetic ideal. Surely, his studies on Fichte and Hemsterhuis, his later affinity for Böhme, and the concerted efforts devoted to developing within himself a more rational, orderly manner of thinking, support this supposition. (1) Yet more concrete evidence is presented in Hardenberg's letters to Friedrich Schlegel. Having completed his law exams in Wittenberg on July 14, 1794, Novalis wrote to Schlegel: "Jetzt hat mein ganzer Charakter einen politisch philoso-phischen Schwung erhalten, und zwar sehr unmerklich,", and in the same epistle he attempts to convince Schlegel that they could perhaps give the same direction to their lives: "Wir können doch eine Bahn gehn" he pleads and asks to be permitted the dream of being like Dion and Plato. (2) Clinging to his philosophical bent with all his being, Novalis wrote two years later from Dürrenberg: "Mein Lieblingsstudium heisst im Grunde wie meine Braut. Sophie heisst sie - Philosophie ist die Seele meines Lebens und der Schlüssel zu meinem eigensten Selbst." (3)

The second sphere of interest having bearing on the prescriptive aspect of poetry deals with the task of the poet, the manner in which he is to achieve this harmony-- through the unification of reality and ideality, ratio and intuition; the utilization of both powers of observation and imagination; the dual concern with the inner and the outer worlds; and the attempt to build a new poetry born of such an amalgamation; a poetry embracing history, philosophy and "Poesie". Yet before turning to this subject, our discussion here will be devoted to Novalis' thoughts on philosophy, and draw on those comments relating to his goal of achieving an integration of philosophy and poetry, a goal this romantic author sought to accomplish within himself as well as within his ideal of art, his long-range view of what poetry is to become in the "Golden Age" of the future. It was Novalis' firm belief that philosophy was necessary to poetry and poetry to philosophy: "Ohne Philosophie unvollkommner Dichter - Ohne Philosophie unvollkommner Denker - Urtheiler." (4)

In his "Hemsterhuis-Studien" of the fall of 1797, Novalis elaborated upon his total view of three salient branches of knowledge--history, philosophy, and poetry: "Die Erste schafft an - Die 2te ordnet und erklärt - Die Dritte hebt jedes Einzelne durch ausgesuchte Kontrastirung mit dem übrigen Ganzen [...]" Little further attention is devoted to the first category, history, however, and the rest of the ex-cursion deals only with the complementary functions of philosophy and poetry, the two studies being absolutely necessary to each other for perfection in either. Whereas philosophy orders and explains the whole, poetry exalts the specific from the general

totality; whereas philosophy makes perfected poetry possible through "Gesetzge-
bung", poetry gives philosophy meaning and life--it is the purpose of philosophy;
whereas philosophy unites the powers of the individual with those of the "Weltall",
poetry fashions "die schöne Gesellschaft oder das innere Ganze." Both spheres
of knowledge, however, share the same function of bringing together individual
and universe by allowing totality to operate as the organ of the individual, and conversely, the individual as the organ of totality. Thus the individual becomes the
object of universal enjoyment, and the universe, the object of individual pleasure.
This unity and mutual sympathy of individual and universe is brought about through
poetry, but Novalis concludes this thought with the phrase: "Durch die Philosophie -
möglich."(5) Thus, the main goal of the reconciling of man and the universe, the
general and the particular, can only be achieved through the interaction of philosophy
and poetry. Each is intimately bound to the fulfillment of the other's task.

To be sure, Novalis did not attempt to fuse poetry and philosophy into one
singular entity and recognized that each had its particular sphere of knowledge and
required different modes of education. Whereas philosophical depth necessitates
the rigors and discipline of academic training, poetic virtuosity has as its prerequisite years of apprenticeship in the art of living: "Lehrjahre sind für den
poetischen - academische Jahre für den philosophischen Jünger" he writes in the
"Vermischte Bermerkungen" of December, 1797/January, 1798 and continues:
"Lehrjahre im vorzüglichen Sinn sind die Lehrjahre der Kunst zu leben."(6) Yet
the study of philosophy often calls forth the same talents, requires the same intensity
of thought and desire for self-knowledge that poetry demands of its disciples, and
thus a familiarity with philosophy and its methods of study and investigation (and the
insights granted to those who indulge in such mental activity) is of inestimable value
to the poetic mind. In one of his "Logololische Fragmente" dating to February, 1798,
Novalis gives philosophy the rank and universality heretofore seen only in his praise
of the omnipotence of "Poesie", and the act of "manumission" to which he refers
would seem to be an integral part of the poetic process:

> Wenn man anfängt über Philosophie nachzudenken - so dünkt uns Philo-
> sophie, wie Gott, und Liebe, Alles zu seyn. Sie ist eine mystische,
> höchstwircksame, durchdringende Idee - die uns unaufhaltsam nach
> allen Richtungen hineintreibt. Der Entschluss zu philosophieren -
> Philosophie zu suchen ist der Act der Manumission - der Stoss auf
> uns Selbst zu.(7)

This individualistic tendency within the process of philosophizing is quite
similar to the subjective aspect of poetry, and indeed, "Der Stoss auf uns Selbst
zu" accompanying the decision to engage in philosophical activity is highly reminiscent of the individualistic nature of the poet's creation. In other words, philosophy leads one to one's inner self, and poetry, having already traversed this inward
path, becomes the expression of what was found there. Both disciplines share a
difficulty, however, in that both are pursued by singular and thus limited human
beings--a poet can hardly depict anything more than his individual philosophy, and
even a philosopher can never completely go beyond the boundaries, the magical
circle, of his individual philosophy. In this limitation, philosophy and poetry are
alike, for it results not from the nature of the discipline, but rather from that of
mortal beings:

Die Darstellung der Philosophie der Philosophie wird immer etwas
von einer Individualphilosophie haben. Der Dichter stellt ebenfalls nur
Individualphilosophie dar, und jeder Mensch wird, so lebhaft er übri-
gens auch die Philosophie der Philosophie anerkennen mag, praktisch
nur mehr oder weniger Individualphilosoph seyn, und, trotz allen Be-
strebens, nie ganz aus dem Zauberkreise seiner Individualphilosophie
heraustreten können. (8)

In the thirteenth fragment of the same collection, Novalis gives a long and
somewhat complicated historical view of the development of the philosophical mind,
"der philosophische Geist", underlying both poet and thinker. Yet an explanation of
this passage is of value, since it clarifies and underscores his belief that the artist
is the fullest manifestation of this philosophical mentality that has undergone change,
progress, and molding, and has expressed itself in the form of various types of
thinkers. The travelings of Novalis' "philosophischer Geist" do not lack some
similarity to Hegel's wandering spirit in its malleability, universality, and ultimate
perfectibility, and Novalis' "Golden Age" can also be seen in analogy to the idealistic
philosopher's vision of the full manifestation of the spirit within historical time. The
passage referred to here divided the history of thought into three major stages of
culture. The first is characterized by the polarity of scholastic thinker and intuitive
poet, the second by the eventual contiguity of these two types or masses, and the
third, by the rise of the "Künstler, der Werckzeug und Genie zugleich ist," the artist
who recognizes in the original separation of the two forms of thought "eine tiefer
liegende Trennung seines eigenen Wesens," a division which can exist only by means
of the possibility for communication, for unification. The first stage of polar antitheses is described in this fashion:

Der rohe, discursive Denker ist der Scholastiker. Der ächte Scholastiker
ist ein mystischer Subtilist. Aus logischen Atomen baut er sein Weltall -
er vernichtet alle lebendige Natur, um ein Gedankenkunststück an ihre
Stelle zu setzen - Sein Ziel ist ein unendlicher Automat. Ihm entgegengesetzt ist der rohe, intuitive Dichter. Er hasst Regel, und feste Gestalt.
Ein wildes, gewaltthätiges Leben herrscht in der Natur - Alles ist belebt.
Kein Gesetz - Willkühr und Wunder überall. Er ist bloss dynamisch. So
regt sich der philosophische Geist zuerst in völlig getrennten Massen. (9)

Obviously, these two types, the discursive thinker and the intuitive poet,
represent the extremes of cold deadening logic and undisciplined lively imagination.
In the second stage, these two bodies begin to affect each other, and from this meet-
ing arise countless eclectics: "So wie in der Vereinigung unendlicher Extreme überhaupt das Endliche, Beschränckte, entsteht, so entstehn nun auch hier Eklektiker
ohne Zahl. Die Zeit der Missverständnisse beginnt." The eclectic, practical philosopher of this age is looked upon with scorn by the pure scholastics of the first
period, since the scholastics regard the worldly, limited approach of the eclectics
as weakness and inconsequence.

Thus this second type of philosopher is not satisfactory either, and it must fall to the product of the third stage, the artist, to bring harmony to the chaos and confusion. The artist is genius and tool, in that he possesses both speculative intellect and practical ability so that can he bridge the gap. He realizes that these extremes are only reflections of the polarities within his own being, his own mental structure, and the secret of their continued existence must lie in a binding principle like the magnetism that separates and yet unites the earth's poles: "Er findet, dass so heterogen auch diese Thätigkeiten sind, sich doch ein Vermögen in ihm vorfinde von Einer zur andern überzugehn, nach Gefallen seine Polaritaet zu verändern - Er entdeckt also in ihnen nothwendige Glieder seines Geistes - er merckt, dass beyde in einem Gemeinsamen Princip vereinigt seyn müssen."(10) It would seem that the poet alone holds the key to life, but if we read on, we see that this ability residing in the crowning glory of cultural development is based on philosophy: "Die vollständige Darstellung des durch diese Handlung zum Bewusstseyn erhobenen ächt geistigen Lebens ist die Philosophie kat exochin." And the reason?

Hier entsteht jene lebendige Reflexion, die sich bey sorgfältiger Pflege nachher zu einem unendlich gestalteten geistigen Universo von selbst ausdehnt - der Kern oder Keim einer alles befassenden Organisation - Es ist der Anfang einer wahrhaften Selbstdurchdringung des Geistes die nie endigt. (11)

This sentence contains the essence of Novalis' belief in the interrelatedness of philosophy and poetry, of their mutual interdependence. Only through the study of philosophy can the intellect be sufficiently trained in the art of lively reflection which forms the kernel of all organization, the beginning of expansion from one infinitesimally small seed to a spiritual universe. Is not this the practice and aim of poetry?

As his interest in philosophy increased, so did the desire to bring together what Novalis saw as the antinomies of life, and although he always granted poetry supreme dominion over the last puzzles of life, he regarded philosophy as an essential ingredient for the solution of the problem. Philosophy is that mode of thought which seeks to enter the void left by the repulsion of opposite poles away from each other: "[...] so wächst die Philosophie in die Unendlichkeit, nach aussen und nach Innen - Sie strebt gleichsam den unendlichen Raum zwischen den Endgliedern auszufüllen," he writes in the "Logololis Fragmente" of February, 1798. (12) In the following aphorism Novalis places the individual human being with his innate penchant for philosophical thought and his natural wish to harmonize "die höchsten Enden" into the center of the universe:

Die höchsten Aufgaben beschäftigen den Menschen am Frühsten. Aeusserst lebhaft fühlt der Mensch beym ersten Nachdenken das Bedürfnis die höchsten Enden zu vereinigen. Mit steigender Kultur nehmen seine Versuche an Genialitaet ab - aber sie nehmen an Brauchbarkeit zu - wodurch er zu dem Irrthume verleitet wird - gänzlich von den Endgliedern zu abstrahiren, und sein Verdienst blos in Vereinigung näherer Bedingter Glieder zu setzen [...] Jezt fällt ihm endlich ein in sich selbst, als absoluten Mittelpunct dieser getrennten Welten das absolute Vereinigungsglied aufzusuchen - Er sieht auf einmal, dass das

> Problem realiter schon durch seine Existenz gelöst ist--und das
> Bewusstseyn der Gegensetze seiner Existenz die Wissenschaft kat
> exochin sey, die er so lange schon suche. Mit der Entdeckung die-
> ses Bewusstseyns ist das grosse Rätsel im Grunde gelösst. So wie
> sein Leben reale Philosophie ist, so ist seine Philosophie ideales
> Leben - lebendige Theorie des Lebens. (13)

From this statement of discovery, it appears that man has the solution to the riddle
of life within his own being and he need go no further than to the boundaries of his
own individuality to achieve his "reale Philosophie". Yet Novalis is not one to be
content with mere recognition and spurs man on to newer heights. The insight
attained here is not the final stage of progress, but rather the initial step in man's
attempt to embrace the universe and reconcile himself to eternity. He continues: (14)

> Sein Weg ist ihm nun auf Ewigkeiten vorgezeichnet - Seine Beschäftigung
> ist Erweiterung seines Daseyns in die Unendlichkeit - der Traum seiner
> Jugend ist zu einer schönen Wirklichkeit [...] Der scheinbare Wider-
> spruch der ursprünglichen Aufgabe - der Aufgaben - Lösung und Nicht-
> lösung zugleich - ist vollkommen gehoben.

This second step, the expansion of individual existence into infinity, lies
within the domain of poetry, for after reason has been prodded to these discoveries
by philosophy, imagination must be inspired by poetry to achieve harmony--both
reason and imagination are necessary to the task:

> Das Poem des Verstandes ist Philosophie - Es ist der höchste Schwung,
> den der Verstand sich über sich selbst giebt - Einheit des Verstandes
> und der Einbildungskraft. Ohne Philosophie bleibt der Mensch in seinen
> wesentlichsten Kräften uneins - Es sind 2 Menschen - Ein Verständiger -
> und Ein Dichter. (15)

Here we see that philosophy underlies not only one aspect of the duality reason/
imagination, but also serves as the force which unites the two functions--through
philosophy, man's two natures can be integrated. This integration of the personality
is furthermore absolutely necessary to the full development of either aspect: "Ohne
Philosophie unvollkommner Dichter - Ohne Philosophie unvollkommner Denker -
Urtheiler." (16)

It seems that Novalis' attempt to unite philosophy and poetry into a new type
of poetic endeavor would require a new name, something more than just "Poesie",
and indeed, he chose a distinct title for the "Poesie, die da kommen soll," namely,
transcendental poetry. This is to be the poetry of the future, the vehicle for man's
ascent into eternal regions: "Die transscendentale Poesie ist aus Philosophie und
Poesie gemischt [...] Der transscendentale Dichter ist der transscendentale Mensch
überhaupt."(17) Whereas the poets of the past were characterized by their dynamic
approach, the poets of the dawning age are destined to proceed in organic fashion,
but the main distinction between these two generations of artists lies not in the
approach, but rather in consciousness of method. Indeed, among the poets of the

past, some poetized organically and were thus genuine poets, but they were unaware of this: "Wenn sie erfunden ist (the transcendental poetry), so wird man sehn, dass alle ächte Dichter bisher, ohne ihr Wissen, organisch poetisirten - dass aber dieser Mangel an Bewusstseyn dessen, was sie thaten--einen wesentlichen Einfluss auf das Ganze ihrer Wercke hatte [...]" Surprisingly enough, this naive, unknowing attitude has a negative effect, and so although a few works turned out to be "ächt poetisch", most are relegated to the class of the unpoetic creations.(18)

Needless to say, it was Novalis' fervent hope that the transcendental poetry of the future would bring about truly poetic works of art, but it is of particular significance that he does not expect this achievement from the naive, unconscious poet at one with nature and life, but rather from the sentimental type (in Schiller's terminology) who is fully aware of what he is doing and what he wants to achieve. This is not a program for simple "romantic" effusion and unbridled imaginative powers; and from this explanation, one can deduce that Novalis' "Golden Age" of poetry is not to be sought in a renewal of the past, a re-establishment of Homeric innocence and objectivity, but at the pinnacle of human culture envisioned in the future. This apex of man's development embraces both subjective and objective elements, thought and imagination, philosophy and poetry--it is not a compound, but rather a solution in which the elements that comprise the mixture are readily detectable.

In June and July of 1798 Novalis turns from his proposed transcendental poetry to further analysis of what poetry and philosophy contribute to each other's task, and here again, philosophy, although serving a vital function, is nevertheless subordinate to poetry:

Die Poesie ist der Held der Philosophie. Die Philosophie erhebt die Poesie zum Grundsatz. Sie lehrt uns den Werth der Poesie kennen. Philosophie ist die Theorie der Poesie. Sie zeigt uns was die Poesie sey, dass sie Eins und alles sey.(19)

Novalis has indeed a positive attitude towards the future of literature and mankind, and in fashion reminiscent of Lessing indicates his expectation of a thousand-year realm free of vice "wenn die Erziehung zur Vernunft vollendet seyn wird."(20) In another instance he discusses the era when art will have triumphed over raw material:

Princip der Vervollkommnung in der Menschheit - die Menschheit wäre nicht Menschheit - wenn nicht ein tausendjähriges Reich kommen müsste. Das Princip ist in jeder Kleinigkeit des Alltagslebens - in allem sichtbar. Das Wahre erhält sich immer - das Gute dringt durch - der Mensch kommt wieder empor - die Kunst bildet sich - Die Wissenschaft entsteht - und nur das Zufällige, das Individuale verschwindet.(21)

Novalis' golden age is one of literary affluence and splendid poetic perfection, but it is a goal projected into the future, as he notes: "Wir sind jezt nur im Anfang der Schriftsteller Kunst."(22)

V. THE NOVEL AS THE VEHICLE FOR THE FULFILLMENT OF THE HIGHEST TASK OF POETRY

With this investigation into Novalis' concept of poetry and the poet's task, the question remains as to how he hoped to achieve this goal. What vehicle would enable the poet to give fullest expression to his idea, to integrate the poles of philosophy and poetry, reality and ideality, the realms of observation and imagination? How was such an ambitious program to attain fulfillment?

At the end of July, 1798, Friedrich Schlegel wrote to Novalis from Dresden: "Du scheinst zwar zu glauben, dass Deine Hauptidee nur in einem Roman mitteilbar sei. Das gebe ich bis auf das nur zu, denn sie dürfte wohl auf unendlich viele Weise mitteilbar sein, und würde am Ende nicht eine solche Correspondenz ein Roman sein?--(1) Thus this all-encompassing genre, which for Novalis drew its breath from the life experience of the author, was envisioned at the time as the only poetic form capable of realizing his "Hauptidee", only the novel seemed able to embrace all the aspects of his poetic endeavor and synthesize them into a totality. In the "Studium Fragmente" of 1798/1799, Novalis noted that his three major concerns at the time were "1) Die Enzyklopädistik, 2) ein Roman, 3) der Brief an Schlegel", (2) and in a letter to Caroline Schlegel of February, 1799, Novalis claims:

> [...] denn ich habe Lust, mein ganzes Leben an Einen Roman zu
> wenden - der allein eine ganze Bibliothek ausmachen, vielleicht
> Lehrjahre einer Nation enthalten soll. Das Wort Lehrjahre ist falsch -
> es drückt ein bestimmtes Wohin aus. Bei mir soll es aber nichts als -
> UebergangsJahre vom Unendlichen zum Endlichen bedeuten. Ich hoffe
> damit zugleich meine historische und philosophische Sehnsucht zu
> befriedigen. (3)

The work on his novel Heinrich von Ofterdingen was to occupy Novalis until his death, and its goal was not only to satisfy the author's historical and philosophical yearnings, but was to be the "Apotheose der Poesie". Yet Heinrich von Ofterdingen was only one of a series of novels planned by Novalis, as his "Romanstudien" of 1799/1800 reveal, and although his "Dichterische Pläne" include fantasies, religious songs, essays, fairytales, and one or two dramas, the novel is the most prominent genre in its frequency of occurrence and its universality. Thus Novalis can forsee his creation of novels centering in history, religion, morals, social life, or even politics. Historical novels might be based on the Reformation, the wars of the Netherlands, the first Christian era, the Crusades, the destruction of Constantinople, the life of Jesus, or the discovery of America, (4) whereas a more socially oriented novel might parallel Wilhelm Meister and be concerned with more immediate and prosaic human contacts: "[...] den Umgang mit Menschen, über Betragen in Krankheiten, über das Schuldenwesen junger Leute, über das vornehme Leben, über Kleidung, Lebensart, Vergnügungen [...] Ehe."(5) Novalis finds the novel best suited to expressing his ideas on morals; even the events of a single day could result in a "dialogierter Roman". (6)

From these plans and other notations, it is clear that the novel has two aspects. First of all, it draws from life and is in this sense realistic; but secondly, it represents an approximation, a "kontinuierliche Reihe", and in this progression, the novel is idealistic. Many aphorisms illuminate the realistic starting point of the novel and describe it as a parallel to real life. "Ein Roman ist ein Leben als Buch," Novalis writes in the summer of 1798, and his analogy is quite vivid: "Jedes Leben hat ein Motto - einen Titel - einen Verleger - eine Vorrede - Einleitung - Text - Noten - etc. oder kann es haben."(7) In fact, the best way for an individual to understand life himself would be to write a novel throughout the course of his life: "Man sollte, um das Leben und sich selbst kennen zu lernen, einen Roman immer neben- her schreiben."(8) Interestingly enough, Novalis included the story of his own life among his plans for a novel.(9) The materials out of which a novel is composed are taken from real life, from the experiences of the individual, and whether or not one makes something of life's chance events depends on one's poetic talent or the level of "Geist". Even business life can be treated in poetic fashion, and such a transformation of prosaic life is actually projected for Novalis' "bürgerlicher Roman":

> Auch Geschäftsarbeiten kann man poëtisch behandeln. Es gehört ein tiefes poëtisches Nachdenken dazu, um diese Verwandlung vorzu-nehmen. Die Alten haben dies herrlich verstanden. Wie poëtisch be-schreiben sie Kräuter, Maschinen, Häuser, Geräthschaften etc.(10)

He continues to explain the various elements necessary to such a metamorphosis of everyday reality, the manner in which the novelist brings reality and ideality together in his work:

> Eine gewisse Alterthümlichkeit des Stils, eine richtige Stellung und Ordnung der Massen, eine leise Hindeutung auf Allegorie, eine ge-wisse Seltsamkeit, Andacht und Verwunderung, die durch die Schreib-art durchschimmert - dies sind einige wesentliche Züge dieser Kunst, die ich zu meinem bürgerlichen Roman recht nöthig habe.(11)

A similar idea is expressed in an aphorism of the "Allgemeine Brouillon" of 1798-99 in which ideality and reality are related to poetry and philosophy and also to farness and nearness. It is self-evident that nearness and philosophy portray reality, whereas farness and poetry convey vagueness and thus the poetic ideal:

> Die Natur ist unbegreiflich per se. Ruhe und gebildete Unbegreiflich-keit. Die Philosophie ist die Prosa. Ihre Consonanten. Ferne Philo-sophie klingt wie Poesie - weil jeder Ruf in die Ferne Vocal wird. Auf beyden Seiten oder um sie her liegt + und minus Poesie. So Berge, ferne Menschen, ferne Begebenheiten etc. alles wird romantisch, quod idem est--daher ergiebt sich unsre Urpoetische Natur. Poesie der Nacht und Dämmerung.(12)

This tendency towards vagueness and the distant charm of poetry is of course what in the aphorism quoted in the introduction(13) was called "Romantisieren". But this process of romanticizing does not exhaust either Novalis' or Friedrich Schlegel's poetic ambitions, since the drive for vagueness and ideality is counterbalanced by a striving for concreteness, which in the above-mentioned aphorism is represented by philosophy and closeness, or in the "Logololische Fragmente" rendered by the term "Logarithmisieren". (14) In other words, just as "Romantisieren" stands for Schlegel's raising to a higher power, "Logarithmisieren" renders Schlegel's reverse movement of "Radizieren", and thus Novalis' antagonism of "Romantisieren" and "Logarithmisieren" can be taken as an explanation of Schlegel's formula of

$$\sqrt[\frac{1}{0}]{\frac{1}{0}}\ \frac{1}{0}$$

The more realistic orientation of the novelist as compared to the lyric poet is also elaborated in a further aphorism of 1799/1800, and as in chapter three, Novalis' regard of poetry as a craft utilizing materials and tools is evident here:

> Der Romandichter sucht mit Begebenheiten und Dialogen, mit
> Reflexionen und Schilderungen--Poësie hervorzubringen, wie der
> Lyrische Dichter durch Empfindungen, Gedanken und Bilder. Es
> kommt also alles auf die Weise an, auf die künstlerische Wählungs-
> und Verbindungskunst. (15)

In order to perfect his art of depiction, the writer must not only invent "Anekdoten", but should devote himself to the study of the best available examples before attempting his own work: "Man muss, als Schriftsteller alle Arten der Darstellung machen können. Erst lerne man sie genau kennen--untersuche sie sorgfältig - studire die besten, schon vorhandnen Muster - dann lege Hand ans Werck. Allmählich wird man in jeder Art Meister." (16) Novalis seems to have taken up Schlegel's suggestion that even such an actual correspondence as theirs might form the content of a novel, for he comments in 1789/99 that letters or conversations are works for a writer: "Briefe, Unterhaltungen - oder Gespräche - Geschäftsarbeiten - wircksame Broschüren - das sind practisch schriftstellerische Arbeiten," and he mentions the novel or a sermon as a possible poetic form. (17) In an earlier fragment Novalis considers letters as a pleasant diversion, but they can serve a more professional goal as well: "Briefe sollen Erholungen seyn, und ich sollte sie auch als solche für mich bearbeiten. Abends Briefe - leicht, frey, romantisch, mannichfaltig - Vorarbeit zum Roman." (18)

Indeed, everything in life is "Samenkorn", possible material for a novel, and unless life is transformed into a poetic dimension, it is a self-destroying illusion. The novel draws from life, but life requires poetic expression to give it substance, and so poetry and life are interdependent. "Das Leben soll kein uns gegebener, sondern ein von uns gemachter Roman sein" Novalis says in May of 1798, (19) and somewhat later he expands this view and explains how the novel and life are related:

> Der Roman handelt von Leben - stellt <u>Leben</u> dar. Ein Mimus wär er
> nur in Beziehung auf den Dichter. Oft enthält er Begebenheiten einer
> Maskerade - eine masquirte Begebenheit unter masquirten Personen.
> Man hebe die Masken - es sind bekannte Begebenheiten--bekannte
> Personen. Der Roman, als solcher, enthält kein bestimmtes Resultat -

> er ist nicht Bild und Factum eines Satzes. Er ist anschauliche Aus-
> führung - Realisierung einer Idee. (20)

Thus although a novel deals with and even depicts life, it does not strive for a
naturalistic presentation of the real world. The natural world from which the poet
extracts events and characters for his novel is limited, whereas an idea can be
infinite. So the novel is a realization of an idea rather than a true reproduction of
the world, and like an idea, enjoys unlimited scope. Novalis continues:

> Aber eine Idee lässt sich nicht, in einen Satz fassen. Eine Idee ist eine
> unendliche Reihe von Sätzen - eine irrationale Grösse - unsetzbar
> (musikalisch) - incommensurabel [...] Das Gesetz ihrer Fortschrei-
> tung lässt sich aber aufstellen - und nach diesem ist ein Roman zu
> kritisiren. (21)

Novalis' concept of the novel as an infinite series, a continuous progression
is given expression in many fragments and explains how he conceives of this genre's
encompassing reality and ideality. The novel finds its beginnings in real life, but
progresses into infinity, and although its goal is beyond rational understanding,
"incommensurabel", the law of its progression can be ascertained. The task of
literary criticism therefore resides in comparing the work with the law of its development. In this sense, Novalis' "Buch soll [...] ein reales und ideales Muster - und
Keim aller Bücher [werden]." (22) The goal of the novel can only be approximated,
never truly realized, by the author, and thus progression also involves some
regressions:

> Der Gang der Approximation ist aus zunehmenden Progressen und
> Regressen zusammengesetzt. Beide retardiren - Beide beschleunigen -
> beide führen zum Ziel. So scheint im Roman der Dichter bald dem
> Ziel zu nähern, bald wider zu entfernen und nie ist es näher, als
> wenn es am entferntesten zu seyn scheint. (23)

An aphorism from the "Vermischte Bemerkungen" elaborates on the novel's
utilization of life's chance happenings as materials for its infinite goal:

> Alle Zufälle unsers Lebens sind Materialien, aus denen wir machen
> können, was wir wollen. Wer viel Geist hat macht viel aus seinem
> Leben - Jede Bekanntschaft, jeder Vorfall wäre für den durchaus
> Geistigen - erstes Glied einer unendlichen Reihe - Anfang eines un-
> endlichen Romans. (24)

One could strengthen the documentation relating to "Zufall" by quoting from Ofterdingen's conversation with Sylvester (25) comparing "die Fabel" and "das Gewissen"
with "der Geist des Weltgedichts, [...] der Zufall der ewigen romantischen Zu-
sammenkunft, des unendlich veränderlichen Gesamtlebens." It is indeed an act
of mere chance that results in the creation of an individual, and thus the infinite
series that forms his life is actually rooted in chance. For this reason, "Zufall"
and the systematic progression of events in a person's life are not at all contradictory:

> Das Individuum wird das Vollkommenste, das rein Systematische seyn,
> das nur durch einen einzigen absoluten Zufall individualisiert ist - z. B.
> durch seine Geburt. In diesem Zufall müssen alle seine übrigen Zufälle,
> die unendliche Reihe seiner Zustände, eingeschachtelt liegen, oder noch
> besser, als seine Zufälle, seine Zustände determiniert seyn. Ablei-
> tung eines individuellen Lebens aus einem einzigen Zufalle - einem
> einzigen Act der Willkühr.

Furthermore, the world we live in can be viewed from a romantic rather than a
prosaic orientation, and life itself is nothing but a colossal novel:

> Nichts ist romantischer als was man gewöhnlich Welt und Schicksal
> nennt. - Wir leben in einem colossalen (im Grossen und Kleinen)
> Roman. Betrachtung der Begebenheiten um uns her. Romantische
> Orientirung, Beurtheilung und Behandlung des Menschenlebens. (26)

In comparing the genres of the novel and the epic poem, Novalis stresses
the progressive nature of both, but there is nevertheless a difference in degree
which bestows the higher value upon the novel: "Der Roman steht schon weit höher -
Jenes dauert fort - dieser (das epische Gedicht) wächst fort - in Jenem ist arythme-
tische, im Roman geometrische Progression." (27) If one asks the question as to
what Novalis actually meant by progression or a continuous series, the answer can
be found in his view of characterization. The novel, perhaps more than any other
genre, deals with characters, poetic depictions of human beings, and the novelist
is progressive insofar as he is able to depict the various aspects of a character.
Writing a novel is "Darstellung eines Gegenstandes in Reihen - Variationsreihen -
Abänderungen etc." or "Dasselbe Individuum in Variationen," (28) and in both
instances, Novalis sees his pattern in Goethe's _Meister_, primarily in the characterizations of Natalie and "die schöne Seele". The term variation is not only applicable
to the depiction of a single individual, however, but to the whole of humanity, since
all human beings are "Variationen Eines vollständigen Individuums." Thus the
complete and ideal character is comprised of elements taken from many real individuals, and it is the novelist's task to gather up the individual variations into a
totality, into a "mächtige Symphonie". (29)

The perfect character would not be an abstract ideal, however, but rather a
transparent, natural appearance, quite familiar to the reader, as Novalis explains
in the "Teplitzer Fragmente": "Der vollkommenste Karacter würde der durchsich-
tige - der von selbst verständliche--der unendlich leicht und natürlich scheinende,
durchaus _Bekannte_, deshalb unbemerckte, übersehene und elastische sein." (30)
Novalis even muses that if one were to travel into the land of novels, one would
meet only familiar persons. (31) Since the individual character is of central importance to his concept of the novel, it is perhaps of interest to note how Novalis viewed
the ideal human being, and in this regard, he is a follower of the German tradition
of "Bildung". The human individual should not be content with his place in life, but
should constantly strive towards universality and perfection, as Novalis indicates

in the "Allgemeine Brouillon": "Wir sollen nicht blos Menschen, wir sollen auch mehr, als Menschen seyn. - Der Mensch ist überhaupt soviel, als Universum--Es ist nichts bestimmtes - Es kann und soll etwas Bestimmtes und Unbestimmtes zugleich seyn,"(32) or in a later fragment of 1799/1800:

> Der vollendete Mensch muss gleichsam zugleich an mehreren Orten und in mehreren Menschen leben - ihm müssen beständig ein weiter Kreis und mannichfache Begebenheiten gegenwärtig seyn. Hier bildet sich dann die wahre, grossartige Gegenwart des Geistes- die den Menschen zum eigentlichen Weltbürger macht und ihn in jedem Augenblicke seines Lebens durch die wohlthätigsten Associationen reizt, stärkt, und in die helle Stimmung einer besonnenen Thätigkeit versetzt. (33)

The construction of a continuous series within a novel is carefully outlined by Novalis in an extensive fragment in the "Anekdoten" of 1798:

> Ein Romanschreiber macht eine Art von Bouts rimes - der aus einer gegebenen Menge von Zufällen und Situationen - eine wohlgeordnete, gesetzmässige Reihe macht - der Ein Individuum zu Einem Zweck durch alle diese Zufälle, die er zweckmässig hindurchführt. Ein eigenthümliches Individuum muss er haben, das die Begebenheiten bestimmt, und von ihnen bestimmt wird. Dieser Wechsel, oder die Veränderungen Eines Individuums - in einer continuirlichen Reihe machen den interessanten Stoff des Romans aus. (34)

One must bear in mind that Novalis' idea of progression is an ordered "gesetzmässige Reihe" rather than an unstructured continuum, as he clearly indicates: "Die Schreibart des Romans muss kein Continuum--es muss ein in jeden Perioden gegliederter Bau seyn. Jedes kleine Stück muss etwas abgeschnittes - begränztes - ein eignes Ganze seyn."(35) The novelist has some freedom in method as long as the overriding goal of unity predominates. He can first think of many events and then imagine an individual through whom they can be enlivened, "eine Menge Reitze, und zu diesen eine besondre, sie mannichfach verändernde und specificirende Constitution," or he can proceed in the opposite fashion and first determine the type of individual to be portrayed, "und zu diesem eine Menge Begebenheiten erfinden;"(36) The greater the writer, however, the more disciplined he will be:

> Je grösser der Dichter, desto weniger Freyheit erlaubt er sich, desto philosophischer ist er. Er begnügt sich mit der willkührlichen Wahl des ersten Moments und entwickelt nachher nur die Anlagen dieses Keims - bis zu seiner Auflösung. Jeder Keim ist eine Dissonanz - ein Missverhältniss was sich nach gerade ausgleichen soll. Dieser erste Moment begreift die Wechselglieder in einem Verhältniss - das nicht so bleiben kann - z. B. bey Meister. (37)

The reference to Goethe's work reveals that Novalis was thinking primarily in terms of the "Bildungsroman" when he elaborated this procedure.

What always remains of central importance, however, is to maintain the poetic quality of the novel, and oddly enough, this aura is not to be granted by estrangement from reality, but rather through a type of local color. "Je persönlicher, localer, temporeller, eigenthümlicher ein Gedicht ist, desto näher steht es dem Centro der Poesie. Ein Gedicht muss ganz unerschöpflich seyn wie ein Mensch und ein guter Spruch," Novalis states, but adds: "Was oben vom Gedicht gesagt ist, gilt auch vom Roman."(38) This should not be interpreted as a naturalistic tendency, for although the words of a novel may depict personal, local, and temporal objects, they must always remain poetic and never depict "platte Natur".(39) The individual and temporal aspects of life must be poetized and made general, but the individual coloring of the universal remains its romanticizing element:

> Alles Nationale, Temporelle, Locale, Individuelle lässt sich
> universalisiren, und so canonisiren und allgemein machen [...]
> Dieses individuelle Colorit des Universellen ist sein romantisirendes
> Element. So ist jeder National, und selbst der persönliche Gott ein
> romantisirtes Universum. Die Persönlichkeit ist das romantische
> Element des Ichs.

As long as the novel has "Plan", "Sinn", and "Ausführung", it can include various styles of expression, and Novalis envisions his own book in this light: "Jedes Stück meines Buchs, das in äusserst verschiedner Manier geschrieben sein kann - in Fragmenten - Briefen - Gedichten - wissenschaftlich strengen Aufsätzen etc."(40) Furthermore, a writer can choose from a variety of elements to establish the center of his work(41): "Ein Buch kann ein sehr verschiednes Interesse haben. Der Autor, der Leser, ein Zweck, eine Begebenheit, seine blosse, individuelle Existenz können die Achse seyn um den es sich dreht."(42)

Yet regardless of approach or style the novelist must poetize the material of his work. He cannot simply convey content, since according to Novalis, "es ist roh und geistlos, sich blos des Inhalts wegen mitzutheilen--der Inhalt, der Stoff muss uns nicht tyrannisieren. Wir müssen uns zweckmässig mittheilen - kunstvoll - besonnen."(43) The real and the ideal must mesh in an artful manner into a totality, and if an author fails to achieve this harmony, he falls prey to Novalis' criticism, as do Wieland and Jean Paul:

> Die Idee eines Ganzen muss durchaus ein ästhetisches Werck be-
> herrschen und modificiren. Selbst in den launigsten Büchern.
> Wieland, Richter und die meisten Comiker fehlen hier sehr oft.
> Es ist so entsetzlich viel überflüssiges und langweiliges, recht
> eigentliche hors d'oeuvres, in ihren Werken. Selten ist der Plan
> und die grosse Vertheilung ästhetisch - Sie haben nur ästhetische
> oder komische Laune, nicht ästhetisch komischen Sinn oder
> Geist.(44)

Art must triumph over raw material, and a novel must always be permeated with poetry:

> Ein Roman muss durch und durch Poesie sein. Die Poesie ist nämlich, wie die Philosophie, eine harmonische Stimmung unsers Gemüts, wo sich alles verschönert, wo jedes Ding seine gehörige Ansicht - alles seine passende Begleitung und Umgebung findet. (45)

Thus the ideal novel incorporates the elements of poetry and philosophy, the fusion Novalis set as his general poetic goal, and in this light, his statement: "Alles kann am Ende zur Philosophie werden - So z. B. Cervantes 'Don Quixote'" gains in clarity. (46) The ideal novel represents what poetry and philosophy share in common for Novalis, namely, a harmonious temper of "Gemüt". It would seem that this Böhmean quality forms the essence of the truly poetic novel and allows it to embrace reality and ideality, poetry and philosophy, to achieve the demand: "Natur soll Kunst und Kunst 2te Natur werden" postulated by this romantic author. (47) A truly poetic book is both natural and marvelous, and because of this intermingling it grants a new understanding of the world:

> Es scheint in einem ächt poëtischen Buche alles so natürlich - und doch so wunderbar - Man glaubt es könne nichts anders seyn und als habe man nur bisher in der Welt geschlummert - und gehe einem nun erst der rechte Sinn für die Welt auf. (48)

VI. THE NOVEL AND THE FAIRYTALE:

"ALLE ROMANE, WO WAHRE LIEBE VORKOMMT, SIND MÄRCHEN"

Having ascertained that a poetic novel requires for Novalis "eine harmoni-
sche Stimmung unsers Gemüts" in the previous chapter, it is interesting to note
that among his literary plans for the future, this author points to a new direction
for such expression: "Im Märchen glaub ich am besten meine Gemütsstimmung
ausdrücken zu können. Alles ist ein Märchen."(1) The fairytale was certainly not
a new literary form for Novalis, since he incorporated it into his incomplete "Natur-
roman" Die Lehrlinge zu Sais(2) and gave this genre a distinctive position in his
most ambitious endeavor, Heinrich von Ofterdingen. Yet it was only towards the
end of his life that he granted it such importance and envisioned it as a further
development of the novel, rather than a mere ingredient. It is not a question of the
fairytale's replacing the novel, but rather becoming a deeper extension of it; however, only certain types of novels are capable of evolving into the fairytale: "Alle
Romane, wo wahre Liebe vorkommt, sind Mährchen--magische Begebenheiten."(3)
Thus the inner qualities of "Gemüt" and "Liebe" seem to create the necessary
atmosphere for not only the natural and wonderful elements of the poetic novel, but
also the magical occurrences which give the novel a new dimension, that of the
fairytale.

Critics have argued as to the correct interpretation of the mysterious and
complex fairytale of Klingsohr at the end of the first part of Heinrich von Ofterdingen,
but no one would dispute the assumption that this "Märchen" is of such significance
to the novel that it can even be seen as the climax to "Die Erwartung" and the key to
Heinrich's further development into a poet. Although the novel was interrupted by
the young author's death, Novalis himself revealed his plans for the second part of
his major work. He wrote to Friedrich Schlegel in April, 1800, that having completed
the first section, he would soon send this portion of Ofterdingen to his friend for his
evaluation and indicated what he attempted to carry out:

> Es sollte mir lieb seyn, wenn Ihr Roman und Märchen in einer
> glücklichen Mischung zu bemerken glaubtet, und der erste Theil
> euch eine noch innigere Mischung im 2ten Theile profezyte. Der
> Roman soll allmälich in Märchen übergehn.(4)

In a later correspondence of June, 1800, Novalis elaborated upon the intention underlying his work. Although he accepted Schlegel's criticism of awkwardness in transition
and clumsiness "in der Behandlung des wandelnden und bewegten Lebens" evident in
Ofterdingen, he intended to strive for "geschmeidige Prosa" and hoped that the second
part might be an improvement over the first:

> Der 2te Theil wird der Commentar des Ersten. Die Antipathie gegen
> Licht und Schatten, die Sehnsucht nach klaren, heissen, durch-
> dringenden Aether, das Unbekannt Heilige, die Vesta, in Sofieen,
> die Vermischung des Romantischen aller Zeiten, der Petrificirende
> und Petrificirte Verstand, Arctur, der Zufall, der Geist des Lebens,
> Einzelne Züge blos, als Arabesken - so betrachte nun mein Märchen.(5)

Furthermore, the second part was to be much more poetic than the first, even in its form. It is clear in this description that Novalis saw no contradiction between the novel and the fairytale, but considered the latter to possess more poetic qualities. The magical atmosphere of this type of prose seems to provide the proper stimulation for Heinrich's poetic growth and increasing depth of insight as he travels through the world. The final blossoming of Heinrich's character is to result in a "innere Verklärung des Gemüths,"(6) after which he is able to penetrate the riddle with which he is confronted: "Heinrich errät den Sinn der Welt."(7) These insights indicate that the fairytale gives the author the opportunity to depict more internal occurrences than the ordinary novel, and the emphasis certainly appears to be on the magical, unknown, indefinite aspects of the world, much to the neglect of rational qualities. Chance rather than plan, spirit rather than intellect, and darkness rather than light are to come into the fore in this poetic form. Yet the world of the fairytale cannot be seen as a completely one-sided entity, for it is the purpose of the fairytale to bring together conflicting elements, to overcome the struggle of antinomies, to harmonize, in other words, to redeem the world. It is in "Märchen und Gedichten" that one will finally recognize "die alten wahren Weltgeschichten".(8) Klingsohr's "Märchen" too ends on a harmonious note, and the flowering of poetry is not viewed as a victory over the forces of cold rationality, but as an end to the long struggle: "Gegründet ist das Reich der Ewigkeit, In Lieb' und Frieden endigt sich der Streit."(9)

Novalis considered the fairytale as the "Canon der Poesie" and claimed that everything poetic should be "mährchenhaft".(10) The fairytale is viewed as a dramatic form of narration, a quality it seems to share with <u>Wilhelm Meister</u>, an astonishing parallel in view of Novalis' reference to Goethe's novel as a "Candide, gerichtet gegen die Poesie" during one period of his Goethe criticism. Yet this sharp statement was directed against the content of <u>Wilhelm Meister</u> and not its poetic style, for Novalis viewed the book as unpoetic, "so poetisch auch die Darstellung sei." Even in his earlier praise of Goethe's novel as the "Roman ohne Beiwort", Novalis thought that this giant of German letters could be surpassed in content and power, but never really in artistic form. It would seem that although his attitude towards the material of <u>Wilhelm Meister</u> underwent some change, Novalis always retained high admiration for Goethe's poetic talent. Thus in their excellence of poetic depiction, "Märchen und 'Meister'" are placed together "Toujours en étant de Poesie"(11) and also serve as the two examples for Novalis' concept of Romanticism:

ROMANTIK. Absolutisirung - Universalisirung - Classification des individuellen Moments, der individuellen Situation etc. ist das eigentliche Wesen des Romantisirens. Vid. Meister. Mährchen.(12)

It is not clear from this quotation, however, whether "Märchen" means the general category or Goethe's <u>Märchen</u>. Cognizance should at least be taken of this latter possibility. Fairytales are also compared to Tieck's poetry as "romantische Phantasien aus dem täglichen Leben,"(13) and so it becomes clear that the fairytale is to accomplish the same task as the novel, namely, the fusion of the individual and the universal, the real and the ideal, but to a higher degree. Daily events are to be made absolute, and individual moments universal through the poet's talent. Just as Novalis could see the world as "kolossaler Roman" from the poetic perspective and found nothing more romantic that what we usually call "Welt und Schicksal", he could also view the real world as a fairyland:

> Es liegt nur an der Schwäche unsrer Organe und der Selbstberührung,
> dass wir uns nicht in einer Feenwelt erblicken. Alle Mährchen sind
> nur Träume von jener heymatlichen Welt, die überall und nirgends
> ist. (14)

The fairytale differs from the novel, however, in that it is more associative in its ideas and more closely resembles the dream and music: "Ein Mährchen ist eigentlich wie ein Traumbild - ohne Zusammenhang - Ein Ensemble wunderbarer Dinge und Begebenheiten - z. B. eine musikalische Fantasie - die Harmonischen Folgen einer Aeolsharfe - die Natur selbst."(15) Its musical, dreamlike quality results in an intermingling of sensory perceptions, a fusion of time and space, body and soul, vision and feeling in what Novalis terms a "Simultanerzeugungsprocess". (16) Yet a higher type of fairytale would not reject a more concrete organization as long as it could retain its basic tone:

> Ein höheres Mährchen wird es, wenn ohne den Geist des Märchens
> zu verscheuchen irgendein Verstand - (Zusammenhang, Bedeutung
> etc.) hineingebracht wird. Sogar nüzlich könnte vielleicht ein Mär-
> chen werden. (17)

In other words, Novalis envisions two types of fairytales, one more fantastic, associative, and dreamlike in quality, and the other, a higher type, related to an idea. The first seems to lack a rational or didactic element, whereas the second embraces meaning and poetry. Does not this latter, more elevated "Märchen" also have the synthesis of poetry and philosophy as its goal then? To be sure, Novalis sees the world of the fairytale as mysterious, marvelous, even anarchistic: "In einem ächten Märchen muss alles wunderbar - geheimnissvoll und unzusammenhängend seyn - alles belebt. Jedes auf eine andre Art. Die ganze Natur muss auf eine wunderliche Art mit der ganzen Geisterwelt vermischt seyn. Die Zeit der allgemeinen Anarchie - Gesezlosigkeit - Freyheit - der Naturstand der Natur - die Zeit vor der Welt (Staat)."(18), and in this it stands in opposition to the historical world. As with all polarities, however, an underlying thread of similarity joins the fairytale to the real world:

> Die Welt des Mährchens ist die durchausentegegengesezte Welt der
> Welt der Wahrheit (Geschichte) - und eben darum ihr so durchaus ähn-
> lich - wie das Chaos der vollendeten Schöpfung. (19)

Even the future world envisioned by Novalis is based on a synthesis of opposites of rationality and chaos: "Die künftige Welt ist das Vernünftige Chaos."(20)

The fairytale, even more emphatically than the novel, is projected into the future--its essence is prophesy, its goal idealistic, and its depiction the product of absolute necessity: "Das ächte Mährchen muss zugleich Prophetische Darstellung - idealistische Darstellung - absolut nothwendige Darstellung seyn. Der ächte

Märchendichter ist ein Seher der Zukunft." (21) Interestingly enough, this statement is found in an aphorism entitled "Roman", further evidence for the intimate connection between these two poetic forms. If one asks why the fairytale is granted such an elevated position in Novalis' later thoughts, the answer perhaps lies in his view of history, his ardent desire to welcome in the new dawn of poetry, "das goldene Zeitalter", a future era which is a poetic renewal of the past: "Mit der Zeit muss die Geschichte Märchen werden - sie wird wieder, wie sie anfieng." (22)

APPENDIX

The close relationship of Thomas Mann's novel <u>Der Zauberberg</u> to <u>Wilhelm Meister</u>, emphasized by Mann himself, stimulated critics to consider Schlegel's famous review of Goethe's work and the features he was able to detect in it as "divinatory criticism", pointing already to a yet unwritten modern novel such as the <u>Zauberberg</u>. The discovery of this anticipatory relationship is certainly most interesting; however, upon closer consideration it proves to be somewhat disappointing, since the early romantic enthusiasm for Goethe's novel soon died out. Novalis termed it a "Candide, gegen die Poësie gerichtet", a satire on poetry, a novel consisting of "Stroh und Hobelspäne", and he strongly protested against the realism and empiricism of the work which was not poetic enough for his taste. (1)

Schlegel too was not so one-sidedly positive in his reaction to <u>Wilhelm Meister</u>, as has often been assumed. Even in his printed aphorisms on Goethe's novel, seemingly so full of praise, a sharper eye can detect a critical undertone. "Wer Goethes Meister gehörig charakterisierte, der hätte damit wohl eigentlich gesagt, was es jetzt an der Zeit ist in der Poesie," he said in Aphorism No. 120 of the <u>Lyceum</u>. This certainly appears to be a high laud, but only if one does not know that Schlegel's characterization essentially consists in pointing out an individual work's ideal which was not yet fully realized. He also included <u>Wilhelm Meister</u> together with the French Revolution and Fichte's <u>Wissenschaftslehre</u> among the three greatest tendencies of the age. (2) How much higher could a novel be placed? Here, however, the term tendency must be questioned, and upon closer scrutiny, it appears that it refers to something not yet achieved and still to be carried out. This impression gains in evidence if one looks at his posthumous notebooks. The first to study them was Josef Körner, and the astonishing revelations about Schlegel's reaction to <u>Wilhelm Meister</u> form a great part of his book <u>Romantiker und Klassiker</u>. (3) Eichner, who edited the literary notebooks, thought that Schlegel's attitude towards Goethe's novel was "überraschend kritisch". (4) This is all the more amazing since most of these critical comments date from 1797, a time before Schlegel started working on his laudatory review. The insights of the philosophical notebooks are even more revealing. As early as 1796 Schlegel equated <u>Wilhelm Meister</u> with "eklektische Philosophie", shortly afterwards he had the impression that "Meister nicht mehr wirkt", and in 1797 this novel is equated to "vollkommner Empirismus". (5) To be sure, these seemingly deprecating statements can easily be counterbalanced by positive remarks of the same years. Goethe's <u>Meister</u> is also "Poesie der Poesie" and taken as an example of a flawless progressive novel. (6) These appreciative observations could be heaped and actually culminate in the <u>Wilhelm Meister</u> review of 1798. (7) Yet even this review has an ironic undertone, quickly recognized by Goethe, and this with great pleasure. Caroline Schlegel related this to her brother-in-law when in October, 1798, after a visit to Weimar, she reported that Goethe had indeed comprehended "die belobte Ironie darin" and would be quite happy with it:

> Erst hat er gesagt, es wäre recht gut, recht charmant, und nach
> dieser bei ihm gebräuchlichen Art vom Wetter zu reden, hat er
> auch warm die Weise gebilligt, wie Sie es behandelt, dass Sie
> immer auf den Bau des Ganzen gegangen und sich nicht bei patho-
> logischer Zergliederung der einzelnen Charaktere aufgehalten,

dann hat er gezeigt, dass er es tüchtig gelesen, indem er viele
Ausdrücke wiederholt und besonders eben die ironischen. (8)

How can this ambivalent attitude be explained if one does not accept the too
simple solution that the Romantics were merely deceiving? It appears to be that a
more thorough occupation with Wilhelm Meister by Schlegel and Novalis originated
when Friedrich Schlegel on his journey to Berlin in June of 1797 made that decisive
stop in Weissenfels, where his friend worked as an assessor in the salt mines. In
Schlegel's notebook begun at that time, Gedanken 1797. - auf der Reise nach Berlin,
in Weissenfels, the germs of their discussion can be found. (9) One even comes upon
entries such as: "gar kein Roman, sondern ein Compedium der höhern Oekonomie,"
referring, however, not to Wilhelm Meister, but to Rousseau's Héloise. (10) In their
criticism, the two friends show a similar line of development, which has often been
misunderstood because their usage of the term "romantic" is different from that of
the modern and contemporary critics. When Schlegel and Novalis note "Goethe ist
nicht romantisch", as Schlegel actually does in one of his posthumous aphorisms, (11)
such a statement is obviously a negation--a negation, however, that is not necessarily
an aesthetic rejection. It simply means that Goethe did not write in the romantic
vein, and we know this already from the early "Studiumsaufsatz" as well as from
the Gespräch über die Poesie, where Goethe's quality as "Morgenröte echter Kunst
und reiner Schönheit" was based on the fact that he transcended mere Romanticism
in a higher synthesis of Classicism and Romanticism. This train of thought could be
pursued into many directions. In a similar way, the Romantics could claim that
Goethe was not poetic enough, as Novalis actually did. (12) But we know from Schlegel's and Novalis' posthumous aphorisms that there are many styles aside from the
poetically poetic in which the poet can work. In summary, being called "not romantic"
and "not poetic" by Schlegel and Novalis need not necessarily be taken as a reproach
against a poet, since "romantic" and "poetic" designate merely particular styles of
poetry like philosophical, ethical, psychological, classical, etc. Of course, there
might be a hierarchy among these styles, and at a certain time, the romantic critic
might even conceive of the "poetically poetic" as the highest goal. However, these
predilections shifted, as we have seen, and cannot be taken as absolute.

Also in the case of Novalis, the overrated negative critical remarks on
Wilhelm Meister can easily be balanced by their positive counterparts, and this often
within the same passage. (13) Unfortunately, in some editions of his works, but in
almost all of the critical literature, attention has been given exclusively to the
seemingly derogatory statements, without even asking whether they were really
derogatory. The Novalis editor, Hans-Joachim Mähl, was infuriated by this history
of the Novalis Wilhelm Meister criticism in our critical literature and was ready to
assume deliberate forgery, going back to the first editors of Novalis' works,
Friedrich Schlegel and Ludwig Tieck--a hypothesis that is not only too far-reaching,
but also amusing in its wild assumptions. (14) The worst part about this misconception
about Novalis' Wilhelm Meister criticism is, however, that from a historical point
of view, it was perhaps the main cause for bringing about and keeping alive the wrong
concept of the romantic theory of the novel in the sense of mere "poetizing". This
erroneous track in the sense of a poetic monism was taken already in the romantic
age, while as Mähl correctly remarked, for Novalis, the dualistic approach to poetry
is characteristic:

[...] für den gerade das polare Nebeneinander und Miteinander von
Phantasie und Verstand, von Genie und Talent, von Stoff- und Form-
kräften - nicht zuletzt durch die Beschäftigung mit Goethes Werk -
zum Gegenstand der Reflexion und künstlerischen Selbstausbildung
geworden war. (15)

In critical articles after the turn of the century, the "romantic" poetry of Tieck,
Novalis, and Schlegel is contrasted to Goethe's more earthly beginnings and praised
because of "ihre Idealität, ihr geistiges, verklärtes Leben." (16) Mähl has studied
this process of distortion in literary history, which in many articles of the time,
leads to statements such as this:

[...] der Göthischen Poesie, als der exoterischen, steht die
Tieckische und Novalische als esoterische, wahrhaft geistige und
religiöse entgegen. Göthe's Poesie ist plastisch und symbolisch;
sie ist in ihr eigenes Leben versunken, oder, wenn sie auch als
Symbol eines höheren und universelleren Lebens gedeutet werden
kann, so tritt doch diese ideale Tendenz hinter das objektive, äussere
Leben zurück. In Tieck's und Novalis' Poesieen strahlt dagegen der
innere, verklärte Geist alles Lebens in seiner Reinheit und Freiheit:
ihr Wesen ist idealische Liebe und Phantasie. Göthe hat eben so
wenig, als die griechischen Dichter, Phantasie im ächten Sinne des
Wortes. Phantasie offenbart sich nur in der orientalischen und
romantischen Dichtkunst und denjenigen Poesieen der Neueren, die
romantischen Geist in sich tragen. Auch kennt Göthe die höhere
Liebe nicht [...] (17)

Adam Müller in his <u>Vorlesungen über die deutsche Wissenschaft und Literatur</u> of
1807, soon confronted Goethe and Novalis as the two main representatives of German
poetry in the sense of a "universeller Zwiespalt", that of economy and poetry. (18)
Similar observations can be made with respect to Görres, Molitor, and many other
romantic critics of the time, on the basis of which it is only understandable that
Goethe first in his conversations with Sulpiz Boisserée in 1811 and especially in the
retrospective letter to Zelter, showed strong resentment against the Romantics,
primarily against Novalis, and doubted their sincerity when they had initially praised
him: "Sie liessen mich bey der grossen Umwälzung, die sie wirklich durchsetzten,
notdürftig stehen, zum Verdrusse Hardenbergs, welcher mich auch wollte delirt
(ausgelöscht) haben." (19)

This confrontation of idealistic romantic and realistic Goethean poetry
flourished chiefly in the years 1807-08. At that time, Novalis was long dead. Seeing
a false ideal of romantic poetry being placed on the pedestal to the detriment of
Goethe, Schlegel felt compelled to re-examine the debate about <u>Wilhelm Meister</u> and
to put the question into proper perspective. The occasion for this important pronouncement was given when in 1808 he reviewed "<u>Goethes Werke. Erster bis vierter
Band</u>" for the <u>Heidelbergische Jahrbücher der Literatur</u>. (20) Indeed, aside from a
detailed characterization of Goethe's "Lieder", a conclusive evaluation of <u>Wilhelm
Meister</u> in its relationship to Romanticism forms the most interesting part of this

long article. Concentrating in this section of the review on the idea of "Bildung",
Schlegel develops a new understanding of this term so essential to the German novel,
not only in its former manifestations such as Meister, but in the true spirit of
divinatory criticism. He thus provides a basis for bringing the investigation of the
present topic to an integration.

Schlegel first emphasizes the enormous and fruitful influence of Wilhelm
Meister on the whole of German literature:

> Der Meister aber hat auf das Ganze der deutschen Literatur, sichtbar
> wie wenige andere gewirkt, und recht eigentlich Epoche gemacht,
> indem er dieselbe mit der Bildung und dem Geist der höheren Gesell-
> schaft in Berührung setzte, und die Sprache nach einer ganz neuen
> Seite hin mehr bereicherte, als es vielleicht in irgend einer Gattung
> durch ein einzelnes Werk auf einmal geschehen ist. (21)

Obviously aware of the many objections that had been raised against this work in the
wake of Novalis' criticism, Schlegel first dismisses the protest against the lack of
morality: "Was den ersten Punkt anbetrifft, so erinnern wir nochmals an die zu ein-
förmige Feierlichkeit der Klopstockschen Art und Ansicht der Dinge, und das Bedürfnis einer nicht so gar eng beschränkten Freiheit für die Entwicklung der Poesie."
Yet the main criticism came from the aesthetic point of view and consisted in the
assumption, seemingly deriving from Novalis, that it was a "Werk gegen die Poesie".
Schlegel understood only too well that the poetry deemed lacking by these critics was
only that sentimental and lacrymose poetry he had already devalued in his Brief über
den Roman, whereas the whole atmosphere of the novel was genuinely poetic, "eine
durchaus poetische". Yet he does not only want to reject the objections, but to understand and to solve them and asks himself as a critic:

> Worin liegt denn aber der Grund des Zwiespaltes, der so vielen,
> die sich stark von dem Werk angezogen fühlten und sich ganz mit
> demselben durchdrungen hatten, doch zuletzt übrig blieb, und sie
> wieder davon zurückstiess? (22)

The reason for this dissension cannot be derived from the work's being unpoetic,
an assumption Schlegel has just dismissed, since the idea of "Bildung", the central
motif of Wilhelm Meister, is viewed as a definitely poetic characteristic: "Diese
Bildung nun, so wenig sie ganz vollständig in dem Werke entwickelt ist, muss un-
streitig als eine durchaus künstlerische, ja poetische, gedacht werden [...]". No, the
work is not anti-poetic, but anti-romantic, and Schlegel is certain that one could
say "es sei ein Roman gegen das Romantische, der uns auf dem Umweg des Modernen (wie durch die Sünde zur Heiligkeit) zum Antiken zurückführe." (23) Wilhelm
Meister, in other words, is a work that is by nature equally poetic as it is unromantic.

Schlegel now has to justify this novel against the widespread reproaches of
its being anti-poetic and reveal them as meaning only anti-romantic. The main point
of his argument is the idea of "Bildung", "der Hauptbegriff, wohin alles in dem Werke

zielt und wie in einen Mittelpunkt zusammengeht."(24) He distinguishes two types
of formation, the classical and the modern one. Classical "Bildung" was interior
and solitary, "ging streng und unerbittlich auf ein Ewiges, auf ein mehr oder minder
richtig erkanntes Unsichtbares," and must be considered its highest form: "Es gibt
aber noch eine andre, mehr äusserliche und gesellige Bildung, die nicht eine so
hohe Richtung und Würde hat, oft sogar in etwas ganz Leeres sich auflöst." In certain comic instances of Goethe's novel, "Bildung" appears in this lesser sense, but
on the whole, strives for the highest form:

> Wie leicht aber würde derjenige, der den höhern, ja den höchsten
> Begriff der Bildung dem Werke absprechen wollte, durch das Ganze
> sowohl als durch Stellen desselben zu widerlegen sein! Das wahre
> und falsche Bildung in dem Buche oft so nah an einander grenzen,
> so ganz in einander verfliessen, dürfte auch kein Tadel sein, denn
> es ist dies die eigentliche Beschaffenheit der feinern Gesellschaft,
> die hier dargestellt werden soll.(25)

The second point in Schlegel's apology of Wilhelm Meister against flat romantic
criticisms is that a novel should never be judged on the basis of mere genre evaluations:

> Es besteht dieses Missverständnis darin, dass man den Roman zu
> einer Gattung der Poesie macht, und sich dadurch zu Vergleichungen
> verführen lässt, die immer unstatthaft sind, und den wahren Ge-
> sichtspunkt durchaus verrücken, weil jeder Roman ein Individuum
> für sich ist, und gerade darin das Wesen desselben besteht.(26)

A critic should be aware that a good novel is a "Zeitroman", not only in depicting its
age, but also in deriving from it. In the first regard, Wilhelm Meister presents its
era so objectively, "dass man schwerlich eine reichere und wahrhaftere Darstellung
dieser Zeit erwarten, oder auch nur begehren kann."(27) In the second, Schlegel
goes so far as to think of the novel as a creation produced mutually by the poet and
his age, "denn der Roman ist oftmals, wie das epische Gedicht, nicht bloss das
Werk des Künstlers und seiner Absicht, sondern das gemeinschaftliche Erzeugnis
des Dichters und des Zeitalters, dem er sich und sein Werk widmet."(28)

What then is the distinction of Wilhelm Meister on this basis? Schlegel
achieves this characterization by comparing Goethe's work to the highest attain-
ment of the novel in former times, Don Quixote. This Spanish example is for him
the ultimate novelistic composition in the romantic style inaugurated by Ariosto,
and if an author wanted to create a romantic novel, Schlegel would advise him
"den Cervantes nicht weniger wie den Ariost selbst, als Vorbild und ältern Ge-
fährten seiner Phantasie gegenwärtig zu erhalten."(29) This was certainly not
what Goethe had in mind when he wrote Wilhelm Meister, the excellences of which
lie in another realm, that of the modern age:

> Der Meister aber in seiner Verbindung und Vermischung von dar-
> stellender Kunst und Künstler-Ansicht und Bildung gehört durchaus
> der modernen Poesie an, die von der romantischen wesentlich

geschieden, und wie durch eine grosse Kluft getrennt ist. Das unter-
scheidende Merkmal der modernen Dichtkunst ist ihr genaues
Verhältnis zur Kritik und Theorie, und der bestimmende Einfluss
der letzteren. (30)

A better endorsement of the chief thrust of this study could not have been
found. After having refuted the contemporary prejudice according to which <u>Wilhelm
Meister</u> was unromantic and thus unpoetic, by demonstrating that the work had
excellences of its own, being unromantic, but nevertheless beautiful and poetic in
a modern sense, Schlegel concludes:

So lasse man denn auch den <u>Meister</u> als ein in seiner Art einziges
Individuum für sich bestehen, und enthalte sich aller verwirrenden
Vergleichungen, deren das vortreffliche Werk zu seinem Lobe
ohnehin nicht bedarf. (31)

If this leading "romantic" critic excludes Goethe's <u>Wilhelm Meister</u> from
being romantic, but nevertheless considers it one of the greatest examples of modern
novel writing, then we should be careful not to use the term "romantic" in the flat
understanding of "Poesie des Gefühls" against which Schlegel defended Goethe's work.
A thorough understanding of what Schlegel and Novalis attempted in their theory of the
novel reveals fundamental ideas that have been, probably more unwittingly than
knowingly, incorporated into poetic works of later ages. Indeed, these theoretical
concepts found more embodiment, more life in literary productions of modern times
than they did within the epoch of their origin and thus might indeed appear as
"divinatory criticism".

FOOTNOTES

INTRODUCTION

1   Kritische Friedrich Schlegel Ausgabe, ed. Ernst Behler (Paderborn, 1958 ff.),
in the following referred to as KA II, p. 182. Schlegel's aphorisms in the Lyceum
(KA II, p. 147 ff.) and the Athenäum (KA, II p. 165 ff.) will be quoted only by
their number.

2   Literary Notebooks (1797-1801), ed. Hans Eichner (London, 1957), in the
following referred to as LN No. 289.

3   René Wellek, "The Concept of Romanticism in Literary History," Concepts
of Criticism (New Haven and London, 1963), p. 134 ff.; Ernst Behler, "The
Origins of the Romantic Literary Theory," Colloquia Germanica, I/2 (1968),
p. 155 ff.; Manfred Dick, Die Entwicklung des Begriffs der Poesie in den
Fragmenten des Novalis (Heidelberg, 1966); Romantic and its Cognates. The
European History of a Word, ed. Hans Eichner (Toronto, 1972); Raymond
Immerwahr, Romantisch. Genese und Tradition einer Denkform (Respublica
Literaria, Vol. 7, Frankfurt, 1972); Ernst Behler, "Kritische Gedanken
zum Begriff der europäischen Romantik," Die europäische Romantik (Frank-
furt, 1972), pp. 7-43; Helmut Schanze, Romantik und Aufklärung. Unter-
suchungen zu Friedrich Schlegel und Novalis (Nürnberg, 1966); Karl Konrad
Polheim, Die Arabeske: Ansichten und Ideen aus Friedrich Schlegels Poetik
(München-Paderborn-Wien, 1966); Raimund Belgardt, Romantische Poesie.
Begriff und Bedeutung bei Friedrich Schlegel (The Hague/Paris, 1969);
Franz Norbert Mennemeier, Friedrich Schlegels Poesiebegriff (München,
1971); Heinz-Dieter Weber, Friedrich Schlegels "Transzendentalpoesie"
(München, 1973).

4   Novalis Schriften. Die Werke Friedrich von Hardenbergs. Zweite, nach den
Handschriften ergänzte und verbesserte Auflage, ed. Paul Kluckhohn and
Richard Samuel, 4 vols. (Stuttgart, 1960-1974), in the following referred to
as Schriften; II, p. 647, No. 473.

5   Schriften II, p. 545, No. 105.

6   Ibid.

7   A History of Modern Criticism (New Haven, 1965), IV, p. 1.

8   KA II, p. 315.

9   Especially in the fourth part of his Philosophische Lehrjahre, KA XVIII,
p. 197 ff. Cf. also the commentary to this work, KA XIX [IV 1201] [V 35].

10   KA XIII, p. 357 ff.

11   August Wilhelm Schlegel, "Aus den 'Vorlesungen über schöne Literatur und
Kunst'," edited in Deutsche National Literatur, XVII-XIX (Heilbronn,
1884), p. 291.

12   KA X, p. 232.

13   Cf. the record of the various prose genres in Friedrich Schlegel's
Philosophische Lehrjahre, KA XIX, pp. 801-803.

14   KA III, p. 140.

15   KA III, p. 141.

16   Ibid.

17   Ibid.

18   Schriften III, p. 685, No. 668; KA II, p. 285. August Wilhelm Schlegels
      Vorlesungen über schöne Literatur und Kunst, ed. Jakob Minor, 3 vols.;
      Deutsche Literaturdenkmale, XVII-XIX (Heilbronn, 1884), in the following
      referred to as Schöne Lit. und Kunst, I, p. 261.

19   August Wilhelm von Schlegels sämtliche Werke, ed. Edward Böcking (Leip-
      zig, 1846), in the following referred to as SW; VII, p. 24 ff., 155 ff., 197 ff.

20   SW VII, p. 101, 103.

21   SW XI, p. 409, 206.

22   SW XI, p. 220.

23   Schriften III, p. 685, No. 668.

24   Schriften IV, p. 246, No. 112.

25   Ibid., pp. 246-247, No. 113.

26   Schriften II, p. 536, No. 51.

27   Ibid.

28   Friedrich Schlegel. Seine prosaischen Jugendschriften, ed. Jakob Minor,
      2 vols. (Vienna, 1882), in the following referred to as Jugendschriften; I,
      p. 197.

29   KA XI, p. 57; Jugendschriften I, p. 197.

30   Jugendschriften I, p. 199, 200.

31   LN 14, 596, 40, 100, 584.

32   KA XI, p. 159, 160, 161.

33   LN 1961; KA II, p. 206, No. 247; LN 584.

34   KA II, p. 162, No. 117.

35   LN 1962; KA XVIII, p. 141, No. 232; KA XVIII, p. 143, No. 244. In his book
      Romantik und Aufklärung, Helmut Schanze deals with every particular ele-
      ment of this definition, pp. 87-113.

36   KA XIII, p. 217; KA XVIII, p. 130, No. 97; KA XVIII, p. 347, No. 311.

FOOTNOTES

PART ONE: FRIEDRICH SCHLEGEL

I. The Intellectual Background and the Literary Derivations of Friedrich Schlegel's Theory of the Novel

1   Gwendolyn Bays, The Orphic Vision. Seer Poets from Novalis to Rimbaud (Lincoln, 1964). Wackenroder's Herzensergiessungen of 1796 can also be included within this tendency, as well as Hölderlin, Heinse, Karl Philipp Moritz; and it is at least implicit in Schiller's writings of the early 1790's.

2   Immanuel Kant. Werke in sechs Bänden (Wiesbaden, 1960-1964), IV, p. 249 ff.

3   KA XVIII, Philosophische Lehrjahre, IV, Nos. 2, 8.

4   Cf. Herder's Gott. Einige Gespräche of 1787, the perhaps most important contribution to the controversy about Spinoza of the time. On this controversy itself, cf. the introduction to the English edition of this book: God. Some Conversations. A translation with a critical introduction and notes by Frederic H. Burckhardt (New York, 1940).

5   Cf. Oskar Walzel, Das Prometheussymbol von Shaftesbury zu Goethe (München, 1932); H. Wolf, Versuch einer Geschichte des Geniebegriffs (Heidelberg, 1932); E. Zilsel, Die Entstehung des Geniebegriffs (Tübingen, 1926).

6   On the communal life of the Romantics in Jena and Dresden, cf. Alfred Schlagdenhauffen, Frédéric Schlegel et son groupe. La doctrine de l'Athenaeum (1798-1800) (Paris, 1934), p. 195 ff., p. 291 ff.

7   Friedrich Wilhelm Joseph von Schelling's sämmtliche Werke (Stuttgart, 1856-1861), III, p. 617 f.

8   Ibid., pp. 617, 628.

9   Ibid., p. 623.

10   Ibid., p. 629.

11   Ibid.

12   Franz Rosenzweig, Das älteste Systemprogramm des deutschen Idealismus, Sitzungsberichte der Heidelberger Akademie der Wissenschaften. Philos.-Histor. Klasse 5, 1917 (Heidelberg, 1917). Also available in Hölderlin. Werke, ed. Pigenot (Berlin, 1943), III, p. 623 ff. A new critical edition of this text by Rüdiger Bubner has appeared in Hegel-Studien, Beiheft 9 (Bonn, 1973), pp. 261-265. On the problem of the authorship, cf. Ludwig Strauss, "Hölderlins Anteil an Schellings frühem Systemprogramm," DVJ 5 (1927), pp. 679-747. For the possibility of Hegel's authorship, cf. Otto Pöggeler, "Hölderlin, Hegel und das älteste Systemprogramm," Hegel-Studien, Beiheft 4 (Bonn, 1969), pp. 17-32.

13   Quoted from the above-mentioned Bubner edition, pp. 263-264.

14   Ibid., p. 264.

15   Ibid., pp. 264-265. On the development of the idea of mythology in German Romanticism, cf. Fritz Strich, Die Mythologie in der deutschen Literatur (Halle, 1910), and Alfred Bäumler's introduction to J. J. Bachofen, Der Mythos von Orient und Okzident (München, 1926). Also Die Eröffnung des Zugangs zum Mythos. Ein Lesebuch, ed. Karl Kerényi (Darmstadt, 1967).

16   Schelling, Friedrich Wilhelm Joseph von. Sämmtliche Werke (Stuttgart, 1861) in following referred to as Schelling, pp. 624-625.

17   KA II, p. 311 ff.

18   LN No. 1683. For further references, cf. KA XI, p. 333, No. 391.

19   Photostatic reprint (Stuttgart, 1965). Cf. Kurt Wölfel, "Friedrich von Blanckenburgs Versuch über den Roman," Deutsche Romantheorien, ed. Reinhold Grimm (Bonn, 1968), p. 29 ff.

20   KA II, p. 47 ff. Cf. Hans Eichner, "Friedrich Schlegel's Theory of Romantic Poetry," PMLA 71 (1956), p. 1019 ff.

21   Herders Werke in fünf Bänden (Berlin, 1964), III, p. 246 ff.

22   Schelling, V, p. 683. August Wilhelm Schlegel, Vorlesungen über philosophische Kunstlehre, ed. August Wünsche (Leipzig, 1911), p. 216 ff. René Wellek correctly remarks in A History of Modern Criticism, II, p. 51: "As opposed to Friedrich, August Wilhelm's main interest among the genres was the drama." The Vorschule der Aesthetik is quoted from Jean Paul, Werke, ed. Norbert Miller (München, 1963), V.

23   Georg Wilhelm Friedrich Hegel. Sämtliche Werke. Jubiläumsausgabe in zwanzig Bänden, ed. Herman Glockner (photostatic reprint, Stuttgart, 1964), XIV, p. 395 f.

24   Lukács, 2d edition (Neuwied, 1963), p. 41.

25   Ibid.

26   Ibid., p. 93.

27   Schopenhauer's sämmtliche Werke in fünf Bänden (Insel Verlag edition), I, p. 340.

28   Friedrich Schlegel. Seine prosaischen Jugendschriften, ed. Jakob Minor (Wien, 1882), I, p. 242.

29   Ibid., p. 222 ff.

30   Ibid., p. 290 ff.

31   Ibid., p. 301 f.

32   KA VI, p. 79 f.

33   Hints at these precursors can be found in his lectures on Europäische Literatur (KA XI), as well as in his still unpublished Cologne lectures on Deutsche Sprache und Literatur. Cf. p. 62 f. of this publication; also Erwin Rohde, Der griechische Roman (Berlin, 1914); O. Schissel von Fleschenberg,

Entwicklungsgeschichte des griechischen Romans im Altertum (1913);
S. L. Wolff, The Greek Romances in Elizabethan Prose Fiction (1913).

34   Cf. The Oxford Classical Dictionary, p. 611 f.

35   Ibid., p. 612.

36   " 'Romantic' and Its Cognates in England, Germany, and France before
        1790," pp. 17-97, in Romantic and Its Cognates. The European History
        of a Word. Cf. Immerwahr, Romantisch. Genese und Tradition einer Denk-
        form (Frankfurt, 1972), and Immerwahr, "Die symbolische Form des
        'Briefes über den Roman'," Zeitschrift für deutsche Philologie, 88 (1969)
        p. 49.

37   KA XI, p. 167 ff.

38   Friedrich Schlegels Briefe an seinen Bruder August Wilhelm, ed. Oskar Walzel
        (Berlin, 1890), p. 499 ff., p. 511 f.

39   KA XI, p. 317, No. 366.

40   KA VI, p. 260.

41   KA II, p. 297.

42   Ibid.

43   Benno von Wiese, Novelle (Stuttgart, 1963). Karl Konrad Polheim, Novellen-
        theorie und Novellenforschung (Stuttgart, 1965). Polheim mentions the con-
        nection between Schlegel's concepts of "Novelle" and "Roman", p. 23.

44   In his study "Nachricht von den poetischen Werken des Johannes Boccaccio"
        of 1801, KA II, p. 394, and KA XI, p. 151 and 320 f.; 324 f.

45   LN Nos. 954, 860, 1025, 1365, 1430, 1025.

46   KA II, p. 394.

47   Ibid., p. 395.

48   In his study "Beiträge zur Geschichte der modernen Poesie und Nachricht
        von provenzalischen Manuskripten," of 1803, which appeared in the periodical
        Europa; KA III, p. 19.

49   KA XI, p. 159.

50   Ibid., p. 160.

51   Ibid., p. 161.

52   Ibid.

53   Friedrich Schlegels Briefe an seinen Bruder August Wilhelm, p. 303.

54   Ibid., pp. 318, 303.

55   Gesammelte Werke. 12 vols. (Oldenburg, 1960), IX, p. 435.

56   Ibid., p. 437.

57   Ibid., pp. 443, 444.

58   Ibid., p. 444 f.

59   Ibid., p. 445.

60   Ibid., p. 448.

61   Ibid., p. 451.

62   Ibid., p. 454.

63   Ibid., p. 469.

64   KA II, p. 303.

65   KA VI, p. 274 f.

66   Ibid., p. 275.

II. "Ein Roman ist ein romantisches Buch"

1   LN No. 32. Cf. also Nos. 289, 580, 583, 774, 884, 1569.

2   KA II, p. 335.

3   In his essay "Schiller and the Genesis of German Romanticism," Essays in the History of Ideas, 4th edition (New York, 1948), p. 211 f. Cf. also this author's "The Meaning of 'Romantic' in Early German Romanticism," ibid., p. 183 ff. where Lovejoy contends that Schlegel based his ideal on "two antithetic critical theories," however vindicated "one of them at the expense of the other" (p. 195). On this problem, cf. Ernst Behler, "The Origins of the Romantic Literary Theory," p. 116 f. and KA VIII, pp. Lxxxvii-xcvii.

4   Most conspicuously in the early study "Ueber das Studium der griechischen Poesie," Seine prosaischen Jugendschriften, I, p. 85 ff.

5   LN No. 884.

6   KA II, p. 335. For the most pertinent discussions of this interrelationship of "Roman" and "romantisch" see Karl Konrad Polheim, Die Arabeske, pp. 178-187; Hans Eichner, Friedrich Schlegel (New York, 1970), pp. 44-83; Raymond Immerwahr, Romantik. Genese und Tradition einer Denkform, esp. pp. 144-197; and Raimund Belgardt, pp. 13-29.

7   Ibid., p. 336.

8   LN No. 754.

9   KA VI, p. 293.

10   Deutsches Museum. Eine Zeitschrift, ed. Friedrich Schlegel, 4 Vols. (Wien, 1812-1813), I, p. 447; KA III, p. 256.

11 LN No. 353.

12 August Wilhelm von Schlegel's Vorlesungen über dramatische Kunst und Literatur. Kritische Ausgabe, ed. Giovanni Vittorio Amoretti, 2 Vols. (Bonn-Leipzig, 1923), I, p. 6 f.

13 LN No. 473.

14 KA II, p. 335.

15 Ibid.

16 LN Nos. 444, 953, 714.

17 LN No. 582.

18 LN Nos. 1385, 1388.

19 LN No. 363.

20 KA XI, p. 166.

21 KA II, p. 346.

22 I owe this observation to a comment by Professor Raymond Immerwahr.

23 LN Nos. 96, 2.

24 LN Nos. 556, 643. On Fichte's concept of "transcendental", cf. J. G. Fichte, Gesamtausgabe, ed. Reinhard Lauth and Hans Jacob (Stuttgart, 1965), II, p. 406 ff. and the commentary to Friedrich Schlegel's Philosophische Lehrjahre, KA XIX, [II, 80].

25 LN Nos. 1729, 287.

26 LN No. 863.

27 LN Nos. 692, 840.

28 LN Nos. 798, 691. On this dialectical process, cf. the commentary to Philosophische Lehrjahre, KA XIX, [II, 298]: on its parallel in Novalis' theory in the sense of "Romantisieren" and "Logarithmisieren", this publication p. 105.

29 LN No. 806.

30 LN No. 1041.

31 KA II, Athenäumsfragment No. 238.

32 Cf. Raymond Immerwahr, "The Subjectivity or Objectivity of Friedrich Schlegel's Poetic Irony," The Germanic Review, 26 (1951), p. 173 ff. and Karl Konrad Polheim, Die Arabeske, p. 103 ff., and Heinz-Dieter Weber, Friedrich Schlegels "Transzendentalpoesie", p. 11 ff.

III. The Novel as a Genre of Romantic Poetry : "Mischgedicht"

1   KA XI, p. 160.

2   Ibid.

3   KA XI, p. 158.

4   KA XVIII, Philosophische Lehrjahre, I, No. 88.

5   KA XVIII, p. 23 ff.

6   KA XVIII, Philosophische Lehrjahre, II, No. 58.

7   Ibid., No. 65.

8   Ibid., No. 95.

9   Ibid., No. 512.

10   Ibid., No. 65.

11   KA XVIII, Philosophische Lehrjahre, IV, Nos. 15, 429.

12   Ibid., No. 435.

13   Ibid., Nos. 436, 437.

14   Wilhelm Dilthey, Leben Schleiermachers (Berlin, 1870), p. 229 ff. The four
     spheres of the intellectual worlds are depicted in Schlegel's Ideen of 1800,
     KA II, p. 256 ff., especially in No. 4. Cf. also the commentary on Philoso-
     phische Lehrjahre, KA XIX [IV, 1069].

15   KA XVIII, Philosophische Lehrjahre, IV, Nos. 14, 20.

16   Ibid., No. 24.

17   Ibid., No. 26.

18   Ibid., No. 273.

19   Ibid., No. 1175.

20   KA XVIII, Philosophische Lehrjahre, V, Nos. 1, 151, 186.

21   KA XVIII, Philosophische Lehrjahre, IV, Nos. 434, 442.

22   LN No. 4.

23   LN No. 20; also No. 55.

24   LN No. 20.

25   LN No. 69.

26   LN No. 76.

27   LN No. 213.

28   LN No. 210.

FOOTNOTES

29   LN Nos. 103, 137.

30   On this term, cf. Footnote No. 32 of Chapter II, p. 129 of this publication and the
      literature mentioned there.

31   LN No. 154.

32   In Aphorism No. 418.

33   Ibid.

34   KA II, p. 299.

35   Raymond Immerwahr, "Die symbolische Form des 'Briefes über den Roman',"
      p. 41 ff. In this article, Immerwahr takes issue with Polheim's recent re-
      interpretation of this essay in Die Arabeske, p. 134 ff. On the critical literature
      dealing with this section of Schlegel's theory of the novel, cf. Footnote No. 3 of Chapter IV,
      p. 131 of this publication. See also Belgradt, p. 66 ff. Mennemeier, p. 216 ff., Hans
      Eichner, KA III, pp. xxxi - xxxii, and Ernst Behler, KA VIII, pp. xlv-xiix.

IV. "Brief über den Roman"

1   Schlegel's historical method in dealing with aesthetic problems is best dis-
     cussed by Josef Körner in Friedrich Schlegel, Neue philosophische Schriften
     (Frankfurt, 1935), p. 342 ff. Cf. also René Wellek, A History of Modern
     Criticism, II, p. 7, and Ernst Behler, Friedrich Schlegel (Hamburg, 1966),
     p. 34 ff. Also KA X, p. xvi.

2   KA II, p. 290. Cf. also Deutsches Museum, I, p. 283: "Die beste Theorie
     der Kunst ist ihre Geschichte."

3   The most pertinent literature on this "Brief" is listed in Footnote No. 35 of Chapter
     III, p. 131 of this publication. Formerly, the work has been discussed by Rudolf Haym.
     Die Romantische Schule, 3d edition (Berlin, 1914), p. 751 ff.; Fritz Strich,
     Die Mythologie in der deutschen Literatur von Klopstock bis Wagner, 2 vols.
     (Halle, 1910), II, p. 45 ff; Paul Kluckhohn, Die deutsche Romantik (Bielefeld,
     Leipzig, 1924), p. 47 ff.; Oskar Walzel, Grenzen von Poesie und Unpoesie
     Frankfurt, 1937), p. 141 ff.; Friedrich Gundolf, Romantiker (Berlin, 1930),
     p. 65 ff.; Paul Böckmann, "Die romantische Poesie Brentanos und ihre
     Grundlagen bei Friedrich Schlegel und Tieck," Jahrbuch des freien deutschen
     Hochstifts (1934/35), p. 75 ff.; Alfred Schlagdenhauffen, Fréderic Schlegel
     et son groupe, p. 347 ff.

4   KA II, p. 336.

5   This difference of opinion can first be noticed in Lovejoy's opposition to
     Rudolf Haym in Lovejoy's article "The Meaning of 'Romantic' in Early German
     Romanticism," Essays in the History of Ideas, p. 183 ff. The controversy is
     continued in Hans Eichner, "Friedrich Schlegel's Theory of Romantic Poetry,"
     PMLA 71 (1956), p. 1018 ff. Recently, Raymond Immerwahr has renewed the

FOOTNOTES

argumentation by opposing Eichner's thesis in "Die symbolische Form des 'Briefes über den Roman'," p. 49 ff. Our thesis attempts to bring a solution to the discrepancy in the interpretations of these terms.

6 KA II, p. 336.

7 Ibid., p. 337.

8 Ibid., p. 334.

9 Ibid., p. 336.

10 Ibid., p. 331.

11 Ibid., pp. 331, 333, 335.

12 Ibid., p. 333.

13 Ibid., p. 334.

14 Ibid., p. 333.

15 Ibid.

16 Ibid., p. 331.

17 Ibid., p. 333.

18 Ibid., pp. 330, 331, 330.

19 Ibid., p. 330. The "Lafontaine" Schlegel means here is August Heinrich Julius Lafontaine (1758-1831). The popularity of the German Lafontaine's novels is attested to by a passage in the journal of the young Eichendorff (Cotta edition, Vol. III, p. 204 f.). He is also satirized in Tieck's Zerbino.

20 Ibid., p. 331.

21 Ibid., pp. 330, 331.

22 Ibid., p. 331.

23 Ibid., p. 330 f.

24 Ibid., p. 331.

25 Ibid., p. 331 f.

26 The distinction between the arabesque on a lower and a higher level is an essential aspect of Polheim's interpretation; cf. Die Arabeske, p. 134 ff.

27 KA II, p. 337 f.

28 Ibid., p. 338.

29 Ibid.

30 Ibid., p. 337.

31 Among these interpretations of Lucinde, the following attempts are to be mentioned: Paul Kluckhohn, Die Auffassung der Liebe in der Literatur des 18. Jahrhunderts und in der deutschen Romantik, 3d edition (Tübingen, 1966);

Hans Eichner, KA V, p. xvii ff.; Wolfgang Paulsen, "Friedrich Schlegels Lucinde als Roman," The Germanic Review, 21 (1946), p. 173 ff. Karl Konrad Polheim, Friedrich Schlegel, Lucinde. Ein Roman (Stuttgart, 1963, Reclam) pp. 110-117; and Polheim, "Friedrich Schlegel's 'Lucinde'," Zeitschrift für deutsche Philologie, 88 (1969).

32 The opinion that Schlegel wrote this letter chiefly in order to justify his novel Lucinde has often been maintained and goes back to Rudolf Haym, Die Romantische Schule, pp. 558, 752. Cf. also I. Rouge, Erläuterungen zu Friedrich Schlegels Lucinde (Lausanne, 1904), p. 18; F. Gundolf, Romantiker, p. 45; and Polheim, "Friedrich Schlegels 'Lucinde', "Zeitschrift für deutsche Philologie, 88 (1969), p. 61 ff.

V. The Typology of the Novel

1   LN Nos. 735, 732, 556.

2   Cf. Jaspers' interpretation of Kant in his Plato, Augustin, Kant. Drei Gründer des Philosophierens (München, 1961).

3   LN No. 732.

4   LN No. 248.

5   LN Nos. 377, 380, 548.

6   LN No. 1367.

7   LN Nos. 162, 289, 185.

8   LN No. 282.

9   LN No. 290.

10 LN No. 154.

11 LN No. 340.

12 LN No. 417.

13 "Friedrich Schlegel's Theory of Romantic Poetry," p. 1024.

14 LN No. 378.

15 LN No. 391.

16 LN No. 393.

17 LN No. 436.

18 LN Nos. 379, 383.

19 LN Nos. 386, 406, 410.

20 LN No. 489.

21   LN Nos. 376, 1026.

22   LN No. 562.

23   Cf. this publication, p. 40 f.

24   "Friedrich Schlegel's Theory of Romantic Poetry," p. 1024.

25   LN No. 484.

26   LN Nos. 835, 947, 948.

27   LN No. 372.

28   LN No. 335.

29   LN Nos. 387, 351.

30   LN No. 774.

31   LN Nos. 851, 998.

32   LN No. 511.

33   LN No. 754.

34   LN Nos. 835, 1105.

35   LN No. 1339.

36   LN No. 1355.

37   LN No. 1413.

38   LN Nos. 1351, 1345, 1383, etc.

39   LN No. 1459.

40   LN No. 1218 ff.

41   LN No. 1538.

VI. <u>The Novel as an Ideal of Progressive Poetry: "absoluter Roman" and the Abandonment of the Novel</u>

1   LN No. 293.

2   LN No. 418.

3   LN No. 695.

4   LN Nos. 794, 824, 1356, 903, 1566.

5   LN No. 491.

6   LN No. 434.

7   LN No. 828.

8   LN No. 449.

9   LN No. 1378.

10   LN No. 1447.

11   LN Nos. 731, 1359.

12   LN Nos. 1396, 1544.

13   LN Nos. 1643, 1683.

14   LN No. 1728.

15   LN Nos. 1741, 1743.

16   LN No. 1761.

17   LN No. 1771.

18   LN No. 1804.

19   Cf. our comments on the Cologne lectures, this publication p. 62 ff. See also p. 14.

20   LN No. 1827 ff.

21   LN No. 1864.

22   LN No. 1867.

23   Cf. our comments on the Cologne lectures, this publication p. 62 ff. See also p. 14.

24   LN No. 1898.

25   Cf. LN, p. 192.

26   LN No. 2106.

27   LN No. 2113.

28   Alfred Schlagdenhauffen, p. 332 ff.

29   KA II, p. 312.

30   Ibid., p. 361.

31   KA II, p. 257, No. 11.

32   KA XVIII, Philosophische Lehrjahre, V, Nos. 1, 151; cf. p. 60 of this publication.

33   KA XIX, VIII, No. 142.

34   KA XVIII, Beilage VIII, No. 44; cf. also No. 102.

35   This course of lectures is still unpublished. I quote from the typewritten transcript by Professor Alison Scott, University of Alberta, Edmonton.

36   August Wilhelm von Schlegels Vorlesungen über dramatische Kunst und Literatur, II, p. 109 ff.

37   Scott Manuscript, p. 55.

38   Ibid., pp. 57, 58, 59.

39   Ibid., p. 59 f.

40   Ibid., p. 70 ff.

41   Ibid., p. 72.

42   Ibid.,

43   Ibid., p. 73.

44   Ibid., p. 74.

45   Ibid., p. 75.

46   Ibid., p. 75 f.

47   Ibid., p. 76.

48   Ibid., pp. 83-84.

49   Ibid., p. 92 ff.

50   Ibid., p. 93.

51   Ibid., p. 95.

52   Ibid., p. 96.

53   KA XIX, Philosophische Lehrjahre, Beilage IX. Schlegel's concept of the novel as it is expressed in his review of Goethe's Werke (1808), is the topic of the last chapter of this book.

54   KA XIX, Philosophische Lehrjahre, Beilage IX, No. 34.

55   Ibid., Nos. 66, 55. On Schlegel's praise of the "Lied", cf. his review of Goethe's Werke: KA III, pp. 109-114.

56   KA XIX, Philosophische Lehrjahre, Beilage IX, No. 60. On the rejection of "Künstlerroman", cf. the review of Goethe's Werke, p. 109 f.

57   KA XIX, Philosophische Lehrjahre, Beilage IX, Nos. 62, 72.

58   Ibid., Nos. 78, 69.

59   Ibid., No. 75.

60   Ibid., No. 81.

61   Ibid., Nos. 84, 119, 120.

62   Ibid., No. 145.

63   KA VI, p. 275.

64   Ibid., p. 274.

65   Ibid., p. 274 f.

FOOTNOTES

66   Cf. this publication, pp. 14-15.

67   KA VI, p. 331.

FOOTNOTES

PART TWO: NOVALIS

I. Novalis Criticism in the Light of New Insights

1   Friedrich Schlegel und Novalis. Biographie einer Romantikerfreundschaft
    in ihren Briefen, ed. Max Preitz (Darmstadt, 1957), p. 123.

2   Schriften II, p. 545, No. 105.

3   For investigation into Novalis' philosophical and critical thought cf. Gerhard
    Schulz, "Die Poetik des Romans bei Novalis," Deutsche Romantheorien
    (Frankfurt am Main - Bonn, 1968), pp. 81-111; Hans-Joachim Mähl, "Goethes
    Urteil über Novalis," Jahrbuch des freien Hochstifts (Tübingen, 1967),
    pp. 130-270; Paul Kluckhohn, Das Ideengut der Deutschen Romantik (Tübingen,
    1961); Friedrich Hiebel, Novalis. German Poet--European Thinker--Christian
    Mystic (Chapel Hill, 1959); E. Spenlé, Novalis. Essai sur l'idéalisme roman-
    tique en Allemagne (Paris, 1904); Egon Friedell, Novalis als Philosoph
    (München, 1904); Georg von Lukács, "Novalis," in Die Seele und die Formen
    (Berlin, 1911), pp. 93-177; Henri Lichtenberger, Novalis (Paris, 1912);
    Anni Carlson, Die Fragmente des Novalis (Basel, 1939); Ursula Flickenschildt,
    Novalis' Begegnung mit Fichte und Hemsterhuis (Dissertation: Kiel, 1947);
    Hugo Kuhn, "Poetische Synthesis oder ein kritischer Versuch über romanti-
    sche Philosophie und Poesie des Novalis' Fragmenten," Zeitschrift für
    philosophische Forschung 5 (1950-1951), pp. 161-178, 358-385; Theodor
    Haering, Novalis als Philosoph (Stuttgart, 1954); Manfred Dick, Die Ent-
    wicklung des Gedankens der Poesie in den Fragmenten des Novalis (Bonn,
    1967); Karl-Heinz Volkman-Schluck, "Novalis' magischer Idealismus,"
    Die deutsche Romantik, Poetik, Formen und Motive, ed. Hans Steffen
    (Göttingen, 1967), pp. 45-53; Géza von Molnar, Novalis' Fichte-Studien.
    The Fountain of his Aesthetics (The Hague, 1970).

4   Schriften III, p. 429, No. 820.

5   Ibid.

6   Ibid., pp. 376-377, No. 617.

7   Schriften II, p. 536, No. 47.

8   Ibid., p. 595, No. 318.

9   Schriften III, p. 374, No. 603.

10 Ibid., p. 302, No. 342.

11 Schriften II, p. 545, No. 105.

12 Die Romantische Schule, p. 328.

13 H. A. Korff, Geist der Goethezeit, 7th edition, 4 vols. (Leipzig, 1914-1954),
    III, pp. 249-250.

14 German Romanticism (New York, 1966).

15 A History of Modern Criticism, The Romantic Age, II.

16 "Weltbild und innere Form der Klassik und Romantik im 'Wilhelm Meister' und 'Heinrich von Ofterdingen'," Deutsche Vierteljahrsschrift für Literaturwissenschaft und Geistesgeschichte, XVI (Buchreihe: Halle/Saale, 1929), pp. 187-203.

17 Ibid., p. 203.

18 Das Erlebnis und die Dichtung (Göttingen, 1965), p. 24.

19 Schriften, pp. 3-203, 697, 713, 749, 751, 753, 754.

20 Schriften II, p. 23; pp. 534-535.

21 This idea can be found in Aphorism No. 32 of the Hemsterhuis studies, Schriften II, p. 372, where Novalis discusses the function of history, philosophy, and poetry, illustrating how each relates the individual to the universe; but many other aphorisms to be discussed in this publication also support this thesis.

22 Schriften II, p. 647, No. 473.

23 Schriften IV, pp. 91-92, No. 31.

24 Ibid., p. 92.

25 Ibid., p. 109, No. 34.

26 Ibid., pp. 109-110.

27 Ibid., p. 252, No. 116.

28 Schriften II, pp. 524-526, No. 13.

29 Cf. Korff, pp. 249-250 ff.

30 Schriften II, pp. 372-373, No. 32.

31 Cf. Kurt May, "Weltbild und innere Form der Klassik und Romantik im 'Wilhelm Meister' und 'Heinrich von Ofterdingen'," pp. 187-203 for a thorough discussion of the structure of Heinrich von Ofterdingen. Cf. also G. Gloege, Novalis' "Heinrich von Ofterdingen" als Ausdruck seiner Persönlichkeit (Leipzig, 1911); Oskar Walzel, "Die Formkunst von Hardenbergs Heinrich von Ofterdingen"," Germanisch-Romanische Monatsschrift 7 (1915-1919), pp. 403, 444, 465-479; Heinz Heinrich Borcherdt, "Novalis' Heinrich von Ofterdingen," Der Roman der Goethezeit (Urach-Stuttgart, 1949), pp. 365-382; Armand Nivelle, "Der symbolische Gehalt des Heinrich von Ofterdingen," Revue des langues vivantes 16 (1950), pp. 404-427; Heinz Ritter, "Die Entstehung des Heinrich von Ofterdingen," Euphorion 55 (1961); pp. 163-195; Richard Samuel, "Novalis. Heinrich von Ofterdingen," Der deutsche Roman. Struktur und Geschichte, ed. Benno von Wiese, I (Düsseldorf, 1963), pp. 252-300; Oskar Ehrensperger, Die epische Struktur in Novalis' Heinrich von Ofterdingen (Winterthur, 1965); Helmut Schanze, Index zu Novalis' Heinrich von Ofterdingen (Frankfurt-Bonn, 1968).

FOOTNOTES

II. "Poesie" as the Highest Expression of Human Achievement: Intellect and
Imagination

1   Schriften II, pp. 22-23.

2   Schriften II, p. 237, No. 435.

3   Schriften II, p. 456, Nos. 100, 101.

4   Ibid., p. 564, No. 196.

5   Ibid., pp. 534-535, Nos. 37, 42.

6   Ibid., p. 535.

7   Ibid., p. 537, No. 55.

8   Ibid., p. 568, No. 207.

9   Ibid.

10   Ibid., p. 746, No. 473.

11   Schriften IV, pp. 275, No. 131.

12   Schriften III, p. 654, No. 577.

13   Schriften II, p. 17.

14   Ibid., pp. 16-17. Novalis' enthusiasm stems from spontaneous and un-
inhibited enjoyment derived from Anacreontic lyrics and not from a
theoretical approach to it; he deals with his subject not as a critic, but as
a loving disciple, "von Wonne trunken," whose judgment rests in feelings
rather than intellect. He criticizes those who prefer the wit in modern poets
to the "Naturgefühl" of Anacreontic odes, a criticism directed primarily
against the French and the Germans. He questions this preference: "Und woher
dies? Weil die Franzosen überhaupt weit tändelnder als zärtlich sind, mehr
den Witz lieben als fein Gefühl. Und unsre Lieder sind auch deswegen wenig
inneres Gefühles voll mehr mit Spitzfündigkeiten angefüllt, besitzen wenig
Einfalt und Natur, aber mehr Witz [...]"

15   Ibid., p. 456, No. 100.

16   Ibid., p. 440, No. 70.

17   Ibid., p. 462, No. 105.

18   The aphorisms pertaining directly to the novel will not be discussed here,
but will be dealt with in Chapter 5, Part Two, of this publication.

19   Schriften II, p. 535, No. 44: "Der Inhalt des Dramas ist ein Werden oder ein
Vergehn. Es enthält die Darstellung der Entstehung einer organischen Gestalt aus dem Flüssigen - einer wohlgegliederten Begebenheit aus Zufall - Es
enthält die Darstellung der Auflösung - der Vergehung einer organischen
Gestalt im Zufall. Es kann beydes zugleich enthalten und dann ist es ein
vollständiges Drama. Man sieht leicht, dass der Inhalt desselben eine Ver-
wandlung - ein Läuterungs, Reduktionsprocess seyn müsse. Oedipus in
Colonos ist ein schönes Beyspiel davon - so auch Philoktet."

20 Ibid., p. 544, No. 98.

21 Ibid., p. 564, No. 197.

22 Ibid., p. 572, No. 214.

23 Ibid., p. 575, No. 227.

24 Ibid., p. 592, No. 294.

25 Ibid., p. 632, Nos. 111, 113.

26 Ibid., p. 633, No. 114.

27 Ibid., p. 588, No. 264.

28 Schriften III, p. 309, No. 382.

29 Schriften III, p. 452, No. 959.

30 Ibid., p. 650, No. 553; cf. also p. 683, No. 656: "Poësie = offenbarten Gemütwircksamer (produktiver) Individualitaet."

31 Ibid., p. 650, No. 557.

32 Ibid.

33 Ibid., p. 691, No. 695.

34 Although Novalis promulgated variety and unity, realistic and idealistic elements in his ideal of poetry, he did not recognize this integration within Shakespeare's works and did not understand him: "Shakespeare ist mir dunkler als Griechenland. Den Spass Aristophanes versteh ich, aber den Shakespeares noch lange nicht. Shakespeare versteh ich überhaupt noch sehr unvollkommen," Schriften III, p. 691, No. 695. Cf. also p. 670, No. 611 and p. 681, No. 643; Adam Müller in his Vorlesungen über die deutsche Wissenschaft und Literatur held in Dresden in the winter of 1806 (Kritische, ästhetische und philosophische Schriften (Neuwied/Berlin, 1967) comments on Novalis' failure to understand Shakespeare correctly. He esteems Novalis' critical opinions, since they stem from the innermost part of his soul and "weil sich mit ihnen streiten lässt, weil sie herausfordern zu neuer Betrachtung." (p. 177) Nevertheless Müller criticizes Novalis' attempt to depict Shakespeare's art as proceeding primarily from nature rather than intention (pp. 177-179) and the particular opinion that Shakespeare's historical works depict "Kampf der Poesie mit der Unpoësie," that the base appears witty and exuberant, while greatness seems stiff and sad within his historical plays. Although Shakespeare's Henry IV seems to justify this opinion, the subsequent drama Henry V combines the commonplace and the great, the base and elevated forms of life: "Zwischen diesen beiden Welten schwankend und dann im folgenden Drama, in König Heinrich V, sie beide in ein schönes Ganze vereinigend, schwebt eine Natur von seltner Vortrefflichkeit, von ungewöhnlichem Umfang und Reichtum, der Liebling Shakespeares, wenn er je einen gehabt, der Kronprinz, Sohn Heinrich IV., nachheriger König Heinrich V. Es frägt sich, ist der Streit dieser beiden Welten, wie er sich am schönsten

in dem Gemüt desselben Prinzen von Wales repräsentiert, wirklich, wie Novalis sagt, Kampf zwischen der Poesie und der Unpoesie, erscheint das Grosse wirklich steif und unpoetisch. Hier hat Novalis offenbar die Klage über seine Zeit, den Zweck seiner Werke etwas voreilig auf Shakespeare übertragen." (p. 181).

35   Schriften III, pp. 689-688, No. 681.

36   Ibid., p. 688, No. 682.

37   Ibid.

38   Schriften IV, p. 327, No. 156.

39   Schriften III, p. 690, No. 690.

III. The Poet and his Craft: Ideality and Reality

1   Schriften IV, p. 242, No. 112.

2   Schriften II, p. 422, No. 26.

3   Ibid.

4   Schriften II, pp. 573-574, No. 226. It is likely that Novalis was inspired to this distinction between the perspectives of the poet and the painter by Lessing's essay Laokoon to which he refers in an earlier fragment: II, p. 379, No. 40.

5   Schriften II, p. 452, No. 87.

6   Ibid.

7   In this thought, Novalis anticipates later concepts of the art of poetry as elaborated by Stefan George and Gottfried Benn.

8   Schriften II, p. 592, No. 296.

9   Schriften II, p. 534, No. 38.

10   Ibid., p. 533, No. 33.

11   Ibid., pp. 534-535, No. 41.

12   Ibid., p. 560, No. 165.

13   Ibid., p. 559, No. 153.

14   Ibid., pp. 534-535.

15   Ibid., p. 562, No. 177.

16   Ibid., p. 591, No. 286.

17   Ibid., p. 537, Nos. 52, 53.

18   Ibid., p. 537, No. 56.

19   Ibid., p. 591, No. 281.

20   See p. 84 and p. 85 of this publication for complete quotations.

21   Schriften III, p. 466, No. 1073.

22   Ibid., p. 468, No. 1093.

23   Ibid., p. 563, No. 56.

24   Ibid., p. 655, No. 583.

25   Ibid., p. 683, No. 654.

26   Ibid., p. 685, No. 691.

27   Ibid., p. 689, No. 685.

28   Ibid., p. 685, No. 668.

29   Ibid., p. 685, No. 671. In aphorisms of the "Vermischte Bemerkungen", however, Novalis does recognize the value of literary criticism and indicates that the history of art provides the foundation for the critic's task: "Formeln für Kunstindividuen finden, durch die sie im eigentlichsten Sinn erst verstanden werden, macht das Geschäft des artistischen Kritikers aus - dessen Arbeiten die Geschichte der Kunst vorbereiten," Schriften II, p. 432, No. 52. See also p. 424, No. 29.

30   Walter Feilchenfeld, "Der Einfluss Jacob Böhmes auf Novalis," Germanische Studien, Heft 22 (Berlin, 1922), p. 67.

31   Feilchenfeld, p. 67.

32   Schriften I, p. 436, No. 32.

33   Schriften IV, pp. 322-323, No. 153.

34   In his impressive study of Böhme's influence on Novalis (see Footnote No. 30 above), Walter Feilchenfeld promotes the thesis that while Goethe's influence on Novalis decreased, that of Böhme increased. Through an analysis of Heinrich von Ofterdingen, beginning with the fifth chapter, this critic demonstrates that Novalis went beyond his magic idealism to develop a cosmic world view incorporating the powers of Böhme's "Weltgemüt": "Er kennt die Kräfte des Weltgemüts, weil sie in ihm selbst vernehmlich sind. Er versöhnt die Weltanschauungen Heinrichs und Klingsohrs. Denn er trägt in sich selbst einen Kosmos (Heinrich); dieser Kosmos ist aber nicht das eigenmächtige Werk des Ichs, sondern der überpersönlichen Kräfte (Klingsohr), die die ganze Natur durchdringen. Damit ist der Schwerpunkt in das grosse Weltgemüt verlegt und dem Ich doch nichts genommen. In dem Märchen sehen wir diesen Schritt vollzogen." (p. 82).

35   Feilchenfeld, p. 5.

36   Ibid., p. 12.

37 Ibid., p. 15.

38 Schriften III, p. 689, No. 685.

39 Ibid., p. 693, No. 705.

40 Korff maintains the position that Klingsohr is a "stilisierte Gestalt Goethes" and that Heinrich, the young Romantic, learns the principles of his art from the classical master (III, p. 570 f.). Hans Heinrich Borcherdt in his chapter on "Heinrich von Ofterdingen" in Der Roman der Goethezeit (Urach and Stuttgart, 1949), pp. 363.382, regards Klingsohr as a new image of Goethe attained by Novalis under Böhme's influence, a Goethean teacher for Heinrich, whose teachings, however, he is eventually to outgrow just as Novalis outgrew his original praise of Wilhelm Meister (p. 379). Kurt May states that Klingsohr attempted to combine "Verstand mit dem Enthusiasmus [...] Der mit seiner klassischen Botschaft die romantische aufzuheben schien, enthüllt sich als einer, der über ihre Gegensätze hinweg zu einer höheren verschmelzenden Einheit hinaufstrebt [...]" ("Weltbild und innere Form der Klassik und Romantik im 'Wilhelm Meister' und 'Heinrich von Ofterdingen'," p. 202). Cf. also Schriften I, "Einleitung der Herausgeber," pp. 183-192.

41 Schriften I, p. 282. Klingsohr states his position clearly: "Die Poesie will vorzüglich [...] als strenge Kunst getrieben werden. Als blosser Genuss hört sie auf Poesie zu sein. Ein Dichter muss nicht den ganzen Tag müssig umherlaufen, und auf Bilder und Gefühle Jagd machen. Das ist ganz der verkehrte Weg. Ein reines offenes Gemüt, Gewandtheit im Nachdenken und Betrachten, und Geschicklichkeit alle seine Fähigkeiten in eine gegenseitig belebende Tätigkeit zu versetzen und darin zu erhalten, das sind die Erfordernisse unserer Kunst."

42 Ibid., p. 283.

43 Ibid., p. 285.

44 Ibid., p. 285. See also Schriften IV, pp. 91-98, No. 31 for text of letter.

45 Ibid., p. 286.

46 See p. 84 of this publication.

47 Schriften I, pp. 427-429. Among these topics for further novels we find: "Liebe und Ehrfurcht. und Rache. und Hass. und Furcht. und Wahnsinn. und Alter. und Kindheit. und Schönheit. und Hässlichkeit. und Stolz," and among the characters planned for inclusion in further novels, Novalis lists: "Eltern, Kinder. Verwandte. Halbkinder, Halbmänner, Männer. Greise. Frauen. Mütter. Mägde. Knechte. Alte Diener. Mädchen. Fürsten [...] Schauspieler. Gelehrte, Künstler. Geschäftsleute [...] etc." Possible occasions for poetic depiction include the most conventional ones of life: "Hochzeiten. Kindtaufen. Gefechte. Begegnungen. Trennungen. Sterbebetten. Begräbnisse. Tänze. Spaziergänge. Reisen [...]"

48 Ibid., p. 430.

FOOTNOTES

49   Ibid., p. 286.

50   Ibid., p. 287. For complete fragment cited here regarding man's potential for creation see p. 84 of this publication.

51   See p. 75 of this publication for complete quotation.

52   Schriften III, p. 339, No. 470.

53   Ibid.

54   Gesammelte Werke in zwölf Bänden, Bd. 10, p. 18 f.

55   Cf. also Diana Behler, "Thomas Mann as a Theoretician of the Novel," Colloquia Germanica 1/2 (1974), pp. 52-88.

56   Schriften III, pp. 276-277, No. 210.

57   Schriften II, p. 595, No. 318.

58   Schriften IV, pp. 248-249, No. 115.

IV The Synthesis of Poetry and Philosophy

1   Cf. table of contents, Schriften II, pp. xiv-xvi; Schriften III, pp. v-vii.

2   Friedrich Schlegel und Novalis, Briefwechsel, p. 52, No. 13. These comments were probably in refutation of Schlegel's earlier belief that Novalis' path was "vielleicht nicht bloss divergierend von dem meinigen, sondern diametral entgegengesetzt," a statement to which Novalis steadfastly refused to give credence. (p. 49, No. 12)

3   Ibid., p. 59, No. 16. It is interesting to note that Novalis gives Fichte the credit for awakening this new interest in philosophy: "Er ists, der mich weckte und indirekte zuschürt," (p. 59) yet ever-conscious of his tendency to go overboard into one direction, Novalis assures Schlegel: "Glaub aber nicht, dass ich, wie sonst, leidenschaftlich bloss Eins verfolge und nicht vor meine Füsse sehe [...] Ich fühle in allem immer mehr die erhabnen Glieder eines wunderbaren Ganzen--in das ich hineinwachse, das zur Fülle meines Ichs werden soll." In an ensuing letter, Schlegel further relates their occupation with philosophy to Fichte: "Wie schön wäre es, wenn wir so allein beisammen sitzen könnten ein paar Tage und philosophierten, oder wie wirs immer nannten - fichtisieren!" (p. 85, No. 31).

4   Schriften II, p. 531, No. 29; cf. also Kluckhohn, Ideengut, pp. 174-175.

5   See p. 73 of this publication for complete quotation.

6   Schriften II, p. 412, No. 4.

7   Ibid., p. 523, No. 7.

8   Ibid., p. 523, No. 8

9   Ibid., p. 524, No. 13.

10   Ibid., p. 525, No. 13.

11   Ibid., pp. 525-526, No. 13.

12   Ibid., p. 527, No. 18.

13   Ibid., pp. 527-528, No. 19.

14   Ibid., p. 528.

15   Ibid., p. 531, No. 29.

16   Ibid.

17   Ibid., p. 535, Nos. 43, 47.

18   Ibid., p. 535, No. 43. See pp. 77-78 of this publication for further
     elaboration on Novalis' view of organic poetry.

19   Ibid., pp. 590-591, No. 280.

20   Ibid., p. 281, No. 623.

21   Ibid., p. 291, No. 651.

22   Ibid., p. 283, No. 633.

V. <u>The Novel as the Vehicle for the Fulfillment of the Highest Task of Poetry</u>

1   <u>Friedrich Schlegel und Novalis, Briefwechsel</u>, p. 123.

2   Schriften III, pp. 277-278, No. 218.

3   Ibid., IV, pp. 281, No. 133. Gerhard Schulz presents a carefully documented
     analysis of Novalis' concept of the novel in his study "Die Poetik des Romans
     bei Novalis," <u>Deutsche Romantheorien</u>, pp. 81-111; see also J. O. E.
     Donner, <u>Der Einfluss Wilhelm Meisters auf den Roman der</u>
     <u>Romantiker</u> (Helsingford, 1893), Clemens Heselhaus, "Die Wilhelm
     Meister-Kritik der Romantiker und die romantische Romantheorie,"
     in <u>Nachahmung und Illusion</u>, Kolloquium Giessen, June, 1963, ed. H. R.
     Jauss (München, 1964), pp. 113-210, and Kluckhohn, <u>Ideengut</u>, p. 180 ff.

4   Schriften II, p. 434, No. 18.

5   Ibid., p. 435, No. 24.

6   Ibid., p. 434, No. 20; p. 436, No. 33.

7   Ibid., p. 599. No. 341.

8   Ibid., p. 544, No. 97.

9   Schriften I, p. 435, No. 22.

10   Schriften III, p. 654, No. 579.

11   Ibid.

12   Schriften III, p. 302, No. 342.

13   Schriften II, p. 545, No. 105.

14   Ibid.

15   Schriften III, p. 649, No. 549.

16   Schriften II, p. 558, No. 265.

17   Schriften III, p. 465, No. 1069.

18   Ibid., p. 308, No. 373.

19   Schriften II, p. 563, No. 188.

20   Ibid., p. 570, No. 212.

21   Ibid.

22   Schriften III, p. 363, No. 557.

23   Schriften II, p. 456, No. 98.

24   Ibid., p. 436, No. 65.

25   Schriften I, p. 331.

26   Schriften III, p. 434, No. 853.

27   Schriften II, p. 534, No. 34.

28   Ibid., p. 647, No. 472; p. 561, No. 175.

29   Ibid., p. 564, No. 199.

30   Ibid., p. 601, No. 352.

31   Ibid., p. 435, No. 28.

32   Schriften III, p. 471, No. 1112.

33   Ibid., p. 560, No. 34.

34   Schriften II, p. 580, No. 242.

35   Schriften III, p. 562, No. 45.

36   Schriften II, p. 580, No. 242. The diversity and seemingly unlimited potential
      of the novel greatly attracted Novalis, and he thought about the various ap-
      proaches a writer might take in depicting the interaction of events and an
      individual which is so characteristic of this genre. Basically, he visualizes
      four types of action: 1) a change in events through the individual, 2) a change
      in the individual through events, 3) individual and events alternated by
      changing, or 4) individual and events independent of each other. Furthermore,
      events can be presented as a series of related actions of a reasonable person

or fate, as a series of isolated chance events, or a mixture of the two. The first type could be depicted in the form of 1) a struggle, 2) a society, or 3) dual worlds having the common feature of being poetic and picturesque. If the second method is chosen, however, the novelists might describe 1) a struggle with unhappiness or misfortune, 2) a unity with good fortune, or 3) a combination of the first two categories. (p. 580, No. 242).

37   Ibid., p. 581, No. 242.

38   Schriften III, p. 664, No. 603.

39   Ibid., p. 681, No. 640.

40   Schriften II, p. 237, No. 434; Schriften III, p. 240, No. 948.

41   Schriften III, p. 271, No.169.

42   Schriften II, p. 282, No. 632.

43   Ibid., p. 281, No. 619.

44   Ibid., p. 277, No. 587.

45   Schriften II, p. 291, No. 651; Schriften III, p. 286, No. 25.

46   Schriften III, p. 682, No. 643.

47   Schriften II, p. 646, No. 468.

48   Schriften III, p. 558, No. 21.

VI. The Novel and the Fairytale

1   Schriften I, p. 431, No. 2. Marianne Thalmann discusses many of Novalis' fairytales as they appear in Heinrich von Ofterdingen and Die Lehrlinge zu Sais as well as the underlying concept and aphoristic statements in her book Das Märchen und die Moderne, 2d edition (Stuttgart-Berlin-Köln-Mainz, 1961), pp. 17-33, and indicates that Novalis' fairytale is "eine in die Zukunft gerichtete Dichtung [...] Es kann einen Endzustand vorwegnehmen und einen Urzustand wiederholen. Es erlaubt das Gewesene und das Kommende über das Gegenwärtige zu setzen, die mechanische Zeit zu ignorieren und zu einer inneren Zeit überzugehen. Der abstrakte Charakter der Märchenstruktur ergibt die edelste Form der Darstellung für ein goldenes Zeitalter, aus dem die Welt vertrieben ist und in das sie auf reiferer Stufe zurückkehrt-- ein Gedanke, der aller Erkenntnis bei Novalis zu Grunde liegt. Daher auch dieses unumwundene Bekenntnis: 'Im Märchen glaube ich am besten meine Gemütsstimmung ausdrücken zu können." (pp. 20-21). Cf. also Hiebel, Novalis; Max Diez, "Metapher und Märchengestalt," I-VIII, PMLA, 48 (1933), pp. 488-507; Albert Reble, Märchen und Wirklichkeit bei Novalis," Deutsche Vierteljahrsschrift, 19 (1941), pp. 70-109, especially with regard to Novalis' philosophical inspirations through Kant and Fichte and his theory

of the fairytale. See also p. 93 ff. for discussion of how reality and the fairytale are intertwined in <u>Heinrich von Ofterdingen</u>; Borcherdt in his discussion of <u>Ofterdingen</u> in <u>Roman der Goethezeit</u> regards the fairytale as the "Gipfelung des Romans." (p. 377) Cf. also Max Diez, "Metapher und Märchengestalt. III Novalis und das allegorische Märchen," PMLA 48 (1933), pp. 488-507.

2   Schriften I, p. 91. "Das Märchen von Hyazinth und Rosenblüte."

3   Schriften III, p. 255, No. 80.

4   Schriften IV, p. 330, No. 158.

5   Ibid., p. 333, No. 163.

6   Schriften III, p. 652, No. 568.

7   Schriften I, p. 344.

8   Ibid., pp. 344-345.

9   Ibid., p. 315.

10   Schriften III, p. 449, No. 940.

11   Schriften II, p. 643, No. 455.

12   Schriften III, p. 256, No. 87.

13   Schriften I, p. 431, No. 1.

14   Schriften II, p. 564, No. 196.

15   Schriften III, p. 454, No. 986.

16   Ibid., p. 458, No. 1011.

17   Ibid., p. 455, No. 986.

18   Ibid., p. 280, No. 234.

19   Ibid., p. 281.

20   Ibid.

21   Ibid.

22   Ibid.

FOOTNOTES

APPENDIX: "DIVINATORY CRITICISM"? THE ROMANTIC REACTION TO WILHELM MEISTER

1   Schriften III, p. 646, No. 536; p. 647.

2   KA II, p. 198, No. 216. Schlegel comments himself on the ambiguous
     meaning of the term "Tendenz" in his satire Ueber die Unverständlichkeit,
     KA II, p. 366 f. Cf. also KA II, p. ixxvi f.

3   Josef Körner, Romantiker und Klassiker. Die Brüder Schlegel in ihren
     Beziehungen zu Schiller und Goethe (Berlin, 1924), p. 90 ff.

4   KA II, p. ixxiii.

5   KA XVIII, Philosophische Lehrjahre, I, No. 88; II, Nos. 222, 1065.

6   Ibid. II, Nos. 75, 80.

7   KA II, p. 126 ff.

8   Caroline. Briefe aus der Frühromantik, according to G. Waitz, augmented
     by E. Schmidt (Leipzig, 1913), I, p. 461.

9   KA XVIII, p. 23.

10   KA XVIII, Philosophische Lehrjahre, II, No. 381.

11   LN No. 1809.

12   Schriften III, p. 646, No. 536.

13   Cf. Schriften II, p. 404 ff., No. 445. In this passage "Ueber Goethe" Novalis
     mentions that Goethe "ist ganz practischer Dichter. Er ist in seinen Wercken--
     was der Engländer in seinen Waaren ist--höchst einfach, nett, bequem, und
     dauerhaft. Er hat in der deutschen Litteratur das gethan, was Wedgwood in
     der englischen Kunstwelt gethan hat - Er hat, wie die Engländer, einen na-
     türlich oeconomischen und einen durch Verstand erworbenen edelen Geschmack.'
     As has been noted earlier, Novalis appears to have been critical of Goethe,
     but in the same essay, he refers to Wilhelm Meister as the "Roman schlecht-
     weg, ohne Beywort." He then states that Goethe must be surpassed, but only
     as the ancients could be surpassed, "an Gehalt und Kraft, an Mannichfaltigkeit
     und Tiefsinn" and not really as an artist. Even in his most critical comment,
     calling Meister "ein fatales und albernes Buch [...] undichterisch im höchsten
     Grade, was den Geist betrifft," Novalis still recognizes the poetic depiction
     of the work. (Schriften III, p. 646, No. 536.)

14   Mähl, "Goethes Urteil über Novalis," p. 130 ff., pp. 174, 183, 185, 188
     (where the blame is put on Tieck), 221, 268.

15   Ibid., p. 149.

16   In F. Ast's Zeitschrift für Wissenschaft und Kunst, I, 1, p. 142 ff. Cf.
     Mähl, p. 202 f.

17   Zeitschrift für Wissenschaft und Kunst, p. 52 f. Cf. Mähl, p. 211 f.

18   Vorlesungen über die deutsche Wissenschaft und Literatur (1806), p. 51 f.
Cf. Mähl, p. 231 f. Müller, however, attempted to solve this opposition in
his lectures, especially in the fifth.

19   Eduard Firmenich-Richartz, Die Brüder Boisserée, Sulpiz und Melchior
Boisserée als Kunstsammler. Ein Beitrag zur Geschichte der Romantik
(Jena, 1916), I, p. 386. Goethes Werke (Sophienausgabe, Weimar, 1887-1919).
IV, Briefwechsel, 49, p. 118 f.

20   KA III, pp. 109-114. This review has recently been studied by Clemens
Heselhaus in "Die Wilhelm Meister-Kritik der Romantiker und die Romanti-
sche Romantheorie," Nachahmung und Illusion, ed. H. R. Jauss (München,
1964), pp. 113-127. Cf. also Henry Hatfield, "Wilhelm Meister's Lehrjahre
und 'Progressive Universalpoesie'," The Germanic Review, 36 (1961);
Raymond Immerwahr, "Friedrich Schlegel's Essay 'On Goethe's Meister',"
Monatshefte, 49 (1957); Joachim Müller, "Das Goethe-Bild in Friedrich
Schlegels Literaturtheorie," Festschrift Heinrich Besseler (Leipzig, 1962).

21   KA III, p. 128.

22   Ibid., pp. 128-130.

23   Ibid., pp. 130-131.

24   Ibid., p. 131.

25   Ibid., p. 133.

26   Ibid., p. 134.

27   Ibid., p. 136-137

28   Ibid.

29   Ibid., p. 138.

30   Ibid.

31   Ibid., p. 141.

BIBLIOGRAPHY

Sources

Balzac, Honoré. La Comédie Humaine. Bibliothèque de la Pléiade, 1935-1960.

Baumgart, Reinhart. Das Ironische und die Ironie in den Werken Thomas Manns. München, 1964.

Caroline. Briefe aus der Frühromantik, ed. G. Waitz, augmented by E. Schmidt, 2 vols. Leipzig, 1913.

Deutsche National Literatur, Volume 143: August Wilhelm und Friedrich Schlegel. In Auswahl herausg. von Oskar Walzel, 369 ff. Stuttgart, 1891.

Deutsches Museum. Eine Zeitschrift, ed. Friedrich Schlegel. 4 vols. Wien, 1812-1813.

Europa. Eine Zeitschrift, ed. Friedrich Schlegel. Frankfurt, 1803-1805. Photostatic reprint, Darmstadt, 1963.

Fichte, J. G. Gesamtausgabe, ed. Reinhard Lauth and Hans Jacob. Stuttgart, 1965.

Friedrich Schlegel. Neue philosophische Schriften, ed. Josef Körner. Frankfurt, 1935.

Friedrich Schlegel und Novalis. Biographie einer Romantikerfreundschaft in ihren Briefen, ed. Max Preitz. Darmstadt, 1957.

Friedrich Schlegels Briefe an seinen Bruder August Wilhelm, ed. Oskar Walzel. Berlin, 1890.

Goethes Werke, Sophienausgabe. Weimar, 1887-1919.

Hegel, Georg Wilhelm Friedrich. Sämtliche Werke. Jubiläumsausgabe in zwanzig Bänden, ed. Hermann Glockner. Photostatic reprint, Stuttgart, 1964.

Heine, Heinrich. Sämtliche Werke, ed. Ernst Elster. Leipzig and Wien, 1890.

Herder, J. G. God. Some Conversations. A translation with a critical introduction and notes by Frederic H. Burckhardt. New York, 1940.

Herders Werke. 5 vols. Berlin, 1964.

Hölderlin, Friedrich. Werke, ed. Norbert von Hellingrath, continued by Friedrich Seebass and Ludwig Pigenot. Berlin, 1943.

Jean Paul. Werke, ed. Nobert Miller. München, 1963.

Kant, Immanuel. Werke. 6 vols. Wiesbaden, 1960-1964.

Lessings Gedanken und Meinungen. Aus dessen Schriften zusammengestellt und erläutert von Friedrich Schlegel. 3 vols. Leipzig, 1804.

Mann, Thomas. Gesammelte Werke. 12 vols. Oldenburg, 1960.

Müller, Adam. Vorlesungen über die deutsche Wissenschaft und Literatur, in: Kritische, ästhetische und philosophische Schriften. Kritische Ausgabe, ed. Walter Schroeder and Werner Siebert. Neuwied/Berlin, 1967.

Nietzsche, Friedrich. Sämtliche Werke. 12 vols. Stuttgart, 1964.

<u>Novalis Schriften</u>. Die Werke Friedrich von Hardenbergs. Zweite, nach den Hand-
schriften ergänzte, erweiterte und verbesserte Auflage. 4 vols, ed. Paul
Kluckhohn and Richard Samuel. Stuttgart, 1960-1976.

Schelling, Friedrich Wilhelm Joseph von. <u>Sämmtliche Werke</u>. Stuttgart, 1861.

Schlegel, August Wilhelm. "Aus den 'Vorlesungen über schöne Literatur und Kunst'",
edited in <u>Deutsche National Literatur</u>. Vols. 17-19. Heilbronn (1844), 287-296.

_____. <u>Vorlesungen über philosophische Kunstlehre</u>, ed. August Wünsche.
Leipzig, 1911.

_____. <u>Vorlesungen über dramatische Kunst und Literatur</u>. Kritische Ausgabe,
ed. and commented by Giovanni Vittorio Amoretti. 2 vols. Bonn-Leipzig, 1923.

Schlegel, Friedrich. <u>Seine prosaischen Jugendschriften</u>, ed. Jakob Minor, Wien,
1882.

_____. <u>Literary Notebooks</u> (1797-1801), ed. with introduction and commentary by
Hans Eichner. London, 1957.

_____. <u>Kritische Ausgabe</u>, ed. Ernst Behler. Paderborn, 1958 ff.

_____. <u>Dialogue on Poetry and Literary Aphorisms</u>, translated, introduced,
and annotated by Ernst Behler and Roman Struc. University Park and London,
1968.

_____. <u>Kölner Vorlesungen</u>. Unpublished manuscript, transcript by Professor
Alison Scott, University of Alberta, Edmonton.

Schopenhauer, Arthur, <u>Sämmtliche Werke,</u> ed. Julius Frauenstädt, 1919.

Tieck, Ludwig. <u>Erinnerungen aus dem Leben des Dichters nach dessen mündlichen
und schriftlichen Mitteilungen</u>. 2 parts. Leipzig, 1955.

<u>The Oxford Classical Dictionary</u>, ed. N.G.L. Hammond and H. H. Scullard, 2d
edition. Oxford at the Clarendon Press, 1970.

Secondary Literature

Allemann, Beda. <u>Ironie und Dichtung</u>. Pfullingen, 1956.

Altenberg, Paul. <u>Die Romane Thomas Manns</u>. Bad Homburg, 1961.

Bachofen, Johann Jacob. <u>Der Mythos von Orient und Okzident</u>, introduced by Alfred
Bäumler. München, 1926.

Bays, Gwendolyn. <u>The Orphic Vision</u>. Seer Poets from Novalis to Rimbaud. Lincoln,
1964

Behler, Ernst. <u>Friedrich Schlegel</u>. Hamburg, 1966.

_____ . "The Origins of the Romantic Literary Theory," <u>Colloquia Germanica</u>.
1/2 (1968), 109 - 126.

_____. "Die Theorie der romantischen Ironie," Zeitschrift für deutsche Philologie, 88 (1969), 90-114.

_____. "Kritische Gedanken zum Begriff der europäischen Romantik," Die europäische Romantik. (Frankfurt, 1972), 7-43.

Belgardt, Raimund. Romantische Poesie. Begriff und Bedeutung bei Friedrich Schlegel. The Hague-Paris, 1966.

Böckmann, Paul. "Die romantische Poesie Brentanos und ihre Grundlagen bei Friedrich Schlegel und Tieck," Jahrbuch des freien deutschen Hochstifts, 1934-1935.

Borcherdt, Hans Heinrich. Der Roman der Goethezeit. Urach and Stuttgart, 1949.

Bubner, Rüdiger. "Das älteste Systemprogramm des deutschen Idealismus," Hegel-Studien, Beiheft 9 (Bonn, 1973), 261-265.

Carlson, Anni. Die Fragmente des Novalis. Basel, 1939.

Daemmrich, Horst S. "Friedrich Schiller and Thomas Mann: Parallels in Aesthetics," The Journal of Aesthetics and Art Criticism, 24 (1965).

Deutsche Romantheorien. Beiträge zu einer historischen Poetik des Romans in Deutschland, ed. Reinhold Grimm. Bonn, 1968.

Dick, Manfred. Die Entwicklung des Begriffs der Poesie in den Fragmenten des Novalis. Bonn, 1966.

Die Eröffnung des Zugangs zum Mythos. Ein Lesebuch, ed. Karl Kerényi. Darmstadt, 1967.

Diez, Max. "Metapher und Märchengestalt," I-VIII, PMLA, 48 (1933), 488-507.

Dilthey, Wilhelm. Leben Schleiermachers. Berlin, 1870.

_____. Das Erlebnis und die Dichtung. Göttingen, 1965.

Donner, J. O. E. Der Einfluss Wilhelm Meisters auf den Roman der Romantiker. Helsingford, 1893.

Ehrensperger, Oskar. Die epische Struktur in Novalis' "Heinrich von Ofterdingen". Winterthur, 1965.

Eichner, Hans. "Aspects of Parody in the Works of Thomas Mann," The Modern Language Review, 47 (1952), 30-48.

_____. "Friedrich Schlegel's Theory of Romantic Poetry," PMLA, 71 (1956), 1018 ff.

_____. "Thomas Mann und die deutsche Romantik," Das Nachleben der Romantik in der modernen deutschen Literatur. Heidelberg, (1969), 152-173.

_____. Friedrich Schlegel. New York, 1970.

Feilchenfeld, Walter. "Der Einfluss Jacob Böhmes auf Novalis," Germanische Studien, Heft 22. Berlin, 1922.

Firmenich-Richartz, Eduard. Die Brüder Boisserée, Vol. 1, Sulpiz und Melchior Boisserée als Kunstsammler. Ein Beitrag zur Geschichte der Romantik. Jena, 1916.

Fleschenberg, O. Schissel von. Entwicklungsgeschichte des griechischen Romans im Altertum. Halle a. S., 1913.

Flickenschildt, Urusula. Novalis' Begegnung mit Fichte und Hemsterhuis. Dissertation. Kiel, 1947.

Friedell, Egon. Novalis als Philosoph. München, 1904.

Gloege, G. Novalis' "Heinrich von Ofterdingen" als Ausdruck seiner Persönlichkeit. Leipzig, 1911.

Gundolf, Friedrich. Romantiker. Berlin, 1930.

Haring, Theodor. Novalis als Philosoph. Stuttgart, 1954.

Hamburger, Käthe. Thomas Mann und die Romantik. Eine problemgeschichtliche Studie. Berlin, 1932.

Hatfield, Henry. "Castorp's Dream and Novalis," History of Ideas News Letter, Vol. I, No. 1 (1954), 9-11.

_____. "Wilhelm Meister's Lehrjahre und 'Progressive Universalpoesie'," The Germanic Review, 36 (1961).

Haym, Rudolf. Die Romantische Schule, 3d edition. Berlin, 1914.

Heine, Roland. Transzendentalpoesie. Studien zu Friedrich Schlegel, Novalis und E. T. A. Hoffmann. Bonn, 1974.

Helbling, Carl. Die Gestalt des Künstlers in der neueren Dichtung. Eine Studie über Thomas Mann, Bern. 1922.

Heller, Erich. The Ironic German. A Study of Thomas Mann. Boston, 1958.

_____. "Conversation on the Magic Mountain," Thomas Mann. A Collection of Critical Essays, ed. Henry Hatfield. Englewood Cliffs (1964), 62-95.

Heselhaus, Clemens. "Die Wilhelm Meister-Kritik der Romantiker und die romantische Romantheorie," in Nachahmung und Illusion, Kolloquium Giessen, June, 1963, ed. H. R. Jauss. München (1964), 113-210.

Hiebel, Friedrich. Novalis. German Poet--European Thinker--Christian Mystic. Chapel Hill, 1959.

Holdheim, Wolfgang. Theory and Practice of the Novel. A study on André Gide. Geneva, 1968.

Holthusen, Hans Egon. Die Welt ohne Transzendenz. Hamburg, 1949.

Immerwahr, Raymond. "The Subjectivity or Objectivity of Friedrich Schlegel's Poetic Irony," The Germanic Review, 26 (1951), 173 ff.

BIBLIOGRAPHY

_____. "Friedrich Schlegel's Essay 'On Goethe's Meister'," Monatshefte, 49 (1957).

_____. "Die symbolische Form des 'Briefes über den Roman'," Zeitschrift für deutsche Philologie, 88 (1969), 49 ff.

_____. " 'Romantic' and its Cognates in England, Germany, and France before 1790," Romantic and its Cognates. The European History of a Word, ed. Hans Eichner, Toronto, 1972.

_____. Romantisch. Genese und Tradition einer Denkform (Respublic Literaria, Vol. 7). Frankfurt, 1972.

Jaspers, Karl. Plato, Augustin, Kant. Drei Gründer des Philosphierens. München, 1961.

Joël, Karl. Nietzsche und die Romantik. Jena-Leipzig, 1905.

Kaufmann, Fritz. Thomas Mann. The World as Will and Representation. Boston, 1957.

Kayser, Wolfgang. Das Groteske. Seine Gestaltung in Malerei und Dichtung. Oldenburg and Hamburg, 1957.

Kluckhohn, Paul. Die deutsche Romantik. Bielefeld-Leipzig, 1924.

_____. Das Ideengut der deutschen Romantik. Tübingen, 1961.

_____. Die Auffassung der Liebe in der Literatur des 18. Jahrhunderts und in der deutschen Romantik, 3d edition. Tübingen, 1966.

Koopmann, Helmut. Die Entwicklung des intellektuellen Romans bei Thomas Mann. Bonn, 1962.

Korff, H. A. Geist der Goethezeit. 7th edition. 4 vols. Leipzig, 1914-1954.

Körner, Josef. Romantiker und Klassiker. Die Brüder Schlegel in ihren Beziehungen zu Schiller und Goethe. Berlin, 1924.

_____. Friedrich Schlegel. Neue philosophische Schriften. Frankfurt, 1935.

Kuhn, Hugo. "Poetische Synthesis oder ein kritischer Versuch über romantische Philosophie und Poesie des Novalis' Fragmenten," Zeitschrift für Philosophische Forschung 5 (1950-1951), 161-178; 358-385.

Lang, Renée. André Gide et la pensée allemande. Paris, 1949.

Lichtenberger, Henri. Novalis. Paris, 1912.

Lovejoy, A. "The Meaning of 'Romantic' in Early German Romanticism," Essays in the History of Ideas. 4th edition. New York (1948), 183 ff.

_____. "Schiller and the Genesis of German Romanticism," Essays in the History of Ideas. 4th edition. New York (1948), 211 ff.

Lukács, Georg. Die Seele und die Formen. Berlin, 1911.

_____. Die Theorie des Romans. Ein geschichtsphilosophischer Versuch über die Formen der grossen Epik. Neuwied, 1963.

Mähl, Hans-Joachim. Die Idee des goldenen Zeitalters im Werk des Novalis. Heidelberg, 1966.

_____. "Goethes Urteil über Novalis," Jahrbuch des freien Hochstifts. Tübingen (1967), 130-270.

May, Kurt. "Weltbild und innere Form der Klassik und Romantik im 'Wilhelm Meister' und 'Heinrich von Ofterdingen'," Deutsche Vierteljahrsschrift für Literaturwissenschaft und Geistesgeschichte, 16 (Buchreihe: Halle/Saale, 1929), 187-203.

Mennemeier, Franz Norbert. Friedrich Schlegels Poesiebegriff. München, 1971.

Molnar, Géza von. Novalis' Fichte-Studien. The Fountain of his Aesthetics. The Hague, 1970.

Müller, Joachim. "Das Goethe-Bild in Friedrich Schlegels Literaturtheorie," Festschrift Heinrich Besseler. Leipzig, 1962.

Naumann, Hans. Die deutsche Dichtung der Gegenwart, 2d edition. Stuttgart, 1924.

Nivelle, Armand. "Der symbolische Gehalt des Heinrich von Ofterdingen," Revue des langues vivantes 16 (1950), 404.427.

Nündel, Ernst. "Der Bogen und die Leier. Thomas Manns Aeusserungen zur künstlerischen Tätigkeit," Der Deutschunterricht, 2 (1969), 42 ff.

Paulsen, Wolfgang. "Friedrich Schlegels Lucinde als Roman," The Germanic Review, 21 (1946), 173 ff.

Pöggeler, Otto. "Hegel, der Verfasser des ältesten Systemprogramms des deutschen Idealismus," Hegel-Studien, Beiheft 4 (Bonn, 1969), 17-32.

_____. "Hölderlin, Hegel und das älteste Systemprogramm," Hegel-Studien, Beiheft 9 (Bonn, 1973), 211-259.

Polheim, Karl Konrad Friedrich Schlegel, Lucinde. Ein Roman. Stuttgart, 1963.

_____. Novellentheorie und Novellenforschung. Stuttgart, 1965.

_____. Die Arabeske: Ansichten und Ideen aus Friedrich Schlegels Poetik. München-Paderborn-Wien, 1966.

_____. "Friedrich Schlegels 'Lucinde'," Zeitschrift für deutsche Philologie, 88 (1969), 61 ff.

Reble, Albert. "Märchen und Wirklichkeit bei Novalis," Deutsche Vierteljahrsschrift, 19 (1941), 70-109.

Ritter, Heinz. "Die Entstehung des Heinrich von Ofterdingen," Euphorion 55 (1961), 163-195.

BIBLIOGRAPHY

Rohde, Erwin. Der griechische Roman. Berlin, 1914.

Romantic and its Cognates. The European History of a Word, ed. Hans Eichner, Toronto, 1972.

Rosenzweig, Franz. Das älteste Systemprogramm des deutschen Idealismus. Sitzungs-berichte der Heidelberger Akademie der Wissenschaften. Philos.-Histor. Klasse 5. Heidelberg, 1917.

Rouge, I. Erläuterungen zu Friedrich Schlegels Lucinde. Lausanne, 1904.

Sagave, Pierre Paul. Réalité sociale et idéologie réligieuse dans les romans de Thomas Mann. Paris, 1954.

Samuel, Richard. "Novalis. Heinrich von Ofterdingen," Der deutsche Roman. Struktur und Geschichte, Vol. I, ed. Benno von Wiese. Düsseldorf (1963), 252-300.

Schanze, Helmut. Romantik und Aufklärung. Untersuchungen zu Friedrich Schlegel und Novalis. Nürnberg, 1966.

_____. Index zu Novalis' Heinrich von Ofterdingen. Frankfurt-Bonn, 1968.

Scharfschwerdt, Jürgen. Thomas Mann und der deutsche Bildungsroman. Köln, 1967.

Schirokauer, Arno. "Bedeutungswandel des Romans," Zur Poetik des Romans. Wege der Forschung, Vol. 35, Darmstadt (1965), 15-31.

Schlagdenhauffen, Alfred. Fréderic Schlegel et son groupe. La doctrine de l'Athenaeum (1798-1800). Paris, 1934.

Schlegel, August Wilhelm. Sämtliche Werke, ed. Edward Böcking. Leipzig, 1846.

Schulz, Gerhard. "Die Poetik des Romans bei Novalis," Deutsche Romantheorien. Frankfurt am Main/Bonn (1968), 81-111.

Seidlin, Oskar. "Der junge Joseph und der alte Fontane," Festschrift für Richard Alewyn. Köln-Graz (1967), 389 ff.

Sontheimer, Kurt. Thomas Mann und die Deutschen. Frankfurt, 1965.

Spenlé, E. Novalis. Essai sur l'idéalisme romantique en Allemagne. Paris, 1904.

Strauss, Ludwig. "Hölderlins Anteil an Schellings frühem Systemprogramm," Deutsche Vierteljahrsschrift 5 (1927), 679-747.

Strich, Fritz. Die Mythologie in der deutschen Literatur von Klopstock bis Wagner. 2 vols. Halle, 1910.

Thalmann, Marianne. Das Märchen und die Moderne. 2d edition. Stuttgart-Berlin-Köln-Mainz, 1961.

Volkman-Schluck, Karl-Heinz. "Novalis' magischer Idealismus," Die deutsche Romantik, Poetik, Formen und Motive, ed. Hans Steffen. Göttingen (1967), 45-53.

BIBLIOGRAPHY

Walzel, Oskar. "Die Formkunst von Hardenbergs Heinrich von Ofterdingen,"
Germanisch-Romanische Monatsschrift 7 (1915-1919), 403, 444, 465-579.

_____. Das Prometheussymbol von Shaftesbury zu Goethe. München, 1932.

_____. Grenzen von Poesie und Unpoesie. Frankfurt, 1937.

_____. German Romanticism. New York, 1966.

Weber, Heinz-Dieter. Friedrich Schlegels "Transzendentalpoesie". München, 1973.

Weigand, Hermann J. The Magic Mountain. Chapel Hill, 1964.

Wellek, René. A History of Modern Criticism. 4 vols. New Haven, 1955-1965.

_____. "The Concept of Romanticism in Literary History," Concepts of
Criticism. New Haven and London (1963), 134 ff.

Wiese, Benno von. Novelle. Stuttgart, 1963.

Wolf, H. Versuch einer Geschichte des Geniebegriffs. Heidelberg, 1932.

Wölfel, Kurt. "Friedrich von Blanckenburgs Versuch über den Roman," Deutsche
Romantheorien. Bonn (1968), 29-60.

Wolff, Samuel Lee. The Greek Romances in Elizabethan Prose Fiction. New York, 1913.

Zilsel, Edgar. Die Entstehung des Geniebegriffs. Ein Beitrag zur Ideengeschichte der
Antike und des Frühkapitalismus. Tübingen, 1926.

INDEX OF NAMES